AF291891

CONTENTS

4

INTRODUCTION

The Instant Omni Toaster Oven Air Fryer is ideal for home cooks who need quick, nutritious, simple dinners consistently—at the bit of a catch. Its extra-enormous limit fits six cuts of toast or a 12" pizza, and lets you air fry, dry out, cook, toast, heat, and sear all the nourishment you have to take care of your family and your companions.

Brisk and in any event, warming guarantees firm, brilliant outcomes without fail. With an assortment of one-contact cooking choices, there's no compelling reason to compute temperature, weight, or time. Select one of the seven Smart Programs and click start. Be that as it may, for you foodies out there, the Omni Toaster Oven gives the adaptability to alter settings to tweak your culinary experience.

This air fry toaster oven likewise accompanies all the embellishments your requirement for rotisserie cooking. The superior convection oven, alongside the rotisserie work, conveys succulent, flavorful rotisserie dishes.

So get together those different apparatuses coating your counter and account for the Omni Toaster Oven today.

Understanding Instant Omni Plus Toaster Oven

The Instant Omni plus toaster oven is the perfect oven to use in the home kitchen or in a professional setting. Its range of cooking programs and easy to use control panel will definitely make cooking a convenient job for you.

This toaster oven is a breeze for those who want to cook large servings at a time. It is an advanced version of the previously launched Instant Omni, and it provides greater capacity and additional cooking functions.

Advantages of Using Instant Omni

The following features of the Instant Omni make this toaster a must to keep cooking appliance:

Eight Smart Functions

This toaster oven combines all the cooking functions of an oven, broiler, air fryer, and a toaster. Imagine you have one single appliance that can carry out all such functions.

Each smart program comes with a preset temperature and timer settings, which are also adjustable as per the needs.

Two Cooking Modes

One feature that makes Instant Omni a toaster oven different from other toaster ovens is its two cooking modes. This feature is rare or impossible to find in other toaster ovens. There are two cooking modes which can be used to cook different types of meals. The two modes are:

Rotate

Using this mode, a user can cook or roast its chicken, duck, or any other meat on the rotisserie. The heat is provided to the food as it rotates on the rotisserie stick.

Convection

This mode is suitable for all other cooking functions in which food is placed in a fixed position. The heat is produced and regulated inside the oven through convection.

XL Capacity

The size of Instant Omni takes it to the top of the list when compared to other toaster ovens. Its great capacity to accommodate all food types, whether you want to cook a whole chicken inside or what to Air fryer a large batch of French fries, the appliance is capable of carrying them all at a time. So, it is perfect to use for large families. The XL capacity of the Instant Omni can cook the following in a single layer:

- 12" Pizza
- Six Toast Slices

Easy to Read Display screen

The display panel of the Instant Omni is easy to understand. It has a display at the center, which is surrounded by the touch keys for all the smart programs, the cooking modes, and the on/off functions.

There are separate knobs attached at the two ends of the touch panel, which can be used to adjust the cooking programs, time, and temperature manually.

Intuitive Customizable Programs

All the smart programs of Instant Omni are customizable. Even when the cooking program is running, the settings can be changed using the temperature and time knobs.

The adjustable programs allow the users to switch from one cooking settings to another with its super flexible heating system.

Even-Heat: Toasts Both Sides

Due to its convection heating mechanism, the Instant Omni toaster oven is capable of heating the food from all sides. This feature ensures even heating. When bread slices or bagels are toasted inside this toaster oven, they are cooked both from the top and the bottom. Without flipping a single slice, a user can get evenly cooked and crispy toasts.

When it comes to electric appliances, it is important to inspect all the parts of the appliance before giving it a test run. The Instant Omni toaster oven comes with the following basic elements and the accessories.

The Oven Base Unit

- Rack tray
- Crumb Tray
- Oven Door
- Rotisserie Catch
- Rotisserie Spit & Forks Rotisserie Lift
- Air Fry Basket
- Baking pan
- Baking trays
- Power plug

Inside the Instant Omni plus oven, there are three grooves on both sides. These grooves are used to insert three rack trays in the oven. The uppermost grooves can be used to insert the trays when the food needs to be broiled.

The center grooves are for Air frying and roasting purposes.

The lowermost level is used to place the food which needs to be baked, reheated, or dehydrated. Crumb tray is inserted at the bottom to protect the bottom of the oven from the food particle during cooking.

The rotisserie stick can be inserted and used to fix the meat of chicken. This stick can be fixed on the inner side of the center portion of the oven into the rotisserie catch. Air fryer basket can be placed on the lower rack when required.

Control Panel

The control panel of the appliance is fixed on the front top portion of the oven. The center black panel consists of the touch screen, which shows all the functions. This panel is placed in between two knobs which are used to adjust the time and cooking temperature:

Smart Program Keys: The seven smart program keys are located at the bottom of the black panel. Any of the programs can be selected by rotating the preset dial.

Display: right above the keys, there is a display which lights in blue colored figures indicating the time, temperature, and other indicators like Start, Cancel, Door, Warm, Flip or turn, etc.

Cooking Modes: There are two keys to the cooking modes, indicated by the: Rotate and Convection marks.

Start and Cancel Key: At the two corners of the display screen, there are keys to start or cancel a selected program.

Dials: The Temp/time dial can be used to adjust the cooking time and temperature. Rotate the dial to the right to increase the value of rotate it to the left to decrease the values. The Preset dial is used to switch the cooking modes.

APPETIZERS AND SIDE DISHES

1.   Parmesan Cabbage Wedges

Servings:4
Cooking Time: 30 Minutes
Ingredients:

- ½ head cabbage, cut into wedges
- 4 tbsp butter, melted
- 2 cup Parmesan cheese, grated
- Salt and black pepper to taste
- 1 tsp smoked paprika

Directions:

1. Preheat on AirFry function to 330 F. Line a baking sheet with parchment paper. Brush the cabbage wedges with butter and season with salt and pepper.
2. Coat the cabbage with the Parmesan cheese and arrange on the baking sheet; sprinkle with paprika. Press Start and cook for 15 minutes. Flip the wedges over and cook for an additional 10 minutes. Serve with yogurt dip.

2.   Cauliflower Mash

Servings: 4
Cooking Time: 6 Minutes
Ingredients:

- 1½ cups water
- ½ teaspoon turmeric
- 1 tablespoon butter
- 1 cauliflower, separated into florets
- Salt and ground black pepper, to taste
- 3 chives, diced

Directions:

1. Put water in the pot immediately, place the cabbage - flower in the basket for cooking, immediately cover the pot and cook 6 minutes to steam.
2. Release the pressure naturally for 2 minutes and quickly release the rest.
3. Transfer the cauliflower to a bowl and mash with a potato masher. Add salt, pepper, butter and saffron, mix, transfer to a blender and mix well. Serve with chives sprinkled on top.
- **Nutrition Info:** Calories: 70, Fat: 5, Fiber: 2, Carbohydrate: 5, Proteins: 2

3.   Bbq Chicken Wings

Servings: 4
Cooking Time: 19 Minutes
Ingredients:

- 2 lbs. chicken wings
- 1 teaspoon olive oil
- 1 teaspoon smoked paprika
- 1 teaspoon garlic powder
- Salt and ground black pepper, as required
- ¼ cup BBQ sauce

Directions:

1. In a large bowl combine chicken wings, smoked paprika, garlic powder, oil, salt, and pepper and mix well.
2. Press "Power Button" of Air Fry Oven and turn the dial to select the "Air Fry" mode.
3. Press the Time button and again turn the dial to set the cooking time to 19 minutes.
4. Now push the Temp button and rotate the dial to set the temperature at 360 degrees F.
5. Press "Start/Pause" button to start.
6. When the unit beeps to show that it is preheated, open the lid.
7. Arrange the chicken wings in "Air Fry Basket" and insert in the oven.
8. After 12 minutes of cooking, flip the wings and coat with barbecue sauce evenly.
9. Serve immediately.
- **Nutrition Info:** Calories 468 Total Fat 18.1 g Saturated Fat 4.8 g Cholesterol 202mg Sodium 409 mg Total Carbs 6.5 g Fiber 0.4 g Sugar 4.3 g Protein 65.8 g

4.   Creamy Broccoli Casserole

Servings: 6
Cooking Time: 30 Minutes
Ingredients:

- 16 oz frozen broccoli florets, defrosted and drained
- 1/2 tsp onion powder
- 10.5 oz can cream of mushroom soup
- 1 cup cheddar cheese, shredded
- 1/3 cup almond milk
- For topping:
- 1 tbsp butter, melted
- 1/2 cup cracker crumbs

Directions:

1. Fit the oven with the rack in position
2. Add all ingredients except topping ingredients into the 1.5-qt casserole dish.
3. In a small bowl, mix together cracker crumbs and melted butter and sprinkle over the casserole dish mixture.
4. Set to bake at 350 F for 35 minutes. After 5 minutes place the casserole dish in the preheated oven.
5. Serve and enjoy.
- **Nutrition Info:** Calories 203 Fat 13.5 g Carbohydrates 11.9 g Sugar 3.6 g Protein 6.9 g Cholesterol 26 mg

5.   Beef Enchilada Dip

Servings: 8
Cooking Time: 10 Minutes
Ingredients:

- 2 lbs. ground beef
- ½ onion, chopped fine
- 2 cloves garlic, chopped fine
- 2 cups enchilada sauce

- 2 cups Monterrey Jack cheese, grated
- 2 tbsp. sour cream

Directions:
1. Place rack in position
2. Heat a large skillet over med-high heat. Add beef and cook until it starts to brown. Drain off fat.
3. Stir in onion and garlic and cook until tender, about 3 minutes. Stir in enchilada sauce and transfer mixture to a small casserole dish and top with cheese.
4. Set oven to convection bake on 325°F for 10 minutes. After 5 minutes, add casserole to the oven and bake 3-5 minutes until cheese is melted and mixture is heated through.
5. Serve warm topped with sour cream.
- **Nutrition Info:** Calories 414, Total Fat 22g, Saturated Fat 10g, Total Carbs 15g, Net Carbs 11g, Protein 39g, Sugar 8g, Fiber 4g, Sodium 1155mg, Potassium 635mg, Phosphorus 385mg

6. Whole Chicken With Bbq Sauce

Servings: 3
Cooking Time: 25 Minutes
Ingredients:
- 1 whole small chicken, cut into pieces
- 1 tsp salt
- 1 tsp smoked paprika
- 1 tsp garlic powder
- 1 cup BBQ sauce

Directions:
1. Coat the chicken with salt, paprika, and garlic. Place the chicken pieces skin-side down in the greased baking tray. Cook in the oven for around 15 minutes at 400 F on Bake function until slightly golden. Remove to a plate and brush with barbecue sauce. Return the chicken to the oven skin-side up and cook for 5 minutes at 340 F. Serve with more barbecue sauce.

7. Spicy Brussels Sprouts(2)

Servings: 4
Cooking Time: 15 Minutes
Ingredients:
- 1 lb Brussels sprouts, cut in half
- 1 1/2 tbsp olive oil
- 1 tbsp gochujang
- 1/2 tsp salt

Directions:
1. Fit the oven with the rack in position 2.
2. In a large mixing bowl, mix together olive oil, gochujang, and salt.
3. Add Brussels sprouts into the bowl and toss until well coated.
4. Transfer Brussels sprouts in air fryer basket then place air fryer basket in baking pan.

5. Place a baking pan on the oven rack. Set to air fry at 360 F for 20 minutes.
6. Serve and enjoy.
- **Nutrition Info:** Calories 98 Fat 5.6 g Carbohydrates 11.2 g Sugar 3 g Protein 4 g Cholesterol 0 mg

8. Garlic Potato Chips

Servings: 3
Cooking Time: 30 Minutes + Marinating Time
Ingredients:
- 3 whole potatoes, cut into thin slices
- ¼ cup olive oil
- 1 tbsp garlic
- ½ cup cream
- 2 tbsp rosemary

Directions:
1. Preheat on Air Fry function to 390 F. In a bowl, add oil, garlic, and salt to form a marinade. Stir in the potatoes. Allow sitting for 30 minutes.
2. Lay the potato slices onto the Air Fryer basket and fit in the baking tray. Cook for 20 minutes. After 10 minutes, give the chips a turn. When readt, sprinkle with rosemary and serve.

9. Bok Choy And Butter Sauce(4)

Servings: 4
Cooking Time: 8 Minutes
Ingredients:
- 2 bok choy heads; trimmed and cut into strips
- 1 tbsp. butter; melted
- 2 tbsp. chicken stock
- 1 tsp. lemon juice
- 1 tbsp. olive oil
- A pinch of salt and black pepper

Directions:
1. In a pan that fits your air fryer, mix all the ingredients, toss, introduce the pan in the air fryer and cook at 380°F for 15 minutes.
2. Divide between plates and serve as a side dish
- **Nutrition Info:** Calories: 141; Fat: 3g; Fiber: 2g; Carbs: 4g; Protein: 3g

10. Lemon-thyme Bruschetta

Servings: 10
Cooking Time: 7 Minutes
Ingredients:
- 1 baguette
- 8 ounces ricotta cheese
- 1 lemon
- Salt
- Freshly cracked black pepper
- Honey
- 8 sprigs fresh thyme

Directions:

1. Start by preheating toaster oven to 425°F.
2. Thinly slice baguette, and zest lemon.
3. Mix ricotta and lemon zest together and season with salt and pepper.
4. Toast the baguette slices for 7 minutes or until they start to brown.
5. Spread ricotta mix over slices.
6. Drizzle with honey and top with thyme, then serve.
- **Nutrition Info:** Calories: 60, Sodium: 71 mg, Dietary Fiber: 0.6 g, Total Fat: 2.0 g, Total Carbs: 7.6 g, Protein: 3.5 g.

11. Salty Carrot Chips

Servings:2
Cooking Time: 20 Minutes
Ingredients:
- 3 large carrots, washed and peeled
- Salt to taste

Directions:
1. Using a mandolin slicer, cut the carrots very thinly heightwise. Season with salt to taste. Place in the frying basket and spray them lightly with cooking spray. Select AirFry function, adjust the temperature to 380 F, and press Start. Cook for 14-16 minutes until crispy.

12. Baked Sweet Potatoes

Servings: 6
Cooking Time: 35 Minutes
Ingredients:
- 4 large sweet potatoes, peel and cut into cubes
- 8 sage leaves
- 1 tsp honey
- 2 tsp vinegar
- 1/2 tsp paprika
- 2 tbsp olive oil
- 1/2 tsp sea salt

Directions:
1. Fit the oven with the rack in position
2. Add sweet potato, oil, sage, and salt in a baking dish and mix well.
3. Set to bake at 375 F for 40 minutes. After 5 minutes place the baking dish in the preheated oven.
4. Transfer roasted sweet potatoes into the large bowl and toss with honey, vinegar, and paprika.
5. Serve and enjoy.
- **Nutrition Info:** Calories 92 Fat 5.1 g Carbohydrates 12 g Sugar 1.2 g Protein 0.8 g Cholesterol 0 mg

13. Herbed Radish Sauté(1)

Servings: 4
Cooking Time: 20 Minutes
Ingredients:

- 2 bunches red radishes; halved
- 2 tbsp. parsley; chopped.
- 2 tbsp. balsamic vinegar
- 1 tbsp. olive oil
- Salt and black pepper to taste.

Directions:
1. Take a bowl and mix the radishes with the remaining ingredients except the parsley, toss and put them in your air fryer's basket.
2. Cook at 400°F for 15 minutes, divide between plates, sprinkle the parsley on top and serve as a side dish
- **Nutrition Info:** Calories: 180; Fat: 4g; Fiber: 2g; Carbs: 3g; Protein: 5g

14. Mexican Rice

Servings: 8
Cooking Time: 4 Minutes
Ingredients:
- ½ cup chopped fresh cilantro
- 1 cup of long grain rice
- 1 cup of vegetable broth
- ¼ cup of hot green sauce
- ½ avocado, salt, peeled and chopped
- Salt and freshly ground black pepper, to taste

Directions:
1. Put the rice in the instant pot, add the broth, stir, cover and cook for 4 minutes.
2. Release the pressure naturally for 10 minutes, uncover the Instant Pot, fluff it with a fork and transfer it to a bowl.
3. In a food processor, mix the avocado with the hot sauce and the cilantro and mash until smooth.
4. Pour over the rice, mix well, add salt and pepper, stir again, divide between the plates and serve.
- **Nutrition Info:** Calories: 100, Fat: 2, Fiber: 1, Carbohydrate: 18, Proteins: 2

15. Chicken Nuggets

Servings: 6
Cooking Time: 10 Minutes
Ingredients:
- 2 large chicken breasts, cut into 1-inch cubes
- 1 cup breadcrumbs
- 1/3 tablespoon Parmesan cheese, shredded
- 1 teaspoon onion powder
- ¼ teaspoon smoked paprika
- Salt and ground black pepper, as required

Directions:
1. In a large resealable bag, add all the ingredients.
2. Seal the bag and shake well to coat completely.
3. Press "Power Button" of Air Fry Oven and turn the dial to select the "Air Fry" mode.

4. Press the Time button and again turn the dial to set the cooking time to 10 minutes.
5. Now push the Temp button and rotate the dial to set the temperature at 400 degrees F.
6. Press "Start/Pause" button to start.
7. When the unit beeps to show that it is preheated, open the lid.
8. Arrange the nuggets in "Air Fry Basket" and insert in the oven.
9. Serve warm.
- **Nutrition Info:** Calories 218 Total Fat 6.6 g Saturated Fat 1.8 g Cholesterol 67 mg Sodium 229 mg Total Carbs 13.3 g Fiber 0.9 g Sugar 1.3 g Protein 24.4 g

16. Bok Choy Crisps

Servings: 2
Cooking Time: 10 Minutes
Ingredients:
- 2 tbsp olive oil
- 4 cups packed bok choy
- 1 tsp vegan seasoning
- 1 tbsp yeast flakes
- Sea salt, to taste

Directions:
1. In a bowl, mix oil, bok choy, yeast, and vegan seasoning. Dump the coated kale in the Air fryer basket. Set the temperature of your toaster oven to 360 F on Air Fry function and cook for 5 minutes. Shake after 3 minutes. Serve sprinkled with sea salt.

17. Rosemary Potato Chips

Servings:4
Cooking Time: 30 Minutes
Ingredients:
- 1 pound potatoes, cut into thin slices
- ¼ cup olive oil
- 1 tbsp garlic puree
- ½ cup heavy cream
- 2 tbsp fresh rosemary, chopped

Directions:
1. Preheat on AirFry function to 390 F. In a bowl, mix oil, garlic puree, and salt. Add in the potato slices and toss to coat. Lay the potato slices onto the frying basket and place in the oven. Press Start and cook for 20-25 minutes. Sprinkle with rosemary and serve.

18. Cilantro Roasted Cauliflower(2)

Servings: 4
Cooking Time: 20 Minutes
Ingredients:
- 2 cups chopped cauliflower florets
- 1 medium lime
- 2 tbsp. chopped cilantro
- 2 tbsp. coconut oil; melted
- ½ tsp. garlic powder.

- 2 tsp. chili powder
Directions:
1. Take a large bowl, toss cauliflower with coconut oil. Sprinkle with chili powder and garlic powder. Place seasoned cauliflower into the air fryer basket
2. Adjust the temperature to 350 Degrees F and set the timer for 7 minutes
3. Cauliflower will be tender and begin to turn golden at the edges. Place into serving bowl. Cut the lime into quarters and squeeze juice over cauliflower. Garnish with cilantro.
- **Nutrition Info:** Calories: 73; Protein: 1.1g; Fiber: 1.1g; Fat: 6.5g; Carbs: 3.3g

19. Salty Baked Almonds

Servings: 4
Cooking Time: 25 Minutes
Ingredients:
- 1 cup raw almonds
- 1 egg white, beaten
- ½ teaspoon coarse sea salt

Directions:
1. Spread the almonds in the baking pan in an even layer.
2. Slide the baking pan into Rack Position 1, select Convection Bake, set temperature to 350ºF (180ºC) and set time to 20 minutes.
3. When cooking is complete, the almonds should be lightly browned and fragrant. Remove from the oven.
4. Coat the almonds with the egg white and sprinkle with the salt. Return the pan to the oven.
5. Slide the baking pan into Rack Position 1, select Convection Bake, set temperature to 350ºF (180ºC) and set time to 5 minutes.
6. When cooking is complete, the almonds should be dried. Cool completely before serving.

20. Simple Chicken Breasts

Servings: 4
Cooking Time: 30 Minutes
Ingredients:
- 4 boneless, skinless chicken breasts
- 1 tsp salt and black pepper
- 1 tsp garlic powder

Directions:
1. Spray the breasts and the Air Fryer basket with cooking spray. Rub chicken with salt, garlic powder, and black pepper. Arrange the breasts on the basket. Fit in the baking pan and cook for 20 minutes at 360 F on Bake function until nice and crispy. Serve warm.

21. Egg Roll Wrapped With Cabbage & Prawns

Servings: 4
Cooking Time: 50 Minutes
Ingredients:
- 2 tbsp vegetable oil
- 1-inch piece fresh ginger, grated
- 1 tbsp minced garlic
- 1 carrot, cut into strips
- ¼ cup chicken broth
- 2 tbsp reduced-sodium soy sauce
- 1 tbsp sugar
- 1 cup shredded Napa cabbage
- 1 tbsp sesame oil
- 8 cooked prawns, chopped
- 1 egg
- 8 egg roll wrappers

Directions:
1. Heat vegetable oil in a skillet over medium heat and sauté ginger and garlic for 40 seconds until fragrant. Stir in carrot and cook for another 2 minutes. Pour in chicken broth, soy sauce, and sugar and bring to a boil. Add in cabbage and let simmer until softened, about 4 minutes. Remove skillet from the heat and stir in sesame oil. Let cool for 15 minutes.
2. Strain cabbage mixture and fold in prawns. Whisk the egg in a small bowl. Fill each egg roll wrapper with prawn mixture, arranging the mixture just below the center of the wrapper. Fold the bottom part over the filling and tuck under. Fold in both sides and tightly roll-up.
3. Use the whisked egg to seal the wrapper. Repeat until all egg rolls are ready. Place the rolls into a greased frying basket, spray them with oil and fit in the baking tray. Cook for 12 minutes at 370 F on Air Fry function, turning once halfway through. Serve.

22. French-style Fries

Servings: 4
Cooking Time: 35 Minutes
Ingredients:
- 4 russet potatoes, cut into 3-inch pieces
- 2 tbsp olive oil
- Salt and black pepper to taste

Directions:
1. Preheat on Air Fry function to 360 F. Drizzle the potatoes with olive oil and toss to coat. Place the potatoes in the Air Fryer basket and fit in the baking tray. Cook for 20-25 minutes. Sprinkle with salt and pepper and to serve.

23. Homemade Tortilla Chips

Servings: 4

Cooking Time: 55 Minutes
Ingredients:
- 1 cup flour
- Salt and black pepper to taste
- 1 tbsp golden flaxseed meal
- 2 cups shredded Cheddar cheese

Directions:
1. Melt cheddar cheese in the microwave for 1 minute. Add flour, salt, flaxseed meal, and pepper. Mix well with a fork. On a board, place the dough and knead it with hands while warm until the ingredients are well combined. Divide the dough into 2 and with a rolling pin, roll them out flat into 2 rectangles. Use a pastry cutter to cut out triangle-shaped pieces.
2. Line them in one layer on the Air Fryer basket and spray with cooking spray. Fit in the baking tray and cook for 10 minutes on Air Fry function at 400 F. Serve with a cheese dip.

24. Simple Zucchini Crisps

Servings:4
Cooking Time: 14 Minutes
Ingredients:
- 2 zucchini, sliced into ¼- to ½-inch-thick rounds (about 2 cups)
- ¼ teaspoon garlic granules
- ⅛ teaspoon sea salt
- Freshly ground black pepper, to taste (optional)
- Cooking spray

Directions:
1. Spritz the air fryer basket with cooking spray.
2. Put the zucchini rounds in the basket, spreading them out as much as possible. Top with a sprinkle of garlic granules, sea salt, and black pepper (if desired). Spritz the zucchini rounds with cooking spray.
3. Put the air fryer basket on the baking pan and slide into Rack Position 2, select Roast, set temperature to 392ºF (200ºC), and set time to 14 minutes.
4. Flip the zucchini rounds halfway through.
5. When cooking is complete, the zucchini rounds should be crisp-tender. Remove from the oven. Let them rest for 5 minutes and serve.

25. Tasty Saffron Risotto

Servings: 10
Cooking Time: 10 Minutes
Ingredients:
- 2 tablespoons extra virgin olive oil
- ½ cup onion, peeled and chopped
- 2 tablespoons hot milk
- ½ teaspoon saffron threads, crushed

- 1½ cups Arborio rice
- 3½ cups vegetable stock
- Salt, to taste
- 1 cinnamon stick
- ⅓ cup dried currants
- 1 tablespoon honey
- ⅓ cup almonds, chopped

Directions:
1. In a bowl, mix the milk with the saffron, mix and set aside. Put the Instant Pot in the sauté mode, add the oil and heat.
2. Add the onion, mix and cook for 5 minutes. Add rice, broth, saffron and milk, honey, salt, almonds, cinnamon stick and blackcurrant. Stir, cover the Instant Pot and cook over rice for 5 minutes.
3. Relieve the pressure, add rice to the rice, discard the cinnamon stick, divide it between the plates and serve.
- **Nutrition Info:** Calories: 260, Fat: 7, Fiber: 2, Carbohydrate: 41, Sugar: 1.5, Proteins: 3.9

26. Marinara Chicken Breasts

Servings: 2
Cooking Time: 20 Minutes
Ingredients:
- 2 chicken breasts, ½ inch thick
- 1 egg, beaten
- ½ cup breadcrumbs
- A pinch of salt and black pepper
- 2 tbsp marinara sauce
- 2 tbsp Grana Padano cheese, grated
- 2 slices mozzarella cheese

Directions:
1. Dip the breasts into the egg, then into the crumbs, and arrange on the Air fryer baking sheet. Cook for 6-8 minutes at 400 F on Air Fry function. Turn over and drizzle with marinara sauce, Grana Padano and mozzarella cheeses. Cook for 5 more minutes. Serve.

27. Mustard Cheddar Twists

Servings:4
Cooking Time: 45 Minutes
Ingredients:
- 2 cups cauliflower florets, steamed
- 1 egg
- 3 ½ oz oats
- 1 red onion, diced
- 1 tsp mustard
- 5 oz cheddar cheese
- Salt and black pepper to taste

Directions:
1. Place the oats in a food processor and pulse until they resemble breadcrumbs. Place the steamed florets in a cheesecloth and squeeze out the excess liquid.

2. Transfer to a large bowl. Add in the rest of the ingredients. Mix well. Take a little bit of the mixture and twist it into a straw.
3. Place on a lined baking tray and repeat with the rest of the mixture. Select AirFry function, adjust the temperature to 360 F, and press Start. Cook for 10 minutes, turn over and cook for an additional 10 minutes.

28. Bread Sticks

Servings: 6
Cooking Time: 6 Minutes
Ingredients:
- 1 egg 1/8 teaspoon ground cinnamon
- Pinch of ground nutmeg Pinch of ground cloves
- Salt, to taste
- 2 bread slices
- 1 tablespoon butter, softened
- Nonstick cooking spray
- 1 tablespoon icing sugar

Directions:
1. In a bowl, add the eggs, cinnamon, nutmeg, cloves and salt and beat until well combined.
2. Spread the butter over both sides of the slices evenly.
3. Cut each bread slice into strips.
4. Dip bread strips into egg mixture evenly.
5. Press "Power Button" of Air Fry Oven and turn the dial to select the "Air Fry" mode.
6. Press the Time button and again turn the dial to set the cooking time to 6 minutes.
7. Now push the Temp button and rotate the dial to set the temperature at 355 degrees F.
8. Press "Start/Pause" button to start.
9. When the unit beeps to show that it is preheated, open the lid.
10. Arrange the breadsticks in "Air Fry Basket" and insert in the oven.
11. After 2 minutes of cooking, spray the both sides of the bread strips with cooking spray.
12. Serve immediately with the topping of icing sugar.
- **Nutrition Info:** Calories 41 Total Fat 2.8 g Saturated Fat 1.5 g Cholesterol 32 mg Sodium 72 mg Total Carbs 3 g Fiber 0.1 g Sugar 1.5 g Protein 1.2 g

29. French Beans With Shallots & Almonds

Servings:4
Cooking Time: 25 Minutes
Ingredients:
- 1 ½ pounds French beans
- 2 shallots, chopped
- 2 tbsp olive oil
- ½ cup almonds, toasted

Directions:

1. Preheat on AirFry function to 400 F. Blanch the beans in boiling water for 5-6 minutes. Drain and mix with oil and shallots in a baking sheet. Cook for 10 minutes. Serve with almonds.

30. Roasted Brussels Sprouts

Servings: 6
Cooking Time: 30 Minutes
Ingredients:
- 1-1/2 pounds Brussels sprouts, ends trimmed and yellow leaves removed
- 3 tablespoons olive oil
- 1 teaspoon salt
- 1/2 teaspoon black pepper

Directions:
1. Start by preheating toaster oven to 400°F.
2. Toss Brussels sprouts in a large bowl, drizzle with olive oil, sprinkle with salt and pepper, then toss.
3. Roast for 30 minutes.
- **Nutrition Info:** Calories: 109, Sodium: 416 mg, Dietary Fiber: 4.3 g, Total Fat: 7.4 g, Total Carbs: 10.4 g, Protein: 3.9 g.

31. Bacon & Potato Salad With Mayonnaise

Servings: 6
Cooking Time: 10 Minutes
Ingredients:
- 4 lb boiled and cubed potatoes
- 15 bacon slices, chopped
- 2 cups shredded cheddar cheese
- 15 oz sour cream
- 2 tbsp mayonnaise
- 1 tsp salt
- 1 tsp pepper
- 1 tsp dried herbs, any

Directions:
1. Preheat on Air Fry function to 350 F. Combine the potatoes, bacon, salt, pepper, and herbs in a large bowl. Transfer to the baking pan. Cook for about 7 minutes. Remove and stir in sour cream and mayonnaise and serve.

32. Parsnip And Onion

Servings: 4
Cooking Time: 30 Minutes
Ingredients:
- Salt and ground black pepper, to taste
- 1½ cups beef stock
- 2½ pounds parsnips, peeled and chopped
- 4 tablespoons vegetable shortening
- 1 yellow onion, peeled and sliced thin
- 1 thyme sprig

Directions:
1. Put the Instant Pot in sauté mode, add 3 tablespoons of fat and heat. Add the parsnips, mix and cook for 15 minutes. Add broth and thyme, stir, cover and cook for 3 minutes in Manual setting.
2. Relieve the pressure, transfer the parsnip mixture to the blender, add salt and pepper to taste and beat. Put the Instant Pot in the sauté mode, add the rest of the fat and heat it. Add the onion, mix and cook for 10 minutes.
3. Transfer the parsnips to the dishes, garnish with sautéed onions and serve.
- **Nutrition Info:** Calories: 130, Fat: 2, Fiber: 3, Carbohydrate: 6.7, Proteins: 10.1

33. Lemony Broccoli

Servings: 6
Cooking Time: 15 Minutes
Ingredients:
- Salt and ground black pepper, to taste
- 5 lemon slices
- 1 head of broccoli, separated into florets
- 1 cup water

Directions:
1. Pour the water into the Instant Pot. Season the broccoli with salt and pepper to taste and add them to the instant pot, add the lemon slices and mix gently.
2. Cover the pan instantly and cook for 15 minutes. Relieve the pressure, divide the broccoli between the plates and serve.
- **Nutrition Info:** Calories: 55, Fat: 0.5, Fiber: 5, Carbohydrate: 11, Proteins: 3.4

34. Easy Home Fries(2)

Servings: 4
Cooking Time: 20 Minutes
Ingredients:
- ½ medium white onion; peeled and diced
- 1 medium green bell pepper; seeded and diced
- 1 medium jicama; peeled.
- 1 tbsp. coconut oil; melted
- ½ tsp. pink Himalayan salt
- ¼ tsp. ground black pepper

Directions:
1. Cut jicama into 1-inch cubes. Place into a large bowl and toss with coconut oil until coated. Sprinkle with pepper and salt. Place into the air fryer basket with peppers and onion.
2. Adjust the temperature to 400 Degrees F and set the timer for 10 minutes. Shake two or three times during cooking. Jicama will be tender and dark around edges. Serve immediately.
- **Nutrition Info:** Calories: 97; Protein: 1.5g; Fiber: 8.0g; Fat: 3.3g; Carbs: 15.8g

35. Air Fry Broccoli Florets

Servings: 2
Cooking Time: 10 Minutes
Ingredients:
- 1 lb broccoli florets
- 1/2 tsp chili powder
- 1/4 tsp turmeric
- 2 tbsp plain yogurt
- 1 tbsp chickpea flour
- 1/2 tsp salt

Directions:
1. Fit the oven with the rack in position 2.
2. Add all ingredients to the bowl and toss well.
3. Place marinated broccoli in a refrigerator for 15 minutes.
4. Place marinated broccoli in an air fryer basket then places an air fryer basket in a baking pan.
5. Place a baking pan on the oven rack. Set to air fry at 390 F for 10 minutes.
6. Serve and enjoy.
- **Nutrition Info:** Calories 114 Fat 1.5 g Carbohydrates 20.5 g Sugar 5.7 g Protein 8.5 g Cholesterol 1 mg

36. Creamy Fennel(1)

Servings: 4
Cooking Time: 20 Minutes
Ingredients:
- 2 big fennel bulbs; sliced
- ½ cup coconut cream
- 2 tbsp. butter; melted
- Salt and black pepper to taste.

Directions:
1. In a pan that fits the air fryer, combine all the ingredients, toss, introduce in the machine and cook at 370°F for 12 minutes
2. Divide between plates and serve as a side dish.
- **Nutrition Info:** Calories: 151; Fat: 3g; Fiber: 2g; Carbs: 4g; Protein: 6g

37. Black Beans

Servings: 8
Cooking Time: 5 Minutes
Ingredients:
- ⅔ cup saltwater, to taste
- 1 cup of black beans, soaked overnight, drained and washed
- 1 piece of dried seaweed
- 1 tablespoon of coriander seed tea
- ½ teaspoon of cumin seeds
- 2 garlic cloves, peeled and chopped

Directions:
1. In the Instant Pot, mix the beans with the seaweed, water, garlic, coriander and cumin. Stir, cover the Instant Pot and cook for 5 minutes in the Bean / Chili setting.

2. Relieve the pressure, remove the seaweed and coriander seeds, divide the beans between the dishes, season with salt and serve.
- **Nutrition Info:** Calories: 330, Fat: 1, Fiber: 16, Carbohydrate: 23, Proteins: 21

38. Crunchy Mozzarella Sticks With Sweet Thai Sauce

Servings:4
Cooking Time: 20 Minutes
Ingredients:
- 12 mozzarella string cheese
- 2 cups breadcrumbs
- 3 eggs
- 1 cup sweet Thai sauce
- 4 tbsp skimmed milk

Directions:
1. Pour the crumbs in a bowl. Crack the eggs into another bowl and beat with the milk. One after the other, dip cheese sticks in the egg mixture, in the crumbs, then egg mixture again and then in the crumbs again. Place the coated cheese sticks on a cookie sheet and freeze for 1 hour.
2. Preheat on AirFry function to 380 F. Arrange the sticks in the frying basket without overcrowding. Press Start and cook for 8 minutes until brown. Serve with sweet Thai sauce.

39. Cod Nuggets

Servings: 5
Cooking Time: 8 Minutes
Ingredients:
- 1 cup all-purpose flour
- 2 eggs
- ¾ cup breadcrumbs
- Pinch of salt
- 2 tablespoons olive oil
- 1 lb. cod, cut into 1x2½-inch strips

Directions:
1. In a shallow dish, place the flour.
2. Crack the eggs in a second dish and beat well.
3. In a third dish, mix together the breadcrumbs, salt, and oil.
4. Coat the nuggets with flour, then dip into beaten eggs and finally, coat with the breadcrumbs.
5. Press "Power Button" of Air Fry Oven and turn the dial to select the "Air Fry" mode.
6. Press the Time button and again turn the dial to set the cooking time to 8 minutes.
7. Now push the Temp button and rotate the dial to set the temperature at 390 degrees F.
8. Press "Start/Pause" button to start.
9. When the unit beeps to show that it is preheated, open the lid.

10. Arrange the nuggets in "Air Fry Basket" and insert in the oven.
11. Serve warm.
- **Nutrition Info:** Calories 323 Total Fat 9.2 g Saturated Fat 1.7 g Cholesterol 115 mg Sodium 245 mg Total Carbs 30.9 g Fiber 1.4 g Sugar 1.2 g Protein 27.7 g

40. Chickpeas With Rosemary & Sage

Servings: 4
Cooking Time: 20 Minutes
Ingredients:
- 2 (14.5-ounce) cans chickpeas, rinsed
- 2 tbsp olive oil
- 1 tsp dried rosemary
- ½ tsp dried thyme
- ¼ tsp dried sage
- ¼ tsp salt

Directions:
1. In a bowl, mix together chickpeas, oil, rosemary, thyme, sage, and salt. Transfer them to the Air Fryer baking dish and spread in an even layer. Cook for 15 minutes at 380 F on Bake function, shaking once halfway through cooking. Serve.

41. Spicy Pumpkin-ham Fritters

Servings: 4
Cooking Time: 10 Minutes
Ingredients:
- 1 oz ham, chopped
- 1 cup dry pancake mix
- 1 egg
- 2 tbsp canned puree pumpkin
- 1 oz cheddar, shredded
- ½ tsp chili powder
- 3 tbsp of flour
- 1 oz beer
- 2 tbsp scallions, chopped

Directions:
1. Preheat on Air Fry function to 370 F. In a bowl, combine the pancake mix and chili powder. Mix in the egg, puree pumpkin, beer, shredded cheddar, ham and scallions. Form balls and roll them in the flour.
2. Arrange the balls into the basket and fit in the baking tray. Cook for 8 minutes. Drain on paper towel before serving.

42. Baked Broccoli

Servings: 6
Cooking Time: 20 Minutes
Ingredients:
- 4 cups broccoli florets
- 3 tbsp olive oil
- 1/2 tsp pepper
- 1/2 tsp garlic powder
- 1 tsp Italian seasoning
- 1 tsp salt

Directions:
1. Fit the oven with the rack in position
2. Spread broccoli in baking pan and drizzle with oil and season with garlic powder, Italian seasoning, pepper, and salt.
3. Set to bake at 400 F for 25 minutes. After 5 minutes place the baking pan in the preheated oven.
4. Serve and enjoy.
- **Nutrition Info:** Calories 84 Fat 7.4 g Carbohydrates 4.4 g Sugar 1.2 g Protein 1.8 g Cholesterol 1 mg

43. Rosemary Roasted Potatoes

Servings:4
Cooking Time: 20 Minutes
Ingredients:
- 1½ pounds (680 g) small red potatoes, cut into 1-inch cubes
- 2 tablespoons olive oil
- 2 tablespoons minced fresh rosemary
- 1 tablespoon minced garlic
- 1 teaspoon salt, plus additional as needed
- ½ teaspoon freshly ground black pepper, plus additional as needed

Directions:
1. Toss the potato cubes with the olive oil, rosemary, garlic, salt, and pepper in a large bowl until thoroughly coated.
2. Arrange the potato cubes in the air fryer basket in a single layer.
3. Put the air fryer basket on the baking pan and slide into Rack Position 2, select Roast, set temperature to 400ºF (205ºC), and set time to 20 minutes.
4. Stir the potatoes a few times during cooking for even cooking.
5. When cooking is complete, the potatoes should be tender. Remove from the oven to a plate. Taste and add additional salt and pepper as needed.

44. Goat Cheese & Pancetta Bombs

Servings: 10
Cooking Time: 25 Minutes
Ingredients:
- 16 oz soft goat cheese
- 2 tbsp fresh rosemary, finely chopped
- 1 cup almonds, chopped into small pieces
- Salt and black pepper
- 15 dried plums, chopped
- 15 pancetta slices

Directions:
1. Line the Air Fryer tray with parchment paper. In a bowl, add goat cheese, rosemary, almonds, salt, pepper, and plums; stir well. Roll into balls and wrap with pancetta slices. Arrange the bombs on the tray and cook for 10 minutes at 400 F. Let cool before serving.

45. Healthy Barley Bread

Servings: 16
Cooking Time: 40 Minutes
Ingredients:
- 2 eggs
- 1/2 tsp baking soda
- 2 tbsp baking powder
- 3 cups barley flour
- 3 tbsp honey
- 1/3 cup olive oil
- 1 1/2 cups buttermilk
- 1 1/4 tsp salt

Directions:
1. Fit the oven with the rack in position
2. In a large bowl, mix together flour, baking powder, baking soda, and salt.
3. In a separate bowl, whisk eggs with honey, oil, and buttermilk.
4. Add egg mixture into the flour mixture and stir until just combined.
5. Pour batter into the greased loaf pan.
6. Set to bake at 350 F for 40 minutes. After 5 minutes place the loaf pan in the preheated oven.
7. Slice and serve.
- **Nutrition Info:** Calories 163 Fat 5.4 g Carbohydrates 26 g Sugar 4.6 g Protein 4.4 g Cholesterol 21 mg

46. Classic French Fries

Servings:6
Cooking Time: 35 Minutes
Ingredients:
- 6 medium russet potatoes
- 2 tbsp olive oil
- Salt to taste

Directions:
1. Preheat on AirFry function to 360 F. Cut potatoes into ¼ by 3-inch pieces. Drizzle oil on the potatoes and toss to coat. Place the potatoes in the frying basket and place in the oven. Press Start and cook for 20-25 minutes. Season with salt and pepper and serve.

47. Browned Ricotta With Capers And Lemon

Servings: 4 To 6
Cooking Time: 8 Minutes
Ingredients:
- 1½ cups whole milk ricotta cheese
- 2 tablespoons extra-virgin olive oil
- 2 tablespoons capers, rinsed
- Zest of 1 lemon, plus more for garnish
- 1 teaspoon finely chopped fresh rosemary
- Pinch crushed red pepper flakes
- Salt and freshly ground black pepper, to taste
- 1 tablespoon grated Parmesan cheese
- In a mixing bowl, stir together the ricotta cheese, olive oil, capers, lemon zest, rosemary, red pepper flakes, salt, and pepper until well combined.

Directions:
1. Spread the mixture evenly in the baking pan.
2. Slide the baking pan into Rack Position 2, select Air Fry, set temperature to 380ºF (193ºC), and set time to 8 minutes.
3. When cooking is complete, the top should be nicely browned. Remove from the oven and top with a sprinkle of grated Parmesan cheese. Garnish with the lemon zest and serve warm.

48. Cheese Scones With Chives

Servings:6
Cooking Time: 25 Minutes
Ingredients:
- 1 cup flour
- Salt and black pepper to taste
- 3 tbsp butter
- 1 tsp fresh chives, chopped
- 1 whole egg
- 1 tbsp milk
- 1 cup cheddar cheese, shredded

Directions:
1. Preheat on AirFry function to 340 F. In a bowl, mix butter, flour, cheddar cheese, chives, milk, and egg to get a sticky dough. Dust a flat surface with flour. Roll the dough into small balls. Place the balls in the frying basket and place in the oven. Press Start and cook for 20 minutes.

49. Apple & Cinnamon Chips

Servings:2
Cooking Time: 25 Minutes
Ingredients:
- 1 tsp sugar
- 1 tsp salt
- 1 whole apple, sliced
- ½ tsp cinnamon
- Confectioners' sugar for serving

Directions:
1. Preheat your oven to 400 F on Bake function. In a bowl, mix cinnamon, salt, and sugar. Add in the apple slices and toss to coat. Transfer to a greased baking tray. Press Start and set the time to 10 minutes. When ready, dust with sugar and serve chilled.

50. Cajun Shrimp

Servings:3
Cooking Time: 15 Minutes
Ingredients:
- ½ pound shrimp, deveined

- ½ tsp Cajun seasoning
- Salt and black pepper to taste
- 1 tbsp olive oil

Directions:
1. Preheat on AirFry function to 390 F. In a bowl, make the marinade by mixing salt, pepper, olive oil, and seasoning. Add in the shrimp and toss to coat. Transfer the prepared shrimp to the frying basket and place in the oven. Press Start and cook for 10-12 minutes.

51. Cinnamon Mixed Nuts

Servings:4
Cooking Time: 25 Minutes
Ingredients:
- ½ cup pecans
- ½ cup walnuts
- ½ cup almonds
- A pinch cayenne pepper
- 2 tbsp sugar
- 2 tbsp egg whites
- 2 tsp cinnamon

Directions:
1. In a bowl, mix the cayenne pepper, sugar, and cinnamon; set aside. In another bowl, beat the egg whites and mix in the pecans, walnuts,and almonds. Add in the spice mixture and stir well.
2. Lightly grease the frying basket with baking tray. Pour in the nuts mixture. Select Toast function, adjust the temperature to 360 F, and press Start. Toast for 10 minutes, then stir the nuts using a wooden vessel, and toast further for 10 minutes. Pour the nuts in a bowl and let cool.

52. Potato Casserole

Servings: 4
Cooking Time: 10 Minutes
Ingredients:
- ¼ cup coconut milk
- 3 pounds sweet potatoes, scrubbed
- 1 cup water
- ⅓ cup brown sugar
- 1 teaspoon ground cinnamon
- ¼ teaspoon allspice
- Salt, to taste
- ½ teaspoon fresh nutmeg, ground
- 2 tablespoons coconut flour
- For the topping:
- ¼ cup pecans, soaked, drained, and ground
- ½ cup walnuts, soaked, drained, and ground
- ¼ cup shredded coconut
- 1 tablespoon chia seeds
- 1 teaspoon ground cinnamon
- 5 tablespoons salted butter
- ½ cup almond flour
- ¼ cup brown sugar

- Salt, to taste

Directions:
1. Chop the potatoes with a fork, place them in the steam basket of the Instant Pot, add the water to the Instant Pot, cover and cook for 20 minutes in manual configuration.
2. In a bowl, mix the almond flour with walnuts, walnuts, coconut, ¼ cup brown sugar, chia seeds, 1 teaspoon of cinnamon, a pinch of salt and butter and mix everything.
3. Relieve the pressure of the Instant Pot naturally, take the potatoes and peel them and add ½ cup of water to the Instant Pot.
4. Chop the potatoes and place them in a pan. Add the disintegrated mixture, mix everything, distribute evenly on the plate, cover, place in the steam basket, cover the Instant Pot again and cook for 10 minutes in manual configuration.
5. Relieve the pressure, remove the dish from the Instant Pot, uncover it, let it cool briefly, cut and serve.
- **Nutrition Info:** Calories: 150, Fat: 9, Fiber: 3, Carbohydrate: 25, Sugar: 10, Proteins: 4

53. Parmesan Dill Pickles

Servings:4
Cooking Time: 20 Minutes
Ingredients:
- 3 cups dill pickles, sliced, drained
- 2 eggs
- 2 tsp water
- 1 cup grated Parmesan cheese
- 1 ½ cups breadcrumbs, smooth
- Black pepper to taste

Directions:
1. Add the breadcrumbs and black pepper to a bowl and mix well. In another bowl, crack the eggs and beat with the water. Add the Parmesan cheese to third bowl.
2. Preheat on AirFry function to 400 F. Dredge the pickle slices in the egg mixture, then in breadcrumbs, and finally in the Parmesan cheese. Place them in the fryer oven. Press Start.AirFry for 8-10 minutes until crispy. Serve with cheese dip.

54. Balsamic-glazed Carrots

Servings:3
Cooking Time: 18 Minutes
Ingredients:
- 3 medium-size carrots, cut into 2-inch × ½-inch sticks
- 1 tablespoon orange juice
- 2 teaspoons balsamic vinegar
- 1 teaspoon maple syrup
- 1 teaspoon avocado oil
- ½ teaspoon dried rosemary
- ¼ teaspoon sea salt

- ¼ teaspoon lemon zest

Directions:
1. Put the carrots in the baking pan and sprinkle with the orange juice, balsamic vinegar, maple syrup, avocado oil, rosemary, sea salt, finished by the lemon zest. Toss well.
2. Slide the baking pan into Rack Position 2, select Roast, set temperature to 392ºF (200ºC), and set time to 18 minutes.
3. Stir the carrots several times during the cooking process.
4. When cooking is complete, the carrots should be nicely glazed and tender. Remove from the oven and serve hot.

55. Buffalo Quesadillas

Servings: 8
Cooking Time: 5 Minutes
Ingredients:
- Nonstick cooking spray
- 2 cups chicken, cooked & chopped fine
- ½ cup Buffalo wing sauce
- 2 cups Monterey Jack cheese, grated
- ½ cup green onions, sliced thin
- 8 flour tortillas, 8-inch diameter
- ¼ cup blue cheese dressing

Directions:
1. Lightly spray the baking pan with cooking spray.
2. In a medium bowl, add chicken and wing sauce and toss to coat.
3. Place tortillas, one at a time on work surface. Spread ¼ of the chicken mixture over tortilla and sprinkle with cheese and onion. Top with a second tortilla and place on the baking pan.
4. Set oven to broil on 400°F for 8 minutes. After 5 minutes place baking pan in position 2. Cook quesadillas 2-3 minutes per side until toasted and cheese has melted. Repeat with remaining ingredients.
5. Cut quesadillas in wedges and serve with blue cheese dressing or other dipping sauce.
- **Nutrition Info:** Calories 376, Total Fat 20g, Saturated Fat 8g, Total Carbs 27g, Net Carbs 26g, Protein 22g, Sugar 2g, Fiber 2g, Sodium 685mg, Potassium 201mg, Phosphorus 301mg

56. Lime Pumpkin Wedges

Servings:4
Cooking Time: 30 Minutes
Ingredients:
- 1 lb pumpkin, cut into wedges
- 1 tbsp paprika
- 1 whole lime, squeezed
- 1 cup paleo dressing
- 1 tbsp balsamic vinegar
- Salt and black pepper to taste
- 1 tsp turmeric

Directions:
1. Preheat on AirFry function to 360 F. Add the pumpkin wedges in a baking tray and press Start. Cook for 20 minutes. In a bowl, mix lime juice, vinegar, turmeric, salt, pepper, and paprika. Pour the mixture over pumpkin and cook for 5 more minutes. Serve.

57. Broiled Prosciutto-wrapped Pears

Servings: 8
Cooking Time: 6 Minutes
Ingredients:
- 2 large, ripe Anjou pears
- 4 thin slices Parma prosciutto
- 2 teaspoons aged balsamic vinegar

Directions:
1. Peel the pears. Slice into 8 wedges and cut out the core from each wedge.
2. Cut the prosciutto into 8 long strips. Wrap each pear wedge with a strip of prosciutto. Place the wrapped pears in the air fryer basket.
3. Put the air fryer basket on the baking pan and slide into Rack Position 2, select Convection Broil, set temperature to High and set time to 6 minutes.
4. After 2 or 3 minutes, check the pears. The pears should be turned over if the prosciutto is beginning to crisp up and brown. Return to the oven and continue cooking.
5. When cooking is complete, remove from the oven. Drizzle the pears with the balsamic vinegar and serve warm.

BREAKFAST RECIPES

58. Eggs In A Hole

Servings: 1
Cooking Time: 7 Minutes
Ingredients:
- 2 eggs
- 2 slices of bread
- 2 tsp butter
- Pepper and salt to taste

Directions:
1. Using a jar punch two holes in the middle of your bread slices. This is the area where you will place your eggs.
2. Preheat your fryer to 330-degree Fahrenheit for about 5 minutes. Spread a tablespoon of butter into the pan and then add bread from the slices.
3. Crack the eggs and place them at the center of the bread slices and lightly season them with salt and pepper.
4. Take out your slices and rebutter the pan with the remaining butter and fry the other part for 3 minutes.
5. Serve while hot.
- **Nutrition Info:** Calories 787 Fat 51g, Carbohydrates 60g, Proteins 22g.

59. Corn & Chorizo Frittata

Servings: 2
Cooking Time: 20 Minutes
Ingredients:
- 4 eggs
- 1 large potato, boiled and cubed
- ½ cup frozen corn
- ½ cup feta cheese, crumbled
- 1 tbsp fresh parsley, chopped
- ½ chorizo, sliced
- 1 tbsp olive oil
- Salt and black pepper to taste

Directions:
1. Preheat on Air Fry function to 375 F. Heat the olive oil in a skillet over medium heat and cook the chorizo cook for 3 minutes. Beat the eggs with salt and pepper in a bowl. Stir in chorizo and the remaining ingredients. Pour the mixture into the baking pan of oven and cook for 10-15 minutes on Bake function. Serve sliced.

60. Zucchini Squash Pita Sandwiches Recipe

Servings:x
Cooking Time:x
Ingredients:
- 1 small Zucchini Squash, (5-6 ounces)
- Salt and Pepper, to taste
- 2 Whole Wheat Pitas
- 1/2 cup Hummus
- 1 1/2 cups Fresh Spinach, (2 handfuls)
- 1/2 cup Diced Red Bell Pepper, (about half a large pepper)
- 1/2 cup Chopped Red Onion, (about 1/4 a large onion)
- 2 teaspoons Olive Oil
- 1/4 teaspoon Dried Oregano
- 1/4 teaspoon Dried Thyme
- 1/4 teaspoon Garlic Powder
- 2 tablespoons Crumbled Feta Cheese, (about 1 ounce)

Directions:
1. Adjust the cooking rack to the lowest placement and preheat toaster oven to 425°F on the BAKE setting.
2. While the oven preheats, quarter the zucchini lengthwise and then cut into 1/2-inch thick pieces. Cut the bell pepper and onion into 1-inch thick pieces.
3. Add the vegetables to a roasting pan. Drizzle with oil and sprinkle over the oregano, garlic powder, and salt and pepper, to taste. Toss to combine.
4. Roast vegetables for 10 minutes. Carefully remove the pan and stir. Return pan to oven and continue cooking until the vegetables have softened and started to brown, about 5 minutes more. Remove from the toaster oven and set aside.
5. Reduce the temperature to 375°F and warm the pitas by placing them directly on the cooking rack for 1 to 2 minutes.
6. Spread warm pitas with hummus. Layer with spinach, roasted vegetables, and crumbled feta.

61. Cinnamon French Toasts

Servings: 2
Cooking Time: 5 Minutes
Ingredients:
- 2 eggs
- ¼ cup whole milk
- 3 tablespoons sugar
- 2 teaspoons olive oil
- 1/8 teaspoon vanilla extract
- 1/8 teaspoon ground cinnamon
- 4 bread slices

Directions:
1. In a large bowl, mix together all the ingredients except bread slices.
2. Coat the bread slices with egg mixture evenly.
3. Press "Power Button" of Air Fry Oven and turn the dial to select the "Air Fry" mode.
4. Press the Time button and again turn the dial to set the cooking time to 6 minutes.
5. Now push the Temp button and rotate the dial to set the temperature at 390 degrees F.

6. Press "Start/Pause" button to start.
7. When the unit beeps to show that it is preheated, open the lid and lightly, grease the sheet pan.
8. Arrange the bread slices into "Air Fry Basket" and insert in the oven.
9. Flip the bread slices once halfway through.
10. Serve warm.
- **Nutrition Info:** Calories: 238 Cal Total Fat: 10.6 g Saturated Fat: 2.7 g Cholesterol: 167 mg Sodium: 122 mg Total Carbs: 20.8 g Fiber: 0.5 g Sugar: 0.9 g Protein: 7.9 g

62. Fried Apple Lemon & Vanilla Turnovers

Servings:x
Cooking Time:x
Ingredients:
- 2 sheets frozen puff pastry
- (17-ounce/480g package), thawed (keep
- cold until use)
- 3 medium Granny Smith apples, peeled
- and diced (about 3 cups)
- 2 tablespoons (30g) unsalted butter
- L cup (70g) dark brown sugar
- 1 teaspoon vanilla extract
- 1 teaspoon lemon juice
- ¾ teaspoon ground cinnamon
- ¼ teaspoon kosher salt
- 1 egg
- 1 tablespoon water
- Turbinado sugar for sprinkling

Directions:
1. Combine filling ingredients in a medium saucepan and cook over medium heat, stirring occasionally, until apples are tender and syrup is thick, about 10 minutes.
2. Transfer apple mixture to a plate and chill in the refrigerator until cool to the touch, about 20 minutes.
3. Scramble egg and water in a small bowl.
4. Place 1 sheet of puff pastry on a clean cutting board; reserve second sheet in the refrigerator.
5. Divide pastry into 4 equal squares. Spoon 2 tablespoons apple mixture onto the center of each square.
6. Brush the edges of each square with egg wash. Fold pastry diagonally over apple mixture and seal the edges with a fork.
7. Place turnovers on a plate and refrigerate while preparing remaining turnovers. Repeat steps 4 to 6 with second sheet of puff pastry.
8. Select AIRFRY/325°F (165°C)/SUPER CONVECTION/20 minutes and press START to preheat oven.
9. Place turnovers on air fry rack. Brush tops with egg wash and sprinkle with turbinado sugar. Make 3 small slits in each turnover.
10. Cook in rack position 4 until puffed and golden brown, about 20 minutes. Serve warm or at room temperature.

63. Cauliflower Tater Tots With Cheddar Cheese

Servings:6
Cooking Time: 35 Minutes
Ingredients:
- 2 lb cauliflower florets, steamed
- 5 oz cheddar cheese, grated
- 1 onion, diced
- 1 cup breadcrumbs
- 1 egg, beaten
- 1 tsp fresh parsley, chopped
- 1 tsp fresh oregano, chopped
- 1 tsp chives, chopped
- 1 tsp garlic powder
- Salt and black pepper to taste

Directions:
1. Mash the cauliflower and place it in a large bowl. Add in the onion, parsley, oregano, chives, garlic powder, cheddar cheese, salt, and pepper. Mix well and form 12 balls out of the mixture.
2. Line a baking sheet with parchment paper. Dip half of the tater tots into the egg and then coat with breadcrumbs. Arrange them on the baking sheet and cook in the preheated oven at 350 F for 15 minutes on AirFry function. Serve.

64. Crunchy Vanilla Granola

Servings: 10
Cooking Time: 30 Minutes
Ingredients:
- 4 cups old fashioned oats
- 1 1/2 tsp vanilla
- 1/4 cup coconut oil
- 1/2 cup honey
- 1/2 tsp cinnamon

Directions:
1. Fit the oven with the rack in position
2. In a mixing bowl, mix oats and cinnamon and set aside.
3. In a small saucepan, add honey and coconut oil and heat over medium-low heat until oil is melted.
4. Remove saucepan from heat. Add vanilla and stir well.
5. Pour honey mixture over oats and stir well.
6. Pour oats mixture onto the parchment-lined baking pan and spread evenly.
7. Set to bake at 300 F for 35 minutes. After 5 minutes place the baking pan in the preheated oven.

8. Serve and enjoy.
- **Nutrition Info:** Calories 350 Fat 9.6 g Carbohydrates 57.1 g Sugar 15.7 g Protein 8.1 g Cholesterol 0 mg

65. Croissant With Ham, Mushroom And Egg

Servings: 1
Cooking Time: 8 Minutes
Ingredients:
- 1 store-bought Croissant
- 3 slices honey shaved ham
- 4 honey cherry tomato, halved
- 4 small button mushrooms, quartered
- 1 Egg
- 1.8 oz. shredded cheddar cheese
- Handful salad greens
- 1/2 Rosemary Sprig, roughly diced (optional)

Directions:
1. Grease a baking dish lightly with margarine.
2. Arrange the ingredients in two layers, placing the cheese in the middle and top layer. Create a space in the center of the ham mixture, break egg in it.
3. Sprinkle some black pepper, salt and rosemary over the mixture and place on the Air fryer basket along with the croissant.
4. Baked in preheated 325°F temperature for 8 minutes. (Take out the croissant from the air fryer basket after 4 minutes).
5. Serve croissant and cheesy baked egg on plate along with some salad greens.
- **Nutrition Info:** Calories 111 Carbohydrates 0.3 g Sugar 0.3 g Protein 6 g Cholesterol 21 mg

66. Eggs In Avocado Cups

Servings: 2
Cooking Time: 10 Minutes
Ingredients:
- 1 avocado, halved and pitted
- 2 large eggs
- Salt and ground black pepper, as required
- 2 cooked bacon slices, crumbled

Directions:
1. Carefully, scoop out about 2 teaspoons of flesh from each avocado half.
2. Crack 1 egg in each avocado half and sprinkle with salt and black pepper.
3. Press "Power Button" of Air Fry Oven and turn the dial to select the "Air Roast" mode.
4. Press the Time button and again turn the dial to set the cooking time to 10 minutes.
5. Now push the Temp button and rotate the dial to set the temperature at 375 degrees F.
6. Press "Start/Pause" button to start.
7. When the unit beeps to show that it is preheated, open the lid and line the "Sheet Pan" with a lightly, grease piece of foil Arrange avocado halves into the "Sheet Pan" and insert in the oven.
8. Top each avocado half with bacon pieces and serve.
- **Nutrition Info:** Calories: 300 Cal Total Fat: 26.6 g Saturated Fat: 6.4 g Cholesterol: 190 mg Sodium: 229 mg Total Carbs: 9 g Fiber: 6.7 g Sugar: 0.9 g Protein: 9.7 g

67. Pumpkin And Yogurt Bread

Servings: 4
Cooking Time: 15 Minutes
Ingredients:
- 2 large eggs
- 8 tablespoons pumpkin puree
- 6 tablespoons banana flour
- 4 tablespoons plain Greek yogurt
- 6 tablespoons oats
- 4 tablespoons honey
- 2 tablespoons vanilla essence
- Pinch of ground nutmeg

Directions:
1. Preheat the Air fryer to 360 ºF and grease a loaf pan.
2. Mix together all the ingredients except oats in a bowl and beat with the hand mixer until smooth.
3. Add oats and mix until well combined.
4. Transfer the mixture into the prepared loaf pan and place in the Air fryer.
5. Cook for about 15 minutes and remove from the Air fryer.
6. Place onto a wire rack to cool and cut the bread into desired size slices to serve.
- **Nutrition Info:** Calories: 212 Cal Total Fat: 3.4 g Saturated Fat: 0 g Cholesterol: 0 mg Sodium: 49 mg Total Carbs: 36 g Fiber: 0 g Sugar: 20.5 g Protein: 6.6 g

68. Egg & Bacon Wraps With Salsa

Servings:3
Cooking Time: 15 Minutes
Ingredients:
- 3 tortillas
- 2 previously scrambled eggs
- 3 slices bacon, cut into strips
- 3 tbsp salsa
- 3 tbsp cream cheese
- 1 cup Pepper Jack cheese, grated

Directions:
1. Preheat on AirFry function to 390 F. Spread 1 tbsp of cream cheese onto each tortilla. Divide the eggs and bacon between the tortillas evenly. Top with salsa and sprinkle some grated cheese over. Roll up the tortillas and press Start. Cook for 10 minutes. Serve.

69. Choco Chip Banana Bread

Servings: 10
Cooking Time: 50 Minutes
Ingredients:
- 2 eggs
- 3 ripe bananas
- 1 tsp vanilla
- 1 cup granulated sugar
- 1/2 cup sour cream
- 1/2 cup butter, melted
- 1/2 cup chocolate chips
- 1 1/2 cups all-purpose flour
- 1 tsp baking soda
- 1 tsp salt

Directions:
1. Fit the oven with the rack in position
2. In a large bowl, add bananas and mash using a fork until smooth.
3. Stir in sour cream and melted butter.
4. Add eggs, vanilla, sugar, and salt and stir well.
5. Add flour, baking soda, and salt and stir until just combined.
6. Add chocolate chips and stir well.
7. Pour batter into the greased 9*8-inch loaf pan.
8. Set to bake at 350 F for 55 minutes, after 5 minutes, place the loaf pan in the oven.
9. Slice and serve.
- **Nutrition Info:** Calories 339 Fat 15.3 g Carbohydrates 48 g Sugar 28.9 g Protein 4.5 g Cholesterol 64 mg

70. Chicken And Yogurt Taquitos

Servings:4
Cooking Time: 12 Minutes
Ingredients:
- 1 cup cooked chicken, shredded
- ¼ cup Greek yogurt
- ¼ cup salsa
- 1 cup shredded Mozzarella cheese
- Salt and ground black pepper, to taste
- 4 flour tortillas
- Cooking spray

Directions:
1. Spritz the air fryer basket with cooking spray.
2. Combine all the ingredients, except for the tortillas, in a large bowl. Stir to mix well.
3. Make the taquitos: Unfold the tortillas on a clean work surface, then scoop up 2 tablespoons of the chicken mixture in the middle of each tortilla. Roll the tortillas up to wrap the filling.
4. Arrange the taquitos in the pan and spritz with cooking spray.
5. Put the air fryer basket on the baking pan and slide into Rack Position 2, select Air Fry, set temperature to 380ºF (193ºC) and set time to 12 minutes.
6. Flip the taquitos halfway through the cooking time.
7. When cooked, the taquitos should be golden brown and the cheese should be melted.
8. Serve immediately.

71. Banana And Oat Bread Pudding

Servings:4
Cooking Time: 16 Minutes
Ingredients:
- 2 medium ripe bananas, mashed
- ½ cup low-fat milk
- 2 tablespoons maple syrup
- 2 tablespoons peanut butter
- 1 teaspoon vanilla extract
- 1 teaspoon ground cinnamon
- 2 slices whole-grain bread, cut into bite-sized cubes
- ¼ cup quick oats
- Cooking spray

Directions:
1. Spritz the baking pan lightly with cooking spray.
2. Mix the bananas, milk, maple syrup, peanut butter, vanilla, and cinnamon in a large mixing bowl and stir until well incorporated.
3. Add the bread cubes to the banana mixture and stir until thoroughly coated. Fold in the oats and stir to combine.
4. Transfer the mixture to the baking pan. Wrap the baking pan in aluminum foil.
5. Slide the baking pan into Rack Position 2, select Air Fry, set temperature to 350ºF (180ºC) and set time to 16 minutes.
6. After 10 minutes, remove the pan from the oven. Remove the foil. Return the pan to the oven and continue to cook for another 6 minutes.
7. When done, the pudding should be set.
8. Let the pudding cool for 5 minutes before serving.

72. Spicy Egg Casserole

Servings: 8
Cooking Time: 45 Minutes
Ingredients:
- 10 eggs
- 1 cup Colby jack cheese, shredded
- 1 cup cottage cheese
- 1 tsp baking powder
- 1/3 cup flour
- 1/2 cup milk
- 4.5 oz can green chilies, chopped
- 1/2 small onion, minced
- 2 tbsp butter
- 1 tsp seasoned salt

Directions:

1. Fit the oven with the rack in position
2. Spray 9*13-inch casserole dish with cooking spray and set aside.
3. Melt butter in a pan over medium heat.
4. Add onion and green chilies and sauté for 5 minutes. Remove pan from heat and set aside.
5. In a small bowl, whisk milk, baking powder, and flour until smooth.
6. In a mixing bowl, whisk eggs with cheese, cottage cheese, and seasoned salt.
7. Add sautéed onion and green chilies, milk, and flour mixture to the eggs and whisk until well combined.
8. Pour egg mixture into the prepared casserole dish.
9. Set to bake at 350 F for 50 minutes. After 5 minutes place the casserole dish in the preheated oven.
10. Serve and enjoy.

- **Nutrition Info:** Calories 219 Fat 13.8 g Carbohydrates 8.4 g Sugar 1.4 g Protein 14.9 g Cholesterol 228 mg

73. Smart Oven Baked Oatmeal Recipe

Servings:x
Cooking Time:x
Ingredients:

- 1 small Ripe Banana, (6 inches long, abut 1/4 cup mashed)
- 1 tablespoon Flax Meal
- 1/2 cup Non-Dairy Milk, plus 2 tablespoons (like Almond Milk or Soy Milk)
- 1 cup Old Fashioned Rolled Oats
- 2 teaspoons Pure Maple Syrup
- 2 teaspoons Olive Oil
- 1/2 teaspoon Ground Cinnamon
- 1/2 teaspoon Pure Vanilla Extract
- 1/4 teaspoon Baking Powder
- 1/8 teaspoon Fine Sea Salt
- 1/4 cup Pecan Pieces, (1 ounce)

Directions:
1. Adjust the cooking rack to the bottom position and preheat toaster oven to 350°F on the BAKE setting. Grease a 7 x 5-inch toaster oven-safe baking dish.
2. In a large bowl, add the banana and mash well. Stir in the flaxseed meal, maple syrup, olive oil, cinnamon, vanilla, baking powder, salt, milk, oats, and pecan pieces. Pour mixture into prepared baking dish.
3. Bake oatmeal until the middle is set and browned on the edges, about 25 to 35 minutes. (For softer scoop able oatmeal bake 25 to 30 minutes, for firm oatmeal bake 30 to 35 minutes.)
4. Let sit at least 10 minutes before slicing and serving.

74. Raspberries Maple Pancakes

Servings: 4
Cooking Time: 15 Minutes
Ingredients:

- 2 cups all-purpose flour
- 1 cup milk
- 3 eggs, beaten
- 1 tsp baking powder
- 1 cup brown sugar
- 1 ½ tsp vanilla extract
- ½ cup frozen raspberries, thawed
- 2 tbsp maple syrup
- A pinch of salt

Directions:
1. Preheat on Bake function to 400 F. In a bowl, mix the flour, baking powder, salt, milk, eggs, vanilla extract, and sugar until smooth. Stir in the raspberries. Do it gently to avoid coloring the batter.
2. Grease a pie pan with cooking spray. Drop the batter onto the pan. Make sure to leave some space between the pancakes. Cook for 10-15 minutes. Drizzle with maple syrup and serve.

75. Peanut Butter And Jelly Banana Boats

Servings: 1
Cooking Time: 15 Minutes
Ingredients:

- 1 banana
- 1/4 cup peanut butter
- 1/4 cup jelly
- 1 tablespoon granola

Directions:
1. Start by preheating toaster oven to 350°F.
2. Slice banana lengthwise and separate slightly.
3. Spread peanut butter and jelly in the gap.
4. Sprinkle granola over the entire banana.
5. Bake for 15 minutes.

- **Nutrition Info:** Calories: 724, Sodium: 327 mg, Dietary Fiber: 9.2 g, Total Fat: 36.6 g, Total Carbs: 102.9 g, Protein: 20.0 g.

76. Pancetta & Hot Dogs Omelet

Servings: 2
Cooking Time: 10 Minutes
Ingredients:

- 4 eggs
- ¼ teaspoon dried parsley
- ¼ teaspoon dried rosemary
- 1 pancetta slice, chopped
- 2 hot dogs, chopped
- 2 small onions, chopped

Directions:
1. In a bowl, crack the eggs and beat well.
2. Add the remaining ingredients and gently, stir to combine.
3. Place the mixture into a baking pan.

4. Press "Power Button" of Air Fry Oven and turn the dial to select the "Air Fry" mode.
5. Press the Time button and again turn the dial to set the cooking time to 10 minutes.
6. Now push the Temp button and rotate the dial to set the temperature at 320 degrees F.
7. Press "Start/Pause" button to start.
8. When the unit beeps to show that it is preheated, open the lid.
9. Arrange pan over the "Wire Rack" and insert in the oven.
10. Cut into equal-sized wedges and serve hot.
- **Nutrition Info:** Calories 282 Total Fat 19.3 g Saturated Fat 6.5 g Cholesterol 351mg Sodium 632 mg Total Carbs 8.2 g Fiber 1.6 g Sugar 4.2 g Protein 18.9 g

77. Egg In A Hole

Servings:1
Cooking Time: 5 Minutes
Ingredients:
- 1 slice bread
- 1 teaspoon butter, softened
- 1 egg
- Salt and pepper, to taste
- 1 tablespoon shredded Cheddar cheese
- 2 teaspoons diced ham

Directions:
1. On a flat work surface, cut a hole in the center of the bread slice with a 2½-inch-diameter biscuit cutter.
2. Spread the butter evenly on each side of the bread slice and transfer to the baking pan.
3. Crack the egg into the hole and season as desired with salt and pepper. Scatter the shredded cheese and diced ham on top.
4. Slide the baking pan into Rack Position 1, select Convection Bake, set temperature to 330ºF (166ºC), and set time to 5 minutes.
5. When cooking is complete, the bread should be lightly browned and the egg should be set. Remove from the oven and serve hot.

78. Basil Parmesan Bagel

Servings:1
Cooking Time: 6 Minutes
Ingredients:
- 2 tbsp butter, softened
- ¼ tsp dried basil
- 1 tsp garlic powder
- 1 tbsp Parmesan cheese, grated
- Salt and black pepper to taste
- 1 bagel

Directions:
1. Preheat on Bake function to 370 F. Cut the bagel in half. Combine the butter, Parmesan cheese, garlic, and basil in a small bowl. Season with salt and pepper. Spread the mixture onto the halved bagel. Place the bagel in the basket and press Start. Cook for 5-6 minutes.

79. Paprika Baked Eggs

Servings:6
Cooking Time: 10 Minutes
Ingredients:
- 6 large eggs
- 1 tsp paprika

Directions:
1. Preheat fryer to 300 F. Lay the eggs in the basket and press Start. Cook for 8 minutes on Bake function. Using tongs, dip the eggs in a bowl with icy water. Let sit for 5 minutes before peeling. Slice, sprinkle with paprika, and serve.

80. Prosciutto & Salami Egg Bake

Servings: 2
Cooking Time: 20 Minutes
Ingredients:
- 1 beef sausage, chopped
- 4 slices prosciutto, chopped
- 3 oz salami, chopped
- 1 cup grated mozzarella cheese
- 4 eggs, beaten
- ½ tsp onion powder

Directions:
1. Preheat on Bake function to 350 F. Whisk the eggs with the onion powder. Brown the sausage in a skillet over medium heat for 2 minutes. Remove to the egg mixture and add in mozzarella cheese, salami, and prosciutto and give it a stir. Pour the egg mixture in a greased baking pan and cook for 10-15 minutes until golden brown on top. Serve.

81. Easy Buttermilk Biscuits

Servings: 16 Biscuits
Cooking Time: 18 Minutes
Ingredients:
- 2½ cups all-purpose flour
- 1 tablespoon baking powder
- 1 teaspoon kosher salt
- 1 teaspoon sugar
- ½ teaspoon baking soda
- 8 tablespoons (1 stick) unsalted butter, at room temperature
- 1 cup buttermilk, chilled

Directions:
1. Stir together the flour, baking powder, salt, sugar, and baking powder in a large bowl.
2. Add the butter and stir to mix well. Pour in the buttermilk and stir with a rubber spatula just until incorporated.
3. Place the dough onto a lightly floured surface and roll the dough out to a disk, ½ inch thick. Cut out the biscuits with a 2-inch

round cutter and re-roll any scraps until you have 16 biscuits. Arrange the biscuits in the baking pan.
4. Slide the baking pan into Rack Position 1, select Convection Bake, set temperature to 325ºF (163ºC) and set time to 18 minutes.
5. When cooked, the biscuits will be golden brown.
6. Remove from the oven to a plate and serve hot.

82. Creamy Mushroom And Spinach Omelet

Servings: 2
Cooking Time: 10 Minutes
Ingredients:
- 4 eggs, lightly beaten
- 2 tbsp heavy cream
- 2 cups spinach, chopped
- 1 cup mushrooms, chopped
- 3 oz feta cheese, crumbled
- 1 tbsp fresh parsley, chopped
- Salt and black pepper to taste

Directions:
1. Spray a baking pan with cooking spray. In a bowl, whisk eggs and heavy cream until combined. Stir in spinach, mushrooms, feta, salt, and pepper.
2. Pour into the basket tray and cook in your for 6-10 minutes at 350 F on Bake function until golden and set. Sprinkle with parsley, cut into wedges, and serve.

83. Buttery Orange Toasts

Servings:6
Cooking Time: 15 Minutes
Ingredients:
- 12 bread slices
- ½ cup sugar
- 1 stick butter
- 1 ½ tbsp vanilla extract
- 1 ½ tbsp cinnamon
- 2 oranges, zested

Directions:
1. Mix butter, sugar, and vanilla extract and microwave the mixture for 30 seconds until it melts. Add in orange zest. Spread the mixture onto bread slices. Lay the bread slices on the cooking basket and cook in the oven for 5 minutes at 400 F on Toast function. Serve warm.

84. Brioche Breakfast Pudding

Servings: 8
Cooking Time: 45 Minutes
Ingredients:
- 1 loaf brioche bread, cut in cubes
- ½ tbsp. coconut oil, soft
- 4 cups milk

- 1 can coconut milk
- 6 eggs
- ½ cup sugar
- 2 tsp vanilla
- ¼ tsp salt
- 1 cup coconut, shredded
- ½ cup chocolate chips

Directions:
1. Place rack in position 1 of the oven. Grease an 8x11-inch baking pan with coconut oil.
2. Add the bread cubes to the pan, pressing lightly to settle.
3. In a large bowl, whisk together milk, coconut milk, eggs, sugar, vanilla, and salt until combined.
4. Stir in coconut and chocolate chips. Pour evenly over bread. Cover with plastic wrap and refrigerate 2 hours or overnight.
5. Set oven to bake on 350°F for 50 minutes. After 5 minutes, add the pudding to the oven and bake 40-45 minutes, or until top is beginning to brown and it passes the toothpick test.
6. Remove to wire rack and let cool 5-10 minutes before serving.
- **Nutrition Info:** Calories 476, Total Fat 24g, Saturated Fat 15g, Total Carbs 51g, Net Carbs 48g, Protein 14g, Sugar 30g, Fiber 3g, Sodium 398mg, Potassium 443mg, Phosphorus 288mg

85. Creamy Vanilla Berry Mini Pies

Servings: 4
Cooking Time: 20 Minutes
Ingredients:
- 4 pastry dough sheets
- 2 tbsp mashed strawberries
- 2 tbsp mashed raspberries
- ¼ tsp vanilla extract
- 2 cups cream cheese, softened
- 1 tbsp honey

Directions:
1. Preheat fryer on Bake function to 375 F. Divide the cream cheese between the dough sheets and spread it evenly. In a small bowl, combine the berries, honey, and vanilla. Spoon the mixture into the pastry sheets. Pinch the ends of the sheets to form puff. Place the puffs in a lined baking dish. Place the dish in the toaster oven and cook for 15 minutes. Serve chilled.

86. Breakfast Sandwich

Servings: 1
Cooking Time: 7minutes
Ingredients:
- 2 Bacon Slices
- 1 Egg
- 1 English muffin Salt& Pepper to taste

Directions:

1. Beat the egg into a soufflé cup and add salt and pepper to taste.
2. Heat the air fryer to 390°F and place the soufflé cup, English muffin and bacon into the tray.
3. Cook all the ingredients for 6-10 minutes. Assemble sandwich and enjoy.
- **Nutrition Info:** Calories 113 Fat 8.2 g Carbohydrates 0.3 g Sugar 0.2 g Protein 5.4 g Cholesterol 18 mg

87. Moist Orange Bread Loaf

Servings: 10
Cooking Time: 50 Minutes
Ingredients:

- 4 eggs
- 4 oz butter, softened
- 1 cup of orange juice
- 1 orange zest, grated
- 1 cup of sugar
- 2 tsp baking powder
- 2 cups all-purpose flour
- 1 tsp vanilla

Directions:

1. Fit the oven with the rack in position
2. In a large bowl, whisk eggs and sugar until creamy.
3. Whisk in vanilla, butter, orange juice, and orange zest.
4. Add flour and baking powder and mix until combined.
5. Pour batter into the greased 9*5-inch loaf pan.
6. Set to bake at 350 F for 55 minutes, after 5 minutes, place the loaf pan in the oven.
7. Slice and serve.
- **Nutrition Info:** Calories 286 Fat 11.3 g Carbohydrates 42.5 g Sugar 22.4 g Protein 5.1 gCholesterol 90 mg

88. Mushroom Leek Frittata

Servings: 4
Cooking Time: 32 Minutes
Ingredients:

- 6 eggs
- 6 oz mushrooms, sliced 1 cup leeks, sliced
- Salt

Directions:

1. Preheat the air fryer to 325 F.
2. Spray air fryer baking dish with cooking spray and set aside.
3. Heat another pan over medium heat. Spray pan with cooking spray.
4. Add mushrooms, leeks, and salt in a pan sauté for 6 minutes.
5. Break eggs in a bowl and whisk well.
6. Transfer sautéed mushroom and leek mixture into the prepared baking dish.

7. Pour egg over mushroom mixture.
8. Place dish in the air fryer and cook for 32 minutes.
9. Serve and enjoy.
- **Nutrition Info:** Calories 116 Fat 7 g Carbohydrates 5.1 g Sugar 2.1 g Protein 10 g Cholesterol 245 mg

89. Air Fried French Toast

Servings: 4
Cooking Time: 6 Minutes
Ingredients:

- 2 slices of sourdough bread
- 3 eggs
- 1 tablespoon of margarine
- 1 tsp. of liquid vanilla
- 3 tsp.s of honey
- 2 tablespoons of Greek yogurt Berries

Directions:

1. Preheat the air fryer to 356°F.
2. Pour the vanilla in the eggs and whisk to mix. Spread the margarine on all sides of the bread and soak in the eggs to absorb.
3. Put the bread into the air fryer basket and cook for 3 minutes Turn the bread over and cook for another 3 minutes.
4. Transfer to a place, top with yogurt and berries with a sprinkle of honey.
- **Nutrition Info:** Calories 99 Fat 8.2 g Carbohydrates 0.2 g Sugar 0.2 g Protein 6 g Cholesterol 18 mg

90. Congee With Eggs With Fresh Chives

Servings:x
Cooking Time:x
Ingredients:

- 3 cups water
- 1-2 tsp hot chili oil or sesame oil
- ½ tsp kosher salt
- 2 eggs
- 1 Tbsp coarsely chopped fresh cilantro
- 1 Tbsp minced fresh chives

Directions:

1. Place the rice in a strainer and rinse well.
2. Add the rice, water, and salt to oven and cover. Place over medium-high heat and bring to a boil. As soon as the water boils, reduce the heat to low and stir the mixture. Cover and simmer for 45 minutes. After 45 minutes, the rice should be very soft and the porridge should have a silky consistency. If not, cook for another 10 minutes or so.
3. While the porridge cooks, whisk together the two eggs in a small bowl.
4. When the rice is cooked, pour the egg into the porridge in a thin stream. If you want a custardy texture, whisk the mixture quickly while you pour in the egg. If you prefer ribbons of egg, stir more slowly.

5. Cook for a minute or two or until the egg is done.
6. Stir in the cilantro and chives, and drizzle over the oil.

91. Salsa Verde Golden Chicken Empanadas

Servings: 12 Empanadas
Cooking Time: 12 Minutes
Ingredients:
- 1 cup boneless, skinless rotisserie chicken breast meat, chopped finely
- ¼ cup salsa verde
- $^2/_3$ cup shredded Cheddar cheese
- 1 teaspoon ground cumin
- 1 teaspoon ground black pepper
- 2 purchased refrigerated pie crusts, from a minimum 14.1-ounce (400 g) box
- 1 large egg
- 2 tablespoons water
- Cooking spray

Directions:
1. Spritz the air fryer basket with cooking spray. Set aside.
2. Combine the chicken meat, salsa verde, Cheddar, cumin, and black pepper in a large bowl. Stir to mix well. Set aside.
3. Unfold the pie crusts on a clean work surface, then use a large cookie cutter to cut out 3½-inch circles as much as possible.
4. Roll the remaining crusts to a ball and flatten into a circle which has the same thickness of the original crust. Cut out more 3½-inch circles until you have 12 circles in total.
5. Make the empanadas: Divide the chicken mixture in the middle of each circle, about 1½ tablespoons each. Dab the edges of the circle with water. Fold the circle in half over the filling to shape like a half-moon and press to seal, or you can press with a fork.
6. Whisk the egg with water in a small bowl.
7. Arrange the empanadas in the pan and spritz with cooking spray. Brush with whisked egg.
8. Put the air fryer basket on the baking pan and slide into Rack Position 2, select Air Fry, set temperature to 350ºF (180ºC) and set time to 12 minutes.
9. Flip the empanadas halfway through the cooking time.
10. When cooking is complete, the empanadas will be golden and crispy.
11. Serve immediately.

92. Easy Apple Pie Baked Oatmeal

Servings: 4
Cooking Time: 30 Minutes
Ingredients:
- 1 cup rolled oats
- 1/4 tsp nutmeg
- 2 tsp cinnamon
- 2 tbsp maple syrup
- 1/4 cup milk
- 1/2 cup raisins
- 1 banana, sliced
- 2 apples, diced
- 1 cup boiling water

Directions:
1. Fit the oven with the rack in position
2. Add oats and boiling water in a mixing bowl and let sit for 10 minutes.
3. After 10 minutes add remaining ingredients to the bowl and mix well.
4. Pour mixture into the greased baking dish.
5. Set to bake at 350 F for 35 minutes. After 5 minutes place the baking dish in the preheated oven.
6. Serve and enjoy.
- **Nutrition Info:** Calories 253 Fat 2.1 g Carbohydrates 58.8 g Sugar 32.8 g Protein 4.4 g Cholesterol 1 mg

93. Rarebit Air-fried Egg

Servings: 2-4
Cooking Time: 5 Minutes
Ingredients:
- 4 Slices Sourdough
- 4 Eggs
- 1/3 cup ale
- 1 & 1/2 cups cheddar, grated
- 1 tsp. mustard powder
- 1/2 tsp. paprika
- Black Pepper to taste
- 2 tsp. Worcestershire Sauce

Directions:
1. Fry eggs, sunny side up and set to one side. Preheat Air Fryer to 350°F.
2. In a bowl, add together the cheddar, ale, paprika, mustard powder, and Worcestershire sauce.
3. Spread just one side of each slice of sourdough with the cheddar mixture.
4. Place the bread slices into the Air fryer tray. Cook for about 3 minutes until slightly browned.
5. Top the rarebits with fried eggs and spice with pepper to taste.
- **Nutrition Info:** Calories 115 Fat 9.2 g Carbohydrates 0.3 g Sugar 0.3 g Protein 5.4 g Cholesterol 19 mg

94. Banana Coconut Muffins

Servings: 12
Cooking Time: 15 Minutes
Ingredients:
- 1 egg
- 3 ripe bananas, mashed

- 1/2 cup shredded coconut
- 2 cups all-purpose flour
- 2 tsp baking powder
- 1/2 tsp baking soda
- 1 cup of sugar
- 1 tsp vanilla
- 1/2 cup milk
- 1/2 cup applesauce
- 1/2 tsp salt

Directions:
1. Fit the oven with the rack in position
2. Line a 12-cup muffin tray with cupcake liners and set aside.
3. In a mixing bowl, whisk the egg with vanilla, milk, applesauce, and salt until well combined.
4. Add baking powder, baking soda, and sugar and mix well.
5. Add flour and mix until just combined.
6. Add shredded coconut and stir well.
7. Pour mixture into the prepared muffin tray.
8. Set to bake at 350 F for 20 minutes. After 5 minutes place the muffin tray in the preheated oven.
9. Serve and enjoy.
- **Nutrition Info:** Calories 193 Fat 2 g Carbohydrates 41.9 g Sugar 22.1 g Protein 3.4 g Cholesterol 14 mg

95. Pork Momos

Servings:4
Cooking Time: 20 Minutes
Ingredients:
- 2 tablespoons olive oil
- 1 pound (454 g) ground pork
- 1 shredded carrot
- 1 onion, chopped
- 1 teaspoon soy sauce
- 16 wonton wrappers
- Salt and ground black pepper, to taste
- Cooking spray

Directions:
1. Heat the olive oil in a nonstick skillet over medium heat until shimmering.
2. Add the ground pork, carrot, onion, soy sauce, salt, and ground black pepper and sauté for 10 minutes or until the pork is well browned and carrots are tender.
3. Unfold the wrappers on a clean work surface, then divide the cooked pork and vegetables on the wrappers. Fold the edges around the filling to form momos. Nip the top to seal the momos.
4. Arrange the momos in the air fryer basket and spritz with cooking spray.
5. Put the air fryer basket on the baking pan and slide into Rack Position 2, select Air Fry, set temperature to 320ºF (160ºC) and set time to 10 minutes.

6. When cooking is complete, the wrappers will be lightly browned.
7. Serve immediately.

96. Coconut Brown Rice Porridge With Dates

Servings:1 Or 2
Cooking Time: 23 Minutes
Ingredients:
- ½ cup cooked brown rice
- 1 cup canned coconut milk
- ¼ cup unsweetened shredded coconut
- ¼ cup packed dark brown sugar
- 4 large Medjool dates, pitted and roughly chopped
- ½ teaspoon kosher salt
- ¼ teaspoon ground cardamom
- Heavy cream, for serving (optional)

Directions:
1. Place all the ingredients except the heavy cream in the baking pan and stir until blended.
2. Slide the baking pan into Rack Position 1, select Convection Bake, set temperature to 375ºF (190ºC) and set time to 23 minutes.
3. Stir the porridge halfway through the cooking time.
4. When cooked, the porridge will be thick and creamy.
5. Remove from the oven and ladle the porridge into bowls.
6. Serve hot with a drizzle of the cream, if desired.

97. Crustless Broccoli Quiche

Servings:4
Cooking Time: 10 Minutes
Ingredients:
- 1 cup broccoli florets
- ¾ cup chopped roasted red peppers
- 1¼ cups grated Fontina cheese
- 6 eggs
- ¾ cup heavy cream
- ½ teaspoon salt
- Freshly ground black pepper, to taste
- Cooking spray

Directions:
1. Spritz the baking pan with cooking spray
2. Add the broccoli florets and roasted red peppers to the pan and scatter the grated Fontina cheese on top.
3. In a bowl, beat together the eggs and heavy cream. Sprinkle with salt and pepper. Pour the egg mixture over the top of the cheese. Wrap the pan in foil.
4. Put the air fryer basket on the baking pan and slide into Rack Position 2, select Air Fry, set temperature to 325ºF (163ºC) and set time to 10 minutes.

5. After 8 minutes, remove the pan from the oven. Remove the foil. Return to the oven and continue to cook for another 2 minutes.
6. When cooked, the quiche should be golden brown.
7. Rest for 5 minutes before cutting into wedges and serve warm.

98. Mushroom & Pepperoncini Omelet

Servings: 2
Cooking Time: 20 Minutes
Ingredients:
- 3 large eggs
- ¼ c milk
- Salt and ground black pepper, as required
- ½ cup cheddar cheese, shredded
- ¼ cup cooked mushrooms
- 3 pepperoncini peppers, sliced thinly
- ½ tablespoon scallion, sliced thinly

Directions:
1. In a bowl, add the eggs, milk, salt and black pepper and beat well.
2. Place the mixture into a greased baking pan.
3. Press "Power Button" of Air Fry Oven and turn the dial to select the "Air Bake" mode.
4. Press the Time button and again turn the dial to set the cooking time to 20 minutes.
5. Now push the Temp button and rotate the dial to set the temperature at 350 degrees F.
6. Press "Start/Pause" button to start.
7. When the unit beeps to show that it is preheated, open the lid.
8. Arrange pan over the "Wire Rack" and insert in the oven.
9. Cut into equal-sized wedges and serve hot.
- **Nutrition Info:** Calories 254 Total Fat 17.5 g Saturated Fat 8.7 g Cholesterol 311 mg Sodium 793 mg Total Carbs 7.3 g Fiber 0.1 g Sugar 3.8 g Protein 8.2 g

99. Crispy Chicken Egg Rolls

Servings:4
Cooking Time: 23 To 24 Minutes
Ingredients:
- 1 pound (454 g) ground chicken
- 2 teaspoons olive oil
- 2 garlic cloves, minced
- 1 teaspoon grated fresh ginger
- 2 cups white cabbage, shredded
- 1 onion, chopped
- ¼ cup soy sauce
- 8 egg roll wrappers
- 1 egg, beaten
- Cooking spray

Directions:
1. Spritz the air fryer basket with cooking spray.
2. Heat olive oil in a saucepan over medium heat. Sauté the garlic and ginger in the olive oil for 1 minute, or until fragrant. Add the ground chicken to the saucepan. Sauté for 5 minutes, or until the chicken is cooked through. Add the cabbage, onion and soy sauce and sauté for 5 to 6 minutes, or until the vegetables become soft. Remove the saucepan from the heat.
3. Unfold the egg roll wrappers on a clean work surface. Divide the chicken mixture among the wrappers and brush the edges of the wrappers with the beaten egg. Tightly roll up the egg rolls, enclosing the filling. Arrange the rolls in the pan.
4. Put the air fryer basket on the baking pan and slide into Rack Position 2, select Air Fry, set temperature to 370ºF (188ºC) and set time to 12 minutes.
5. Flip the rolls halfway through the cooking time.
6. When cooked, the rolls will be crispy and golden brown.
7. Transfer to a platter and let cool for 5 minutes before serving.

100. Oatmeal Muffins

Servings: 2-4
Cooking Time: 15 Minutes
Ingredients:
- 2 Eggs
- 31/2 ounce oats
- 3 ounce margarine, melted
- 1/2 cup flour
- 1/4 tsp. vanilla essence
- 1/2 cup icing sugar Pinch baking powder
- 1 tablespoon raisins
- Cooking spray

Directions:
1. Combine sugar and margarine until soft. Whisk together the eggs and vanilla essence. Add it to the sugar/margarine mix until soft peaks forms.
2. Combine flour, raisins, baking powder and oats in a separate bowl. Add it to the mixed ingredients.
3. Grease the muffin molds lightly with cooking spray and fill with the batter mixture. Preheat the Air fryer at 350°F.
4. Place the muffin molds into the air fryer tray. Let it cook for 12 minutes.
- **Nutrition Info:** Calories 108 Fat 9.0 g Carbohydrates 0.3 g Sugar 0.3 g Protein 6.3 g Cholesterol 21 mg

101. Mushroom Spinach Egg Muffins

Servings: 12
Cooking Time: 20 Minutes
Ingredients:
- 12 eggs
- 1/2 cup fresh basil

- 1 cup mushrooms, diced
- 1 cup spinach, chopped
- 3/4 cup feta cheese, crumbled
- Pepper
- Salt

Directions:
1. Fit the oven with the rack in position
2. Spray a muffin tray with cooking spray and set aside.
3. In a bowl, whisk eggs with pepper and salt.
4. Add basil, mushrooms, spinach, and cheese and stir well.
5. Pour egg mixture into the prepared muffin tray.
6. Set to bake at 400 F for 25 minutes. After 5 minutes place the muffin tray in the preheated oven.
7. Serve and enjoy.
- **Nutrition Info:** Calories 90 Fat 6.4 g Carbohydrates 1 g Sugar 0.8 g Protein 7.2 g Cholesterol 172 mg

102.Sweet Pineapple Oatmeal

Servings: 6
Cooking Time: 45 Minutes
Ingredients:
- 2 cups old-fashioned oats
- 1/2 cup coconut flakes
- 1 cup pineapple, crushed
- 2 eggs, lightly beaten
- 1/3 cup yogurt
- 1/3 cup butter, melted
- 1/2 tsp baking powder
- 1/3 cup brown sugar
- 1/2 tsp vanilla
- 2/3 cup milk
- 1/2 tsp salt

Directions:
1. Fit the oven with the rack in position
2. In a mixing bowl, mix together oats, baking powder, brown sugar, and salt.
3. In a separate bowl, beat eggs with vanilla, milk, yogurt, and butter.
4. Add egg mixture into the oat mixture and stir to combine.
5. Add coconut and pineapple and stir to combine.
6. Pour oat mixture into the greased 8-inch baking dish.
7. Set to bake at 350 F for 50 minutes, after 5 minutes, place the baking dish in the oven.
8. Serve and enjoy.
- **Nutrition Info:** Calories 304 Fat 16.4 g Carbohydrates 33.2 g Sugar 13.6 g Protein 7.5 g Cholesterol 85 mg

103.Fluffy Frittata With Bell Pepper

Servings:x
Cooking Time:x

Ingredients:
- 8 eggs
- 2 Tbsp whole milk
- 1 Tbsp butter
- Coarse salt, freshly ground pepper, to taste
- ½ zucchini diced
- 1 bell Pepper seeded and diced

Directions:
1. Preheat oven to 400°F.
2. Heat oven over medium heat. Add butter.
3. In a bowl, add remaining ingredients. Pour mixture into oven.
4. When eggs are half set and edges begin to pull away, place frittata in
5. the oven and bake for about 10 minutes, or until center is no longer jiggly.
6. Cut into wedges or slide out onto serving plate.

104.Soft Banana Oat Muffins

Servings: 12
Cooking Time: 20 Minutes
Ingredients:
- 1 egg
- 1 cup banana, mashed
- 1 tsp vanilla
- 1/3 cup applesauce
- 3/4 cup milk
- 1/4 tsp nutmeg
- 1/2 tsp cinnamon
- 1 tsp baking soda
- 2 tsp baking powder
- 1/4 cup brown sugar
- 1/4 cup white sugar
- 1 cup old fashioned oats
- 1 1/2 cups whole wheat flour
- 1/2 tsp salt

Directions:
1. Fit the oven with the rack in position
2. Line a 12-cup muffin tray with cupcake liners and set aside.
3. In a mixing bowl, mix flour, nutmeg, cinnamon, baking soda, baking powder, sugar, oats, flour, and salt.
4. In a separate bowl, whisk eggs with milk, vanilla, and applesauce. Add mashed banana and stir to combine.
5. Add flour mixture into the egg mixture and mix until just combined.
6. Pour mixture into the prepared muffin tray.
7. Set to bake at 400 F for 25 minutes. After 5 minutes place the muffin tray in the preheated oven.
8. Serve and enjoy.
- **Nutrition Info:** Calories 165 Fat 1.7 g Carbohydrates 33 g Sugar 10.5 g Protein 4.4 g Cholesterol 15 mg

105.Breakfast Cheese Sandwiches

Servings:2
Cooking Time: 8 Minutes
Ingredients:
- 1 teaspoon butter, softened
- 4 slices bread
- 4 slices smoked country ham
- 4 slices Cheddar cheese
- 4 thick slices tomato

Directions:
1. Spoon ½ teaspoon of butter onto one side of 2 slices of bread and spread it all over.
2. Assemble the sandwiches: Top each of 2 slices of unbuttered bread with 2 slices of ham, 2 slices of cheese, and 2 slices of tomato. Place the remaining 2 slices of bread on top, butter-side up.
3. Lay the sandwiches in the baking pan, buttered side down.
4. Slide the baking pan into Rack Position 1, select Convection Bake, set temperature to 370ºF (188ºC), and set time to 8 minutes.
5. Flip the sandwiches halfway through the cooking time.
6. When cooking is complete, the sandwiches should be golden brown on both sides and the cheese should be melted. Remove from the oven. Allow to cool for 5 minutes before slicing to serve.

106.Spinach Egg Breakfast

Servings: 4
Cooking Time: 20 Minutes
Ingredients:
- 3 eggs
- 1/4 cup coconut milk
- 1/4 cup parmesan cheese, grated 4 oz spinach, chopped
- 3 oz cottage cheese

Directions:
1. Preheat the air fryer to 350 F.
2. Add eggs, milk, half parmesan cheese, and cottage cheese in a bowl and whisk well. Add spinach and stir well.
3. Pour mixture into the air fryer baking dish.
4. Sprinkle remaining half parmesan cheese on top.
5. Place dish in the air fryer and cook for 20 minutes.
6. Serve and enjoy.
- **Nutrition Info:** Calories 144 Fat 8.5 g Carbohydrates 2.5 g Sugar 1.1 g Protein 14 g Cholesterol 135 mg

107.Amazing Apple & Brie Sandwich

Servings:1
Cooking Time: 10 Minutes
Ingredients:
- 2 bread slices
- ½ apple, thinly sliced
- 2 tsp butter
- 2 oz brie cheese, thinly sliced

Directions:
1. Spread butter on the outside of the bread slices. Arrange apple slices on the inside of one bread slice. Place brie slices on top of the apple. Top with the other slice of bread. Press Start on the oven and cook for 5 minutes at 350 F on Bake function. Cut diagonally and serve.

108.Flavorful Zucchini Frittata

Servings: 4
Cooking Time: 25 Minutes
Ingredients:
- 6 eggs
- 2 cups zucchini, grated & squeeze out excess liquid
- 1 cup cheddar cheese, shredded
- 1 cup ham, chopped
- 1/4 cup heavy cream
- 2 tbsp butter
- 1/4 tsp pepper
- 1 tsp salt

Directions:
1. Fit the oven with the rack in position
2. Melt butter in a pan over medium heat.
3. Add zucchini in the pan and sauté until tender. Remove pan from heat.
4. In a bowl, whisk eggs and cream. Stir in zucchini, cheese, ham, pepper, and salt.
5. Pour mixture into the greased baking dish.
6. Set to bake at 325 F for 30 minutes. After 5 minutes place the baking dish in the preheated oven.
7. Serve and enjoy.
- **Nutrition Info:** Calories 349 Fat 27.5 g Carbohydrates 4.3 g Sugar 1.7 g Protein 21.8 gCholesterol 320 mg

109.Baja Fish Tacos

Servings: 6 Tacos
Cooking Time: 17 Minutes
Ingredients:
- 1 egg
- 5 ounces (142 g) Mexican beer
- ¾ cup all-purpose flour
- ¾ cup cornstarch
- ¼ teaspoon chili powder
- ½ teaspoon ground cumin
- ½ pound (227 g) cod, cut into large pieces
- 6 corn tortillas
- Cooking spray
- Salsa:
- 1 mango, peeled and diced
- ¼ red bell pepper, diced
- ½ small jalapeño, diced
- ¼ red onion, minced

- Juice of half a lime
- Pinch chopped fresh cilantro
- ¼ teaspoon salt
- ¼ teaspoon ground black pepper

Directions:
1. Spritz the air fryer basket with cooking spray.
2. Whisk the egg with beer in a bowl. Combine the flour, cornstarch, chili powder, and cumin in a separate bowl.
3. Dredge the cod in the egg mixture first, then in the flour mixture to coat well. Shake the excess off.
4. Arrange the cod in the basket and spritz with cooking spray.
5. Put the air fryer basket on the baking pan and slide into Rack Position 2, select Air Fry, set temperature to 380ºF (193ºC) and set time to 17 minutes.
6. Flip the cod halfway through the cooking time.
7. When cooked, the cod should be golden brown and crunchy.
8. Meanwhile, combine the ingredients for the salsa in a small bowl. Stir to mix well.
9. Unfold the tortillas on a clean work surface, then divide the fish on the tortillas and spread the salsa on top. Fold to serve.

110.Banana Cake With Peanut Butter

Servings:2
Cooking Time: 35 Minutes
Ingredients:
- 1 cup + 1 tbsp flour
- 1 tsp baking powder
- ⅓ cup sugar
- 2 bananas, mashed
- ¼ cup vegetable oil
- 1 egg, beaten
- 1 tsp vanilla extract
- ¾ cup chopped walnuts
- ¼ tsp salt
- 2 tbsp peanut butter
- 2 tbsp sour cream

Directions:
1. Preheat on AirFry function to 330 F. In a bowl, combine flour, salt, and baking powder In another bowl, combine bananas, oil, egg, peanut butter, vanilla, sugar, and sour cream.
2. Gently mix the both mixtures. Stir in the chopped walnuts. Pour the batter into a greased baking dish and press Start. Cook for 25 minutes. Serve chilled.

111.Healthy Squash

Servings: 4
Cooking Time: 25 Minutes
Ingredients:

- 2 lbs yellow squash, cut into half-moons
- 1 tsp Italian seasoning
- ¼ tsp pepper
- 1 tbsp olive oil
- ¼ tsp salt

Directions:
1. Add all ingredients into the large bowl and toss well.
2. Preheat the air fryer to 400 F.
3. Add squash mixture into the air fryer basket and cook for 10 minutes.
4. Shake basket and cook for another 10 minutes.
5. Shake once again and cook for 5 minutes more.
- **Nutrition Info:** Calories 70, Fat 4 g, Carbohydrates 7 g, Sugar 4 g, Protein 2 g, Cholesterol 1 mg

112.Perfect Sausage-hash Brown Casserole

Servings: 12
Cooking Time: 45 Minutes
Ingredients:
- 6 eggs
- 16 oz frozen hash browns, defrosted
- 1/2 cup milk
- 2 cups cheddar cheese, shredded
- 1 lb breakfast sausage, browned
- 1/2 tsp pepper
- 1 tsp kosher salt

Directions:
1. Fit the oven with the rack in position
2. Layer hash browns in a greased 9*9-inch casserole dish.
3. Spread sausage on top of hash browns. Sprinkle cheese on top.
4. In a mixing bowl, whisk eggs with milk, pepper, and salt.
5. Pour egg mixture over hash brown mixture.
6. Set to bake at 350 F for 50 minutes. After 5 minutes place the casserole dish in the preheated oven.
7. Serve and enjoy.
- **Nutrition Info:** Calories 323 Fat 24.4 g Carbohydrates 11.7 g Sugar 0.7 g Protein 15.8 g Cholesterol 134 mg

113.Asparagus And Cheese Strata

Servings:4
Cooking Time: 17 Minutes
Ingredients:
- 6 asparagus spears, cut into 2-inch pieces
- 1 tablespoon water
- 2 slices whole-wheat bread, cut into ½-inch cubes
- 4 eggs
- 3 tablespoons whole milk
- 2 tablespoons chopped flat-leaf parsley

- ½ cup grated Havarti or Swiss cheese
- Pinch salt
- Freshly ground black pepper, to taste
- Cooking spray

Directions:
1. Add the asparagus spears and 1 tablespoon of water in the baking pan.
2. Slide the baking pan into Rack Position 1, select Convection Bake, set temperature to 330ºF (166ºC) and set time to 4 minutes.
3. When cooking is complete, the asparagus spears will be crisp-tender.
4. Remove the asparagus from the pan and drain on paper towels.
5. Spritz the pan with cooking spray. Place the bread and asparagus in the pan.
6. Whisk together the eggs and milk in a medium mixing bowl until creamy. Fold in the parsley, cheese, salt, and pepper and stir to combine. Pour this mixture into the baking pan.
7. Select Bake and set time to 13 minutes. Put the pan back to the oven. When done, the eggs will be set and the top will be lightly browned.
8. Let cool for 5 minutes before slicing and serving.

114.Tomato Oatmeal

Servings: 4
Cooking Time: 20 Minutes
Ingredients:
- 1 cup tomatoes, cubed
- 1 cup old fashioned oats
- 2 cups almond milk
- A drizzle of avocado oil
- A pinch of salt and black pepper
- 1 teaspoon cilantro, chopped
- 1 teaspoon basil, chopped
- 2 spring onions, chopped

Directions:
1. In your air fryer, combine the tomatoes with the oats and the other ingredients, toss and cook at 360 degrees F for 20 minutes.
2. Divide the oatmeal into bowls and serve for breakfast.
- **Nutrition Info:** calories 140, fat 2, fiber 3, carbs 8, protein 4

LUNCH RECIPES

115. Lemon Pepper Turkey

Servings: 6
Cooking Time: 45 Minutes
Ingredients:
- 3 lbs. turkey breast
- 2 tablespoons oil
- 1 tablespoon Worcestershire sauce
- 1 teaspoon lemon pepper
- 1/2 teaspoon salt

Directions:
1. Whisk everything in a bowl and coat the turkey liberally.
2. Place the turkey in the Air fryer basket.
3. Press "Power Button" of Air Fry Oven and turn the dial to select the "Air Fry" mode.
4. Press the Time button and again turn the dial to set the cooking time to 45 minutes.
5. Now push the Temp button and rotate the dial to set the temperature at 375 degrees F.
6. Once preheated, place the air fryer basket inside and close its lid.
7. Serve warm.
- **Nutrition Info:** Calories 391 Total Fat 2.8 g Saturated Fat 0.6 g Cholesterol 330 mg Sodium 62 mg Total Carbs 36.5 g Fiber 9.2 g Sugar 4.5 g Protein 6.6

116. Carrot And Beef Cocktail Balls

Servings: 10
Cooking Time: 20 Minutes
Ingredients:
- 1-pound ground beef
- 2 carrots
- 1 red onion, peeled and chopped
- 2 cloves garlic
- 1/2 teaspoon dried rosemary, crushed
- 1/2 teaspoon dried basil
- 1 teaspoon dried oregano
- 1 egg
- 3/4 cup breadcrumbs
- 1/2 teaspoon salt
- 1/2 teaspoon black pepper, or to taste
- 1 cup plain flour

Directions:
1. Preparing the ingredients. Place ground beef in a large bowl.
2. In a food processor, pulse the carrot, onion and garlic; transfer the vegetable mixture to a large-sized bowl.
3. Then, add the rosemary, basil, oregano, egg, breadcrumbs, salt, and black pepper.
4. Shape the mixture into even balls; refrigerate for about 30 minutes.
5. Roll the balls into the flour.
6. Air frying. Close air fryer lid.
7. Then, air-fry the balls at 350 degrees f for about 20 minutes, turning occasionally; work with batches. Serve with toothpicks.
- **Nutrition Info:** Calories 284 Total fat 7.9 g Saturated fat 1.4 g Cholesterol 36 mg Sodium 704 mg Total carbs 46 g Fiber 3.6 g Sugar 5.5 g Protein 17.9 g

117. Turkey And Mushroom Stew

Servings: 4
Cooking Time: 12 Minutes
Ingredients:
- ½ lb. brown mushrooms; sliced
- 1 turkey breast, skinless, boneless; cubed and browned
- ¼ cup tomato sauce
- 1 tbsp. parsley; chopped.
- Salt and black pepper to taste.

Directions:
1. In a pan that fits your air fryer, mix the turkey with the mushrooms, salt, pepper and tomato sauce, toss, introduce in the fryer and cook at 350°F for 25 minutes
2. Divide into bowls and serve for lunch with parsley sprinkled on top.
- **Nutrition Info:** Calories: 220; Fat: 12g; Fiber: 2g; Carbs: 5g; Protein: 12g

118. Spicy Avocado Cauliflower Toast

Servings: 2
Cooking Time: 15 Minutes
Ingredients:
- 1/2 large head of cauliflower, leaves removed
- 3 1/4 teaspoons olive oil
- 1 small jalapeño
- 1 tablespoon chopped cilantro leaves
- 2 slices whole grain bread
- 1 medium avocado
- Salt and pepper
- 5 radishes
- 1 green onion
- 2 teaspoons hot sauce
- 1 lime

Directions:
1. Start by preheating toaster oven to 450°F.
2. Cut cauliflower into thick pieces, about 3/4-inches-thick, and slice jalapeño into thin slices.
3. Place cauliflower and jalapeño in a bowl and mix together with 2 teaspoons olive oil.
4. Add salt and pepper to taste and mix for another minute.
5. Coat a pan with another teaspoon of olive oil, then lay the cauliflower mixture flat across the pan.
6. Cook for 20 minutes, flipping in the last 5 minutes.

7. Reduce heat to toast.
8. Sprinkle cilantro over the mix while it is still warm, and set aside.
9. Brush bread with remaining oil and toast until golden brown, about 5 minutes.
10. Dice onion and radish.
11. Mash avocado in a bowl, then spread on toast and sprinkle salt and pepper to taste.
12. Put cauliflower mix on toast and cover with onion and radish. Drizzle with hot sauce and serve with a lime wedge.
- **Nutrition Info:** Calories: 359, Sodium: 308 mg, Dietary Fiber: 11.1 g, Total Fat: 28.3 g, Total Carbs: 26.4 g, Protein: 6.6 g.

119.Sweet Potato Chips

Servings: 2
Cooking Time: 40 Minutes
Ingredients:
- 2 sweet potatoes
- Salt and pepper to taste
- Olive oil
- Cinnamon

Directions:
1. Start by preheating toaster oven to 400°F.
2. Cut off each end of potato and discard.
3. Cut potatoes into 1/2-inch slices.
4. Brush a pan with olive oil and lay potato slices flat on the pan.
5. Bake for 20 minutes, then flip and bake for another 20.
- **Nutrition Info:** Calories: 139, Sodium: 29 mg, Dietary Fiber: 8.2 g, Total Fat: 0.5 g, Total Carbs: 34.1 g, Protein: 1.9 g.

120.Chicken Potato Bake

Servings: 4
Cooking Time: 25 Minutes
Ingredients:
- 4 potatoes, diced
- 1 tablespoon garlic, minced
- 1.5 tablespoons olive oil
- 1/8 teaspoon salt
- 1/8 teaspoon pepper
- 1.5 lbs. boneless skinless chicken
- 3/4 cup mozzarella cheese, shredded
- parsley chopped

Directions:
1. Toss chicken and potatoes with all the spices and oil in a baking pan.
2. Drizzle the cheese on top of the chicken and potato.
3. Press "Power Button" of Air Fry Oven and turn the dial to select the "Bake" mode.
4. Press the Time button and again turn the dial to set the cooking time to 25 minutes.
5. Now push the Temp button and rotate the dial to set the temperature at 375 degrees F.

6. Once preheated, place the baking pan inside and close its lid.
7. Serve warm.
- **Nutrition Info:** Calories 695 Total Fat 17.5 g Saturated Fat 4.8 g Cholesterol 283 mg Sodium 355 mg Total Carbs 26.4 g Fiber 1.8 g Sugar 0.8 g Protein 117.4 g

121.Garlic Chicken Potatoes

Servings: 4
Cooking Time: 30 Minutes
Ingredients:
- 2 lbs. red potatoes, quartered
- 3 tablespoons olive oil
- 1/2 teaspoon cumin seeds
- Salt and black pepper, to taste
- 4 garlic cloves, chopped
- 2 tablespoons brown sugar
- 1 lemon (1/2 juiced and 1/2 cut into wedges)
- Pinch of red pepper flakes
- 4 skinless, boneless chicken breasts
- 2 tablespoons cilantro, chopped

Directions:
1. Place the chicken, lemon, garlic, and potatoes in a baking pan.
2. Toss the spices, herbs, oil, and sugar in a bowl.
3. Add this mixture to the chicken and veggies then toss well to coat.
4. Press "Power Button" of Air Fry Oven and turn the dial to select the "Bake" mode.
5. Press the Time button and again turn the dial to set the cooking time to 30 minutes.
6. Now push the Temp button and rotate the dial to set the temperature at 400 degrees F.
7. Once preheated, place the baking pan inside and close its lid.
8. Serve warm.
- **Nutrition Info:** Calories 545 Total Fat 36.4 g Saturated Fat 10.1 g Cholesterol 200 mg Sodium 272 mg Total Carbs 40.7 g Fiber 0.2 g Sugar 0.1 g Protein 42.5 g

122.Creamy Green Beans And Tomatoes

Servings: 4
Cooking Time: 20 Minutes
Ingredients:
- 1 pound green beans, trimmed and halved
- ½ pound cherry tomatoes, halved
- 2 tablespoons olive oil
- 1 teaspoon oregano, dried
- 1 teaspoon basil, dried
- Salt and black pepper to the taste
- 1 cup heavy cream
- ½ tablespoon cilantro, chopped

Directions:
1. In your air fryer's pan, combine the green beans with the tomatoes and the other

Ingredients:, toss and cook at 360 degrees F for 20 minutes.
2. Divide the mix between plates and serve.
- **Nutrition Info:** Calories 174, fat 5, fiber 7, carbs 11, protein 4

123.Oregano Chicken Breast

Servings: 6
Cooking Time: 25 Minutes
Ingredients:
- 2 lbs. chicken breasts, minced
- 1 tablespoon avocado oil
- 1 teaspoon smoked paprika
- 1 teaspoon garlic powder
- 1 teaspoon oregano
- 1/2 teaspoon salt
- Black pepper, to taste

Directions:
1. Toss all the meatball Ingredients: in a bowl and mix well.
2. Make small meatballs out this mixture and place them in the air fryer basket.
3. Press "Power Button" of Air Fry Oven and turn the dial to select the "Air Fry" mode.
4. Press the Time button and again turn the dial to set the cooking time to 25 minutes.
5. Now push the Temp button and rotate the dial to set the temperature at 375 degrees F.
6. Once preheated, place the air fryer basket inside and close its lid.
7. Serve warm.
- **Nutrition Info:** Calories 352 Total Fat 14 g Saturated Fat 2 g Cholesterol 65 mg Sodium 220 mg Total Carbs 15.8 g Fiber 0.2 g Sugar 1 g Protein 26 g

124.Chicken Breasts With Chimichurri

Servings: 1
Cooking Time: 35 Minutes
Ingredients:
- 1 chicken breast, bone-in, skin-on
- Chimichurri
- ½ bunch fresh cilantro
- 1/4 bunch fresh parsley
- ½ shallot, peeled, cut in quarters
- ½ tablespoon paprika ground
- ½ tablespoon chili powder
- ½ tablespoon fennel ground
- ½ teaspoon black pepper, ground
- ½ teaspoon onion powder
- 1 teaspoon salt
- ½ teaspoon garlic powder
- ½ teaspoon cumin ground
- ½ tablespoon canola oil
- Chimichurri
- 2 tablespoons olive oil
- 4 garlic cloves, peeled
- Zest and juice of 1 lemon
- 1 teaspoon kosher salt

Directions:
1. Preheat the Air fryer to 300 degree F and grease an Air fryer basket.
2. Combine all the spices in a suitable bowl and season the chicken with it.
3. Sprinkle with canola oil and arrange the chicken in the Air fryer basket.
4. Cook for about 35 minutes and dish out in a platter.
5. Put all the ingredients in the blender and blend until smooth.
6. Serve the chicken with chimichurri sauce.
- **Nutrition Info:** Calories: 140, Fats: 7.9g, Carbohydrates: 1.8g, Sugar: 7.1g, Proteins: 7.2g, Sodium: 581mg

125.Easy Prosciutto Grilled Cheese

Servings: 1
Cooking Time: 5 Minutes
Ingredients:
- 2 slices muenster cheese
- 2 slices white bread
- Four thinly-shaved pieces of prosciutto
- 1 tablespoon sweet and spicy pickles

Directions:
1. Set toaster oven to the Toast setting.
2. Place one slice of cheese on each piece of bread.
3. Put prosciutto on one slice and pickles on the other.
4. Transfer to a baking sheet and toast for 4 minutes or until the cheese is melted.
5. Combine the sides, cut, and serve.
- **Nutrition Info:** Calories: 460, Sodium: 2180 mg, Dietary Fiber: 0 g, Total Fat: 25.2 g, Total Carbs: 11.9 g, Protein: 44.2 g.

126.Rolled Salmon Sandwich

Servings: 1
Cooking Time: 5 Minutes
Ingredients:
- 1 piece of flatbread
- 1 salmon filet
- Pinch of salt
- 1 tablespoon green onion, chopped
- 1/4 teaspoon dried sumac
- 1/2 teaspoon thyme
- 1/2 teaspoon sesame seeds
- 1/4 English cucumber
- 1 tablespoon yogurt

Directions:
1. Start by peeling and chopping the cucumber. Cut the salmon at a 45-degree angle into 4 slices and lay them flat on the flatbread.
2. Sprinkle salmon with salt to taste. Sprinkle onions, thyme, sumac, and sesame seeds evenly over the salmon.
3. Broil the salmon for at least 3 minutes, but longer if you want a more well-done fish.

4. While you broil your salmon, mix together the yogurt and cucumber. Remove your flatbread from the toaster oven and put it on a plate, then spoon the yogurt mix over the salmon.
5. Fold the sides of the flatbread in and roll it up for a gourmet lunch that you can take on the go.
- **Nutrition Info:** Calories: 347, Sodium: 397 mg, Dietary Fiber: 1.6 g, Total Fat: 12.4 g, Total Carbs: 20.6 g, Protein: 38.9 g.

127.Herb-roasted Turkey Breast

Servings: 8
Cooking Time: 60 Minutes
Ingredients:
- 3 lb turkey breast
- Rub Ingredients:
- 2 tbsp olive oil
- 2 tbsp lemon juice
- 1 tbsp minced Garlic
- 2 tsp ground mustard
- 2 tsp kosher salt
- 1 tsp pepper
- 1 tsp dried rosemary
- 1 tsp dried thyme
- 1 tsp ground sage

Directions:
1. Take a small bowl and thoroughly combine the Rub Ingredients: in it. Rub this on the outside of the turkey breast and under any loose skin.
2. Place the coated turkey breast keeping skin side up on a cooking tray.
3. Place the drip pan at the bottom of the cooking chamber of the Instant Pot Duo Crisp Air Fryer. Select Air Fry option, post this, adjust the temperature to 360°F and the time to one hour, then touch start.
4. When preheated, add the food to the cooking tray in the lowest position. Close the lid for cooking.
5. When the Air Fry program is complete, check to make sure that the thickest portion of the meat reads at least 160°F, remove the turkey and let it rest for 10 minutes before slicing and serving.
- **Nutrition Info:** Calories 214, Total Fat 10g, Total Carbs 2g, Protein 29g

128.Coriander Artichokes(3)

Servings: 4
Cooking Time: 12 Minutes
Ingredients:
- 12 oz. artichoke hearts
- 1 tbsp. lemon juice
- 1 tsp. coriander, ground
- ½ tsp. cumin seeds
- ½ tsp. olive oil
- Salt and black pepper to taste.

Directions:
1. In a pan that fits your air fryer, mix all the ingredients, toss, introduce the pan in the fryer and cook at 370°F for 15 minutes
2. Divide the mix between plates and serve as a side dish.
- **Nutrition Info:** Calories: 200; Fat: 7g; Fiber: 2g; Carbs: 5g; Protein: 8g

129.Air Fryer Fish

Servings: 4
Cooking Time: 17 Minutes
Ingredients:
- 4-6 Whiting Fish fillets cut in half
- Oil to mist
- Fish Seasoning
- ¾ cup very fine cornmeal
- ¼ cup flour
- 2 tsp old bay
- 1 ½ tsp salt
- 1 tsp paprika
- ½ tsp garlic powder
- ½ tsp black pepper

Directions:
1. Put the Ingredients: for fish seasoning in a Ziplock bag and shake it well. Set aside.
2. Rinse and pat dry the fish fillets with paper towels. Make sure that they still are damp.
3. Place the fish fillets in a ziplock bag and shake until they are completely covered with seasoning.
4. Place the fillets on a baking rack to let any excess flour to fall off.
5. Grease the bottom of the Instant Pot Duo Crisp Air Fryer basket tray and place the fillets on the tray. Close the lid, select the Air Fry option and cook filets on 400°F for 10 minutes.
6. Open the Air Fryer lid and spray the fish with oil on the side facing up before flipping it over, ensure that the fish is fully coated. Flip and cook another side of the fish for 7 minutes. Remove the fish and serve.
- **Nutrition Info:** Calories 193, Total Fat 1g, Total Carbs 27g, Protein 19g

130.Kale And Pine Nuts

Servings: 4
Cooking Time: 12 Minutes
Ingredients:
- 10 cups kale; torn
- 1/3 cup pine nuts
- 2 tbsp. lemon zest; grated
- 1 tbsp. lemon juice
- 2 tbsp. olive oil
- Salt and black pepper to taste.

Directions:

1. In a pan that fits the air fryer, combine all the ingredients, toss, introduce the pan in the machine and cook at 380°F for 15 minutes
2. Divide between plates and serve as a side dish.
- **Nutrition Info:** Calories: 121; Fat: 9g; Fiber: 2g; Carbs: 4g; Protein: 5g

131.Barbecue Air Fried Chicken

Servings: 10
Cooking Time: 26 Minutes
Ingredients:
- 1 teaspoon Liquid Smoke
- 2 cloves Fresh Garlic smashed
- 1/2 cup Apple Cider Vinegar
- 3 pounds Chuck Roast well-marbled with intramuscular fat
- 1 Tablespoon Kosher Salt
- 1 Tablespoon Freshly Ground Black Pepper
- 2 teaspoons Garlic Powder
- 1.5 cups Barbecue Sauce
- 1/4 cup Light Brown Sugar + more for sprinkling
- 2 Tablespoons Honey optional and in place of 2 TBL sugar

Directions:
1. Add meat to the Instant Pot Duo Crisp Air Fryer Basket, spreading out the meat.
2. Select the option Air Fry.
3. Close the Air Fryer lid and cook at 300 degrees F for 8 minutes. Pause the Air Fryer and flip meat over after 4 minutes.
4. Remove the lid and baste with more barbecue sauce and sprinkle with a little brown sugar.
5. Again Close the Air Fryer lid and set the temperature at 400°F for 9 minutes. Watch meat though the lid and flip it over after 5 minutes.
- **Nutrition Info:** Calories 360, Total Fat 16g, Total Carbs 27g, Protein 27g

132.Spicy Egg And Ground Turkey Bake

Servings: 6
Cooking Time: 10 Minutes
Ingredients:
- 1½ pounds ground turkey
- 6 whole eggs, well beaten
- 1/3 teaspoon smoked paprika
- 2 egg whites, beaten
- Tabasco sauce, for drizzling
- 2 tablespoons sesame oil
- 2 leeks, chopped
- 3 cloves garlic, finely minced
- 1 teaspoon ground black pepper
- 1/2 teaspoon sea salt

Directions:

1. Warm the oil in a pan over moderate heat; then, sweat the leeks and garlic until tender; stir periodically.
2. Next, grease 6 oven safe ramekins with pan spray. Divide the sautéed mixture among six ramekins.
3. In a bowl, beat the eggs and egg whites using a wire whisk. Stir in the smoked paprika, salt and black pepper; whisk until everything is thoroughly combined. Divide the egg mixture among the ramekins.
4. Air-fry approximately 22 minutes at 345 degrees F. Drizzle Tabasco sauce over each portion and serve.
- **Nutrition Info:** 298 Calories; 16g Fat; 4g Carbs; 16g Protein; 9g Sugars; 7g Fiber

133.Bok Choy And Butter Sauce(1)

Servings: 4
Cooking Time: 12 Minutes
Ingredients:
- 2 bok choy heads; trimmed and cut into strips
- 1 tbsp. butter; melted
- 2 tbsp. chicken stock
- 1 tsp. lemon juice
- 1 tbsp. olive oil
- A pinch of salt and black pepper

Directions:
1. In a pan that fits your air fryer, mix all the ingredients, toss, introduce the pan in the air fryer and cook at 380°F for 15 minutes.
2. Divide between plates and serve as a side dish
- **Nutrition Info:** Calories: 141; Fat: 3g; Fiber: 2g; Carbs: 4g; Protein: 3g

134.Delicious Chicken Burgers

Servings: 4
Cooking Time: 30 Minutes
Ingredients:
- 4 boneless, skinless chicken breasts
- 1¾ ounces plain flour
- 2 eggs
- 4 hamburger buns, split and toasted
- 4 mozzarella cheese slices
- 1 teaspoon mustard powder
- ½ teaspoon paprika
- 1 teaspoon Worcestershire sauce
- ¼ teaspoon dried parsley
- ¼ teaspoon dried tarragon
- ¼ teaspoon dried oregano
- 1 teaspoon dried garlic
- 1 teaspoon chicken seasoning
- ½ teaspoon cayenne pepper
- Salt and black pepper, as required

Directions:
1. Preheat the Air fryer to 355 degree F and grease an Air fryer basket.

2. Put the chicken breasts, mustard, paprika, Worcestershire sauce, salt, and black pepper in a food processor and pulse until minced.
3. Make 4 equal-sized patties from the mixture.
4. Place the flour in a shallow bowl and whisk the egg in a second bowl.
5. Combine dried herbs and spices in a third bowl.
6. Coat each chicken patty with flour, dip into whisked egg and then coat with breadcrumb mixture.
7. Arrange the chicken patties into the Air fryer basket in a single layer and cook for about 30 minutes, flipping once in between.
8. Place half bun in a plate, layer with lettuce leaf, patty and cheese slice.
9. Cover with bun top and dish out to serve warm.
- **Nutrition Info:** Calories: 562, Fat: 20.3g, Carbohydrates: 33g, Sugar: 3.3g, Protein: 58.7g, Sodium: 560mg

135.Crisp Chicken Casserole

Servings: 4
Cooking Time: 15 Minutes
Ingredients:
- 3 cup chicken, shredded
- 12 oz bag egg noodles
- 1/2 large onion
- 1/2 cup chopped carrots
- 1/4 cup frozen peas
- 1/4 cup frozen broccoli pieces
- 2 stalks celery chopped
- 5 cup chicken broth
- 1 tsp garlic powder
- salt and pepper to taste
- 1 cup cheddar cheese, shredded
- 1 package French's onions
- 1/4 cup sour cream
- 1 can cream of chicken and mushroom soup

Directions:
1. Place the chicken, vegetables, garlic powder, salt and pepper, and broth and stir. Then place it into the Instant Pot Duo Crisp Air Fryer Basket.
2. Press or lightly stir the egg noodles into the mix until damp/wet.
3. Select the option Air Fryer and cook for 4 minutes.
4. Stir in the sour cream, can of soup, cheese, and 1/3 of the French's onions.
5. Top with the remaining French's onions and close the Air Fryer lid and cook for about 10 more minutes.
- **Nutrition Info:** Calories 301, Total Fat 17g, Total Carbs 17g, Protein 20g

136.Lime And Mustard Marinated Chicken

Servings: 4
Cooking Time: 10 Minutes
Ingredients:
- 1/2 teaspoon stone-ground mustard
- 1/2 teaspoon minced fresh oregano
- 1/3 cup freshly squeezed lime juice
- 2 small-sized chicken breasts, skin-on
- 1 teaspoon kosher salt
- 1teaspoon freshly cracked mixed peppercorns

Directions:
1. Preheat your Air Fryer to 345 degrees F.
2. Toss all of the above ingredients in a medium-sized mixing dish; allow it to marinate overnight.
3. Cook in the preheated Air Fryer for 26 minutes.
- **Nutrition Info:** 255 Calories; 15g Fat; 7g Carbs; 33g Protein; 8g Sugars; 3g Fiber

137.Baked Shrimp Scampi

Servings: 4
Cooking Time: 10 Minutes
Ingredients:
- 1 lb large shrimp
- 8 tbsp butter
- 1 tbsp minced garlic (use 2 for extra garlic flavor)
- 1/4 cup white wine or cooking sherry
- 1/2 tsp salt
- 1/4 tsp cayenne pepper
- 1/4 tsp paprika
- 1/2 tsp onion powder
- 3/4 cup bread crumbs

Directions:
1. Take a bowl and mix the bread crumbs with dry seasonings.
2. On the stovetop (or in the Instant Pot on saute), melt the butter with the garlic and the white wine.
3. Remove from heat and add the shrimp and the bread crumb mix.
4. Transfer the mix to a casserole dish.
5. Choose the Bake operation and add food to the Instant Pot Duo Crisp Air Fryer. Close the lid and Bake at 350°F for 10 minutes or until they are browned.
6. Serve and enjoy.
- **Nutrition Info:** Calories 422, Total Fat 26g, Total Carbs 18g, Protein 29 g

138.Rosemary Lemon Chicken

Servings: 8
Cooking Time: 45 Minutes
Ingredients:
- 4-lb. chicken, cut into pieces
- Salt and black pepper, to taste
- Flour for dredging 3 tablespoons olive oil

- 1 large onion, sliced
- Peel of ½ lemon
- 2 large garlic cloves, minced
- 1 1/2 teaspoons rosemary leaves
- 1 tablespoon honey
- 1/4 cup lemon juice
- 1 cup chicken broth

Directions:
1. Dredges the chicken through the flour then place in the baking pan.
2. Whisk broth with the rest of the Ingredients: in a bowl.
3. Pour this mixture over the dredged chicken in the pan.
4. Press "Power Button" of Air Fry Oven and turn the dial to select the "Bake" mode.
5. Press the Time button and again turn the dial to set the cooking time to 45 minutes.
6. Now push the Temp button and rotate the dial to set the temperature at 400 degrees F.
7. Once preheated, place the baking pan inside and close its lid.
8. Baste the chicken with its sauce every 15 minutes.
9. Serve warm.
- **Nutrition Info:** Calories 405 Total Fat 22.7 g Saturated Fat 6.1 g Cholesterol 4 mg Sodium 227 mg Total Carbs 26.1 g Fiber 1.4 g Sugar 0.9 g Protein 45.2 g

139.Marinated Chicken Parmesan

Servings: 4
Cooking Time: 20 Minutes
Ingredients:
- 2 cups breadcrumbs
- 1 teaspoon dried oregano
- 1/2 teaspoon garlic powder
- 4 teaspoons paprika
- 1/2 teaspoon salt
- 1/2 teaspoon black pepper
- 2 egg whites
- 1/2 cup skim milk
- 1/2 cup flour
- 4 (6 oz.) chicken breast halves, lb.ed
- Cooking spray
- 1 jar marinara sauce
- 3/4 cup mozzarella cheese, shredded
- 2 tablespoons Parmesan, shredded

Directions:
1. Whisk the flour with all the spices in a bowl and beat the eggs in another.
2. Coat the pounded chicken with flour then dip in the egg whites.
3. Dredge the chicken breast through the crumbs well.
4. Spread marinara sauce in a baking dish and place the crusted chicken on it.
5. Drizzle cheese on top of the chicken.

6. Press "Power Button" of Air Fry Oven and turn the dial to select the "Bake" mode.
7. Press the Time button and again turn the dial to set the cooking time to 20 minutes.
8. Now push the Temp button and rotate the dial to set the temperature at 400 degrees F.
9. Once preheated, place the baking pan inside and close its lid.
10. Serve warm.
- **Nutrition Info:** Calories 361 Total Fat 16.3 g Saturated Fat 4.9 g Cholesterol 114 mg Sodium 515 mg Total Carbs 19.3 g Fiber 0.1 g Sugar 18.2 g Protein 33.3 g

140.Persimmon Toast With Sour Cream & Cinnamon

Servings: 1
Cooking Time: 5 Minutes
Ingredients:
- 1 slice of wheat bread
- 1/2 persimmon
- Sour cream to taste
- Sugar to taste
- Cinnamon to taste

Directions:
1. Spread a thin layer of sour cream across the bread.
2. Slice the persimmon into 1/4 inch pieces and lay them across the bread.
3. Sprinkle cinnamon and sugar over persimmon.
4. Toast in toaster oven until bread and persimmon begin to brown.
- **Nutrition Info:** Calories: 89, Sodium: 133 mg, Dietary Fiber: 2.0 g, Total Fat: 1.1 g, Total Carbs: 16.5 g, Protein: 3.8 g.

141.Turkey Meatballs With Manchego Cheese

Servings: 4
Cooking Time: 10 Minutes
Ingredients:
- 1 pound ground turkey
- 1/2 pound ground pork
- 1 egg, well beaten
- 1 teaspoon dried basil
- 1 teaspoon dried rosemary
- 1/4 cup Manchego cheese, grated
- 2 tablespoons yellow onions, finely chopped
- 1 teaspoon fresh garlic, finely chopped
- Sea salt and ground black pepper, to taste

Directions:
1. In a mixing bowl, combine all the ingredients until everything is well incorporated.
2. Shape the mixture into 1-inch balls.
3. Cook the meatballs in the preheated Air Fryer at 380 degrees for 7 minutes. Shake

halfway through the cooking time. Work in batches.
4. Serve with your favorite pasta.
- **Nutrition Info:** 386 Calories; 24g Fat; 9g Carbs; 41g Protein; 3g Sugars; 2g Fiber

142.Country Comfort Corn Bread

Servings: 12
Cooking Time: 20 Minutes
Ingredients:
- 1 cup yellow cornmeal
- 1-1/2 cups oatmeal
- 1/4 teaspoon salt
- 1/4 cup granulated sugar
- 2 teaspoons baking powder
- 1 cup milk
- 1 large egg
- 1/2 cup applesauce

Directions:
1. Start by blending oatmeal into a fine powder.
2. Preheat toaster oven to 400°F.
3. Mix oatmeal, cornmeal, salt, sugar, and baking powder, and stir to blend.
4. Add milk, egg, and applesauce, and mix well.
5. Pour into a pan and bake for 20 minutes.
- **Nutrition Info:** Calories: 113, Sodium: 71 mg, Dietary Fiber: 1.9 g, Total Fat: 1.9 g, Total Carbs: 21.5 g, Protein: 3.4 g.

143.Green Bean Casserole(2)

Servings: 4
Cooking Time: 12 Minutes
Ingredients:
- 1 lb. fresh green beans, edges trimmed
- ½ oz. pork rinds, finely ground
- 1 oz. full-fat cream cheese
- ½ cup heavy whipping cream.
- ¼ cup diced yellow onion
- ½ cup chopped white mushrooms
- ½ cup chicken broth
- 4 tbsp. unsalted butter.
- ¼ tsp. xanthan gum

Directions:
1. In a medium skillet over medium heat, melt the butter. Sauté the onion and mushrooms until they become soft and fragrant, about 3–5 minutes.
2. Add the heavy whipping cream, cream cheese and broth to the pan. Whisk until smooth. Bring to a boil and then reduce to a simmer. Sprinkle the xanthan gum into the pan and remove from heat
3. Chop the green beans into 2-inch pieces and place into a 4-cup round baking dish. Pour the sauce mixture over them and stir until coated. Top the dish with ground pork rinds. Place into the air fryer basket

4. Adjust the temperature to 320 Degrees F and set the timer for 15 minutes. Top will be golden and green beans fork tender when fully cooked. Serve warm.
- **Nutrition Info:** Calories: 267; Protein: 6g; Fiber: 2g; Fat: 24g; Carbs: 7g

144.Air Fried Sausages

Servings: 6
Cooking Time: 13 Minutes
Ingredients:
- 6 sausage
- olive oil spray

Directions:
1. Pour 5 cup of water into Instant Pot Duo Crisp Air Fryer. Place air fryer basket inside the pot, spray inside with nonstick spray and put sausage links inside.
2. Close the Air Fryer lid and steam for about 5 minutes.
3. Remove the lid once done. Spray links with olive oil and close air crisp lid.
4. Set to air crisp at 400°F for 8 min flipping halfway through so both sides get browned.
- **Nutrition Info:** Calories 267, Total Fat 23g, Total Carbs 2g, Protein 13g

145.Herb-roasted Chicken Tenders

Servings: 2
Cooking Time: 10 Minutes
Ingredients:
- 7 ounces chicken tenders
- 1 tablespoon olive oil
- 1/2 teaspoon Herbes de Provence
- 2 tablespoons Dijon mustard
- 1 tablespoon honey
- Salt and pepper

Directions:
1. Start by preheating toaster oven to 450°F.
2. Brush bottom of pan with 1/2 tablespoon olive oil.
3. Season the chicken with herbs, salt, and pepper.
4. Place the chicken in a single flat layer in the pan and drizzle the remaining olive oil over it.
5. Bake for about 10 minutes.
6. While the chicken is baking, mix together the mustard and honey for a tasty condiment.
- **Nutrition Info:** Calories: 297, Sodium: 268 mg, Dietary Fiber: 0.8 g, Total Fat: 15.5 g, Total Carbs: 9.6 g, Protein: 29.8 g.

146.Roasted Grape And Goat Cheese Crostinis

Servings: 10
Cooking Time: 5 Minutes
Ingredients:

- 1 pound seedless red grapes
- 1 teaspoon chopped rosemary
- 4 tablespoons olive oil
- 1 rustic French baguette
- 1 cup sliced shallots
- 2 tablespoons unsalted butter
- 8 ounces goat cheese
- 1 tablespoon honey

Directions:
1. Start by preheating toaster oven to 400°F.
2. Toss grapes, rosemary, and 1 tablespoon of olive oil in a large bowl.
3. Transfer to a roasting pan and roast for 20 minutes.
4. Remove the pan from the oven and set aside to cool.
5. Slice the baguette into 1/2-inch-thick pieces.
6. Brush each slice with olive oil and place on baking sheet.
7. Bake for 8 minutes, then remove from oven and set aside.
8. In a medium skillet add butter and one tablespoon of olive oil.
9. Add shallots and sauté for about 10 minutes.
10. Mix goat cheese and honey in a medium bowl, then add contents of shallot pan and mix thoroughly.
11. Spread shallot mixture onto baguette, top with grapes, and serve.
- **Nutrition Info:** Calories: 238, Sodium: 139 mg, Dietary Fiber: 0.6 g, Total Fat: 16.3 g, Total Carbs: 16.4 g, Protein: 8.4 g.

147.Glazed Lamb Chops

Servings: 4
Cooking Time: 15 Minutes
Ingredients:
- 1 tablespoon Dijon mustard
- ½ tablespoon fresh lime juice
- 1 teaspoon honey
- ½ teaspoon olive oil
- Salt and ground black pepper, as required
- 4 (4-ounce) lamb loin chops

Directions:
1. In a black pepper large bowl, mix together the mustard, lemon juice, oil, honey, salt, and black pepper.
2. Add the chops and coat with the mixture generously.
3. Place the chops onto the greased "Sheet Pan".
4. Press "Power Button" of Ninja Foodi Digital Air Fry Oven and turn the dial to select the "Air Bake" mode.
5. Press the Time button and again turn the dial to set the cooking time to 15 minutes.
6. Now push the Temp button and rotate the dial to set the temperature at 390 degrees F.
7. Press "Start/Pause" button to start.

8. When the unit beeps to show that it is preheated, open the lid.
9. Insert the "Sheet Pan" in oven.
10. Flip the chops once halfway through.
11. Serve hot.
- **Nutrition Info:** Calories: 224 kcal Total Fat: 9.1 g Saturated Fat: 3.1 g Cholesterol: 102 mg Sodium: 169 mg Total Carbs: 1.7 g Fiber: 0.1 g Sugar: 1.5 g Protein: 32 g

148.Orange Chicken Rice

Servings: 4
Cooking Time: 55 Minutes
Ingredients:
- 3 tablespoons olive oil
- 1 medium onion, chopped
- 1 3/4 cups chicken broth
- 1 cup brown basmati rice
- Zest and juice of 2 oranges
- Salt to taste
- 4 (6-oz.) boneless, skinless chicken thighs
- Black pepper, to taste
- 2 tablespoons fresh mint, chopped
- 2 tablespoons pine nuts, toasted

Directions:
1. Spread the rice in a casserole dish and place the chicken on top.
2. Toss the rest of the Ingredients: in a bowl and liberally pour over the chicken.
3. Press "Power Button" of Air Fry Oven and turn the dial to select the "Bake" mode.
4. Press the Time button and again turn the dial to set the cooking time to 55 minutes.
5. Now push the Temp button and rotate the dial to set the temperature at 350 degrees F.
6. Once preheated, place the casserole dish inside and close its lid.
7. Serve warm.
- **Nutrition Info:** Calories 231 Total Fat 20.1 g Saturated Fat 2.4 g Cholesterol 110 mg Sodium 941 mg Total Carbs 30.1 g Fiber 0.9 g Sugar 1.4 g Protein 14.6 g

149.Turkey Meatloaf

Servings: 4
Cooking Time: 20 Minutes
Ingredients:
- 1 pound ground turkey
- 1 cup kale leaves, trimmed and finely chopped
- 1 cup onion, chopped
- ½ cup fresh breadcrumbs
- 1 cup Monterey Jack cheese, grated
- 2 garlic cloves, minced
- ¼ cup salsa verde
- 1 teaspoon red chili powder
- ½ teaspoon ground cumin
- ½ teaspoon dried oregano, crushed
- Salt and ground black pepper, as required

Directions:

1. Preheat the Air fryer to 400 degree F and grease an Air fryer basket.
2. Mix all the ingredients in a bowl and divide the turkey mixture into 4 equal-sized portions.
3. Shape each into a mini loaf and arrange the loaves into the Air fryer basket.
4. Cook for about 20 minutes and dish out to serve warm.

- **Nutrition Info:** Calories: 435, Fat: 23.1g, Carbohydrates: 18.1g, Sugar: 3.6g, Protein: 42.2g, Sodium: 641mg

150.Parmesan Chicken Meatballs

Servings: 4
Cooking Time: 12 Minutes
Ingredients:

- 1-lb. ground chicken
- 1 large egg, beaten
- ½ cup Parmesan cheese, grated
- ½ cup pork rinds, ground
- 1 teaspoon garlic powder
- 1 teaspoon paprika
- 1 teaspoon kosher salt
- ½ teaspoon pepper
- Crust:
- ½ cup pork rinds, ground

Directions:

1. Toss all the meatball Ingredients: in a bowl and mix well.
2. Make small meatballs out this mixture and roll them in the pork rinds.
3. Place the coated meatballs in the air fryer basket.
4. Press "Power Button" of Air Fry Oven and turn the dial to select the "Bake" mode.
5. Press the Time button and again turn the dial to set the cooking time to 12 minutes.
6. Now push the Temp button and rotate the dial to set the temperature at 400 degrees F.
7. Once preheated, place the air fryer basket inside and close its lid.
8. Serve warm.

- **Nutrition Info:** Calories 529 Total Fat 17 g Saturated Fat 3 g Cholesterol 65 mg Sodium 391 mg Total Carbs 55 g Fiber 6 g Sugar 8 g Protein 41g

151.Roasted Delicata Squash With Kale

Servings: 2
Cooking Time: 10 Minutes
Ingredients:

- 1 medium delicata squash
- 1 bunch kale
- 1 clove garlic
- 2 tablespoons olive oil
- Salt and pepper

Directions:

1. Start by preheating toaster oven to 425°F.
2. Clean squash and cut off each end. Cut in half and remove the seeds. Quarter the halves.
3. Toss the squash in 1 tablespoon of olive oil.
4. Place the squash on a greased baking sheet and roast for 25 minutes, turning halfway through.
5. Rinse kale and remove stems. Chop garlic.
6. Heat the leftover oil in a medium skillet and add kale and salt to taste.
7. Sauté the kale until it darkens, then mix in the garlic.
8. Cook for another minute then remove from heat and add 2 tablespoons of water.
9. Remove squash from oven and lay it on top of the garlic kale.
10. Top with salt and pepper to taste and serve.

- **Nutrition Info:** Calories: 159, Sodium: 28 mg, Dietary Fiber: 1.8 g, Total Fat: 14.2 g, Total Carbs: 8.2 g, Protein: 2.6 g.

152.Perfect Size French Fries

Servings: 1
Cooking Time: 30 Minutes
Ingredients:

- 1 medium potato
- 1 tablespoon olive oil
- Salt and pepper to taste

Directions:

1. Start by preheating your oven to 425°F.
2. Clean the potato and cut it into fries or wedges.
3. Place fries in a bowl of cold water to rinse.
4. Lay the fries on a thick sheet of paper towels and pat dry.
5. Toss in a bowl with oil, salt, and pepper.
6. Bake for 30 minutes.

- **Nutrition Info:** Calories: 284, Sodium: 13 mg, Dietary Fiber: 4.7 g, Total Fat: 14.2 g, Total Carbs: 37.3 g, Protein: 4.3 g.

153.Deviled Chicken

Servings: 8
Cooking Time: 40 Minutes
Ingredients:

- 2 tablespoons butter
- 2 cloves garlic, chopped
- 1 cup Dijon mustard
- 1/2 teaspoon cayenne pepper
- 1 1/2 cups panko breadcrumbs
- 3/4 cup Parmesan, freshly grated
- 1/4 cup chives, chopped
- 2 teaspoons paprika
- 8 small bone-in chicken thighs, skin removed

Directions:

1. Toss the chicken thighs with crumbs, cheese, chives, butter, and spices in a bowl and mix well to coat.
2. Transfer the chicken along with its spice mix to a baking pan.
3. Press "Power Button" of Air Fry Oven and turn the dial to select the "Air Fry" mode.
4. Press the Time button and again turn the dial to set the cooking time to 40 minutes.
5. Now push the Temp button and rotate the dial to set the temperature at 350 degrees F.
6. Once preheated, place the baking pan inside and close its lid.
7. Serve warm.
- **Nutrition Info:** Calories 380 Total Fat 20 g Saturated Fat 5 g Cholesterol 151 mg Sodium 686 mg Total Carbs 33 g Fiber 1 g Sugar 1.2 g Protein 21 g

154.Buttery Artichokes

Servings: 4
Cooking Time: 20 Minutes
Ingredients:
- 4 artichokes, trimmed and halved
- 3 garlic cloves, minced
- 1 tablespoon olive oil
- Salt and black pepper to the taste
- 4 tablespoons butter, melted
- ¼ teaspoon cumin, ground
- 1 tablespoon lemon zest, grated

Directions:
1. In a bowl, combine the artichokes with the oil, garlic and the other Ingredients:, toss well and transfer them to the air fryer's basket.
2. Cook for 20 minutes at 370 degrees F, divide between plates and serve as a side dish.
- **Nutrition Info:** Calories 214, fat 5, fiber 8, carbs 12, protein 5

155.Ricotta Toasts With Salmon

Servings: 2
Cooking Time: 4 Minutes
Ingredients:
- 4 bread slices
- 1 garlic clove, minced
- 8 oz. ricotta cheese
- 1 teaspoon lemon zest
- Freshly ground black pepper, to taste
- 4 oz. smoked salmon

Directions:
1. In a food processor, add the garlic, ricotta, lemon zest and black pepper and pulse until smooth.
2. Spread ricotta mixture over each bread slices evenly.
3. Press "Power Button" of Air Fry Oven and turn the dial to select the "Air Fry" mode.

4. Press the Time button and again turn the dial to set the cooking time to 4 minutes.
5. Now push the Temp button and rotate the dial to set the temperature at 355 degrees F.
6. Press "Start/Pause" button to start.
7. When the unit beeps to show that it is preheated, open the lid and lightly, grease the sheet pan.
8. Arrange the bread slices into "Air Fry Basket" and insert in the oven.
9. Top with salmon and serve.
- **Nutrition Info:** Calories: 274 Cal Total Fat: 12 g Saturated Fat: 6.3 g Cholesterol: 48 mg Sodium: 1300 mg Total Carbs: 15.7 g Fiber: 0.5 g Sugar: 1.2 g Protein: 24.8 g

156.Basic Roasted Tofu

Servings: 4
Cooking Time: 45 Minutes
Ingredients:
- 1 or more (16-ounce) containers extra-firm tofu
- 1 tablespoon sesame oil
- 1 tablespoon soy sauce
- 1 tablespoon rice vinegar
- 1 tablespoon water

Directions:
1. Start by drying the tofu: first pat dry with paper towels, then lay on another set of paper towels or a dish towel.
2. Put a plate on top of the tofu then put something heavy on the plate (like a large can of vegetables). Leave it there for at least 20 minutes.
3. While tofu is being pressed, whip up marinade by combining oil, soy sauce, vinegar, and water in a bowl and set aside.
4. Cut the tofu into squares or sticks. Place the tofu in the marinade for at least 30 minutes.
5. Preheat toaster oven to 350°F. Line a pan with parchment paper and add as many pieces of tofu as you can, giving each piece adequate space.
6. Bake 20–45 minutes; tofu is done when the outside edges look golden brown. Time will vary depending on tofu size and shape.
- **Nutrition Info:** Calories: 114, Sodium: 239 mg, Dietary Fiber: 1.1 g, Total Fat: 8.1 g, Total Carbs: 2.2 g, Protein: 9.5 g.

157.Moroccan Pork Kebabs

Servings: 4
Cooking Time: 45 Minutes
Ingredients:
- 1/4 cup orange juice
- 1 tablespoon tomato paste
- 1 clove chopped garlic
- 1 tablespoon ground cumin
- 1/8 teaspoon ground cinnamon

- 4 tablespoons olive oil
- 1-1/2 teaspoons salt
- 3/4 teaspoon black pepper
- 1-1/2 pounds boneless pork loin
- 1 small eggplant
- 1 small red onion
- Pita bread (optional)
- 1/2 small cucumber
- 2 tablespoons chopped fresh mint
- Wooden skewers

Directions:
1. Start by placing wooden skewers in water to soak.
2. Cut pork loin and eggplant into 1- to 1-1/2-inch chunks.
3. Preheat toaster oven to 425°F.
4. Cut cucumber and onions into pieces and chop the mint.
5. In a large bowl, combine the orange juice, tomato paste, garlic, cumin, cinnamon, 2 tablespoons of oil, 1 teaspoon of salt, and 1/2 teaspoon of pepper.
6. Add the pork to this mixture and refrigerate for at least 30 minutes, but up to 8 hours.
7. Mix together vegetables, remaining oil, and salt and pepper.
8. Skewer the vegetables and bake for 20 minutes.
9. Add the pork to the skewers and bake for an additional 25 minutes.
10. Remove ingredients from skewers and sprinkle with mint; serve with flatbread if using.
- **Nutrition Info:** Calories: 465, Sodium: 1061 mg, Dietary Fiber: 5.6 g, Total Fat: 20.8 g, Total Carbs: 21.9 g, Protein: 48.2 g.

158.Boneless Air Fryer Turkey Breasts

Servings: 4
Cooking Time: 50 Minutes
Ingredients:
- 3 lb boneless breast
- ¼ cup mayonnaise
- 2 tsp poultry seasoning
- 1 tsp salt
- ½ tsp garlic powder
- ¼ tsp black pepper

Directions:
1. Choose the Air Fry option on the Instant Pot Duo Crisp Air fryer. Set the temperature to 360°F and push start. The preheating will start.
2. Season your boneless turkey breast with mayonnaise, poultry seasoning, salt, garlic powder, and black pepper.
3. Once preheated, Air Fry the turkey breasts on 360°F for 1 hour, turning every 15 minutes or until internal temperature has reached a temperature of 165°F.

- **Nutrition Info:** Calories 558, Total Fat 18g, Total Carbs 1g, Protein 98g

159.Herbed Radish Sauté(3)

Servings: 4
Cooking Time: 12 Minutes
Ingredients:
- 2 bunches red radishes; halved
- 2 tbsp. parsley; chopped.
- 2 tbsp. balsamic vinegar
- 1 tbsp. olive oil
- Salt and black pepper to taste.

Directions:
1. Take a bowl and mix the radishes with the remaining ingredients except the parsley, toss and put them in your air fryer's basket.
2. Cook at 400°F for 15 minutes, divide between plates, sprinkle the parsley on top and serve as a side dish
- **Nutrition Info:** Calories: 180; Fat: 4g; Fiber: 2g; Carbs: 3g; Protein: 5g

160.Greek Lamb Meatballs

Servings: 12
Cooking Time: 12 Minutes
Ingredients:
- 1 pound ground lamb
- ½ cup breadcrumbs
- ¼ cup milk
- 2 egg yolks
- 1 teaspoon ground coriander
- 1 teaspoon ground cumin
- 3 garlic cloves, minced
- 1 teaspoon dried oregano
- ½ teaspoon salt
- ½ teaspoon black pepper
- 1 lemon, juiced and zested
- ¼ cup fresh parsley, chopped
- ½ cup crumbled feta cheese
- Olive oil, for shaping
- Tzatziki, for dipping

Directions:
1. Combine all ingredients except olive oil in a large mixing bowl and mix until fully incorporated.
2. Form 12 meatballs, about 2 ounces each. Use olive oil on your hands so they don't stick to the meatballs. Set aside.
3. Select the Broil function on the COSORI Air Fryer Toaster Oven, set time to 12 minutes, then press Start/Cancel to preheat.
4. Place the meatballs on the food tray, then insert the tray at top position in the preheated air fryer toaster oven. Press Start/Cancel.
5. Take out the meatballs when done and serve with a side of tzatziki.
- **Nutrition Info:** Calories: 129 kcal Total Fat: 6.4 g Saturated Fat: 0 g Cholesterol: 0 mg

Sodium: 0 mg Total Carbs: 4.9 g Fiber: 0 g Sugar: 0 g Protein: 12.9 g

161.Roasted Beet Salad With Oranges & Beet Greens

Servings: 6
Cooking Time: 1-1/2 Hours
Ingredients:
- 6 medium beets with beet greens attached
- 2 large oranges
- 1 small sweet onion, cut into wedges
- 1/3 cup red wine vinegar
- 1/4 cup extra-virgin olive oil
- 2 garlic cloves, minced
- 1/2 teaspoon grated orange peel

Directions:
1. Start by preheating toaster oven to 400°F.
2. Trim leaves from beets and chop, then set aside.
3. Pierce beets with a fork and place in a roasting pan.
4. Roast beets for 1-1/2 hours.
5. Allow beets to cool, peel, then cut into 8 wedges and put into a bowl.
6. Place beet greens in a sauce pan and cover with just enough water to cover. Heat until water boils, then immediately remove from heat.
7. Drain greens and press to remove liquid from greens, then add to beet bowl.
8. Remove peel and pith from orange and segment, adding each segment to the bowl.
9. Add onion to beet mixture. In a separate bowl mix together vinegar, oil, garlic and orange peel.
10. Combine both bowls and toss, sprinkle with salt and pepper.
11. Let stand for an hour before serving.
- **Nutrition Info:** Calories: 214, Sodium: 183 mg, Dietary Fiber: 6.5 g, Total Fat: 8.9 g, Total Carbs: 32.4 g, Protein: 4.7 g.

162.Eggplant And Leeks Stew

Servings: 4
Cooking Time: 12 Minutes
Ingredients:
- 2 big eggplants, roughly cubed
- ½ bunch cilantro; chopped.
- 1 cup veggie stock
- 2 garlic cloves; minced
- 3 leeks; sliced
- 2 tbsp. olive oil
- 1 tbsp. hot sauce
- 1 tbsp. sweet paprika
- 1 tbsp. tomato puree
- Salt and black pepper to taste.

Directions:

1. In a pan that fits the air fryer, mix all the ingredients, toss, introduce in the fryer and cook at 380°F for 20 minutes
2. Divide the stew into bowls and serve for lunch.
- **Nutrition Info:** Calories: 183; Fat: 4g; Fiber: 2g; Carbs: 4g; Protein: 12g

163.Tomato And Avocado

Servings: 4
Cooking Time: 12 Minutes
Ingredients:
- ½ lb. cherry tomatoes; halved
- 2 avocados, pitted; peeled and cubed
- 1 ¼ cup lettuce; torn
- 1/3 cup coconut cream
- A pinch of salt and black pepper
- Cooking spray

Directions:
1. Grease the air fryer with cooking spray, combine the tomatoes with avocados, salt, pepper and the cream and cook at 350°F for 5 minutes shaking once
2. In a salad bowl, mix the lettuce with the tomatoes and avocado mix, toss and serve.
- **Nutrition Info:** Calories: 226; Fat: 12g; Fiber: 2g; Carbs: 4g; Protein: 8g

164.Chives Radishes

Servings: 4
Cooking Time: 12 Minutes
Ingredients:
- 20 radishes; halved
- 2 tbsp. olive oil
- 1 tbsp. garlic; minced
- 1 tsp. chives; chopped.
- Salt and black pepper to taste.

Directions:
1. In your air fryer's pan, combine all the ingredients and toss.
2. Introduce the pan in the machine and cook at 370°F for 15 minutes
3. Divide between plates and serve as a side dish.
- **Nutrition Info:** Calories: 160; Fat: 2g; Fiber: 3g; Carbs: 4g; Protein: 6g

165.Lamb Gyro

Servings: 4
Cooking Time: 25 Minutes
Ingredients:
- 1 pound ground lamb
- ¼ red onion, minced
- ¼ cup mint, minced
- ¼ cup parsley, minced
- 2 cloves garlic, minced
- ½ teaspoon salt
- ⅛ teaspoon rosemary
- ½ teaspoon black pepper

- 4 slices pita bread
- ¾ cup hummus
- 1 cup romaine lettuce, shredded
- ½ onion sliced
- 1 Roma tomato, diced
- ½ cucumber, skinned and thinly sliced
- 12 mint leaves, minced
- Tzatziki sauce, to taste

Directions:
1. Mix ground lamb, red onion, mint, parsley, garlic, salt, rosemary, and black pepper until fully incorporated.
2. Select the Broil function on the COSORI Air Fryer Toaster Oven, set time to 25 minutes and temperature to 450°F, then press Start/Cancel to preheat.
3. Line the food tray with parchment paper and place ground lamb on top, shaping it into a patty 1-inch-thick and 6 inches in diameter.
4. Insert the food tray at top position in the preheated air fryer toaster oven, then press Start/Cancel.
5. Remove when done and cut into thin slices.
6. Assemble each gyro starting with pita bread, then hummus, lamb meat, lettuce, onion, tomato, cucumber, and mint leaves, then drizzle with tzatziki.
7. Serve immediately.
- **Nutrition Info:** Calories: 409 kcal Total Fat: 14.6 g Saturated Fat: 0 g Cholesterol: 0 mg Sodium: 0 mg Total Carbs: 29.9 g Fiber: 0 g Sugar: 0 g Protein: 39.4 g

166.Kalamta Mozarella Pita Melts

Servings: 2
Cooking Time: 5 Minutes
Ingredients:
- 2 (6-inch) whole wheat pitas
- 1 teaspoon extra-virgin olive oil
- 1 cup grated part-skim mozzarella cheese
- 1/4 small red onion
- 1/4 cup pitted Kalamata olives
- 2 tablespoons chopped fresh herbs such as parsley, basil, or oregano

Directions:
1. Start by preheating toaster oven to 425°F.
2. Brush the pita on both sides with oil and warm in the oven for one minute.
3. Dice onions and halve olives.
4. Sprinkle mozzarella over each pita and top with onion and olive.
5. Return to the oven for another 5 minutes or until the cheese is melted.
6. Sprinkle herbs over the pita and serve.
- **Nutrition Info:** Calories: 387, Sodium: 828 mg, Dietary Fiber: 7.4 g, Total Fat: 16.2 g, Total Carbs: 42.0 g, Protein: 23.0 g.

167.Mushroom Meatloaf

Servings: 4
Cooking Time: 25 Minutes
Ingredients:
- 14-ounce lean ground beef
- 1 chorizo sausage, chopped finely
- 1 small onion, chopped
- 1 garlic clove, minced
- 2 tablespoons fresh cilantro, chopped
- 3 tablespoons breadcrumbs
- 1 egg
- Salt and freshly ground black pepper, to taste
- 2 tablespoons fresh mushrooms, sliced thinly
- 3 tablespoons olive oil

Directions:
1. Preparing the ingredients. Preheat the instant crisp air fryer to 390 degrees f.
2. In a large bowl, add all ingredients except mushrooms and mix till well combined.
3. In a baking pan, place the beef mixture.
4. With the back of spatula, smooth the surface.
5. Top with mushroom slices and gently, press into the meatloaf.
6. Drizzle with oil evenly.
7. Air frying. Arrange the pan in the instant crisp air fryer basket, close air fryer lid and cook for about 25 minutes.
8. Cut the meatloaf in desires size wedges and serve.
- **Nutrition Info:** Calories 284 Total fat 7.9 g Saturated fat 1.4 g Cholesterol 36 mg Sodium 704 mg Total carbs 46 g Fiber 3.6 g Sugar 5.5 g Protein 17.9 g

168.Turkey Legs

Servings: 2
Cooking Time: 40 Minutes
Ingredients:
- 2 large turkey legs
- 1 1/2 tsp smoked paprika
- 1 tsp brown sugar
- 1 tsp season salt
- ½ tsp garlic powder
- oil for spraying avocado, canola, etc.

Directions:
1. Mix the smoked paprika, brown sugar, seasoned salt, garlic powder thoroughly.
2. Wash and pat dry the turkey legs.
3. Rub the made seasoning mixture all over the turkey legs making sure to get under the skin also.
4. While preparing for cooking, select the Air Fry option. Press start to begin preheating.
5. Once the preheating temperature is reached, place the turkey legs on the tray in the

Instant Pot Duo Crisp Air Fryer basket. Lightly spray them with oil.

6. Air Fry the turkey legs on 400°F for 20 minutes. Then, open the Air Fryer lid and flip the turkey legs and lightly spray with oil. Close the Instant Pot Duo Crisp Air Fryer lid and cook for 20 more minutes.
7. Remove and Enjoy.
- **Nutrition Info:** Calories 958, Total Fat 46g, Total Carbs 3g, Protein 133g

169.Simple Turkey Breast

Servings: 10
Cooking Time: 40 Minutes
Ingredients:
- 1: 8-poundsbone-in turkey breast
- Salt and black pepper, as required
- 2 tablespoons olive oil

Directions:
1. Preheat the Air fryer to 360 degree F and grease an Air fryer basket.
2. Season the turkey breast with salt and black pepper and drizzle with oil.
3. Arrange the turkey breast into the Air Fryer basket, skin side down and cook for about 20 minutes.
4. Flip the side and cook for another 20 minutes.
5. Dish out in a platter and cut into desired size slices to serve.
- **Nutrition Info:** Calories: 719, Fat: 35.9g, Carbohydrates: 0g, Sugar: 0g, Protein: 97.2g, Sodium: 386mg

170.Roasted Garlic(2)

Servings: 12 Cloves
Cooking Time: 12 Minutes
Ingredients:
- 1 medium head garlic
- 2 tsp. avocado oil

Directions:
1. Remove any hanging excess peel from the garlic but leave the cloves covered. Cut off ¼ of the head of garlic, exposing the tips of the cloves
2. Drizzle with avocado oil. Place the garlic head into a small sheet of aluminum foil, completely enclosing it. Place it into the air fryer basket. Adjust the temperature to 400 Degrees F and set the timer for 20 minutes. If your garlic head is a bit smaller, check it after 15 minutes
3. When done, garlic should be golden brown and very soft
4. To serve, cloves should pop out and easily be spread or sliced. Store in an airtight container in the refrigerator up to 5 days.
5. You may also freeze individual cloves on a baking sheet, then store together in a freezer-safe storage bag once frozen.
- **Nutrition Info:** Calories: 11; Protein: 2g; Fiber: 1g; Fat: 7g; Carbs: 0g

171.Chicken Wings With Prawn Paste

Servings: 6
Cooking Time: 8 Minutes
Ingredients:
- Corn flour, as required
- 2 pounds mid-joint chicken wings
- 2 tablespoons prawn paste
- 4 tablespoons olive oil
- 1½ teaspoons sugar
- 2 teaspoons sesame oil
- 1 teaspoon Shaoxing wine
- 2 teaspoons fresh ginger juice

Directions:
1. Preheat the Air fryer to 360 degree F and grease an Air fryer basket.
2. Mix all the ingredients in a bowl except wings and corn flour.
3. Rub the chicken wings generously with marinade and refrigerate overnight.
4. Coat the chicken wings evenly with corn flour and keep aside.
5. Set the Air fryer to 390 degree F and arrange the chicken wings in the Air fryer basket.
6. Cook for about 8 minutes and dish out to serve hot.
- **Nutrition Info:** Calories: 416, Fat: 31.5g, Carbohydrates: 11.2g, Sugar: 1.6g, Protein: 24.4g, Sodium: 661mg

DINNER RECIPES

172.Zingy Dilled Salmon

Servings: 2
Cooking Time: 20 Minutes
Ingredients:

- 2 salmon steaks
- Coarse sea salt, to taste
- 1/4 teaspoon freshly ground black pepper, or more to taste
- 1 tablespoon sesame oil
- Zest of 1 lemon
- 1 tablespoon fresh lemon juice
- 1 teaspoon garlic, minced
- 1/2 teaspoon smoked cayenne pepper
- 1/2 teaspoon dried dill

Directions:

1. Preheat your Air Fryer to 380 degrees F. Pat dry the salmon steaks with a kitchen towel.
2. In a ceramic dish, combine the remaining ingredients until everything is well whisked.
3. Add the salmon steaks to the ceramic dish and let them sit in the refrigerator for 1 hour. Now, place the salmon steaks in the cooking basket. Reserve the marinade.
4. Cook for 12 minutes, flipping halfway through the cooking time.
5. Meanwhile, cook the marinade in a small sauté pan over a moderate flame. Cook until the sauce has thickened.
6. Pour the sauce over the steaks and serve.
- **Nutrition Info:** 476 Calories; 18g Fat; 2g Carbs; 47g Protein; 8g Sugars; 4g Fiber

173.Baked Veggie Egg Rolls

Servings: 2
Cooking Time: 20 Minutes
Ingredients:

- 1/2 tablespoon olive or vegetable oil
- 2 cups thinly-sliced chard
- 1/4 cup grated carrot
- 1/2 cup chopped pea pods
- 3 shiitake mushrooms
- 2 scallions
- 2 medium cloves garlic
- 1/2 tablespoon fresh ginger
- 1/2 tablespoon soy sauce
- 6 egg roll wrappers
- Olive oil spray for cookie sheet and egg rolls

Directions:

1. Start by mincing mushrooms, garlic, and ginger and slicing scallions.
2. Heat oil on medium heat in a medium skillet and char peas, carrots, scallions, and mushrooms.
3. Cook 3 minutes, then add ginger. Stir in soy sauce and remove from heat.
4. Preheat toaster oven to 400°F and spray cookie sheet. Spoon even portions of vegetable mix over each egg roll wrapper, and wrap them up.
5. Place egg rolls on cookie sheet and spray with olive oil. Bake for 20 minutes until egg roll shells are browned.
- **Nutrition Info:** Calories: 421, Sodium: 1166 mg, Dietary Fiber: 8.2 g, Total Fat: 7.7 g, Total Carbs: 76.9 g, Protein: 13.7 g.

174.Grilled Chicken Tikka Masala

Servings: 4
Cooking Time: 20 Minutes
Ingredients:

- 1 tsp. Tikka Masala 1 tsp. fine sea salt
- 2 heaping tsps. whole grain mustard
- 2 tsps. coriander, ground 2 tablespoon olive oil
- 2 large-sized chicken breasts, skinless and halved lengthwise
- 2 tsp.s onion powder
- 1½ tablespoons cider vinegar Basmati rice, steamed
- 1/3 tsp. red pepper flakes, crushed

Directions:

1. Preheat the air fryer to 335 °For 4 minutes.
2. Toss your chicken together with the other ingredients, minus basmati rice. Let it stand at least 3 hours.
3. Cook for 25 minutes in your air fryer; check for doneness because the time depending on the size of the piece of chicken.
4. Serve immediately over warm basmati rice. Enjoy!
- **Nutrition Info:** 319 Calories; 20.1g Fat; 1.9g Carbs; 30.5g Protein; 0.1g Sugars

175.Turkey Wontons With Garlic-parmesan Sauce

Servings: 8
Cooking Time: 20 Minutes
Ingredients:

- 8 ounces cooked turkey breasts, shredded 16 wonton wrappers
- 1½ tablespoons margarine, melted
- 1/3 cup cream cheese, room temperature 8 ounces Asiago cheese, shredded
- 3 tablespoons Parmesan cheese, grated
- 1 tsp. garlic powder
- Fine sea salt and freshly ground black pepper, to taste

Directions:

1. In a small-sized bowl, mix the margarine, Parmesan, garlic powder, salt, and black pepper; give it a good stir.
2. Lightly grease a mini muffin pan; lay 1 wonton wrapper in each mini muffin cup. Fill each cup with the cream cheese and turkey mixture.

3. Air-fry for 8 minutes at 335 °F. Immediately top with Asiago cheese and serve warm.
- **Nutrition Info:** 362 Calories; 13.5g Fat; 40.4g Carbs; 18.5g Protein; 1.2g Sugars

176.Herbed Carrots

Servings: 8
Cooking Time: 14 Minutes
Ingredients:
- 6 large carrots, peeled and sliced lengthwise
- 2 tablespoons olive oil
- ½ tablespoon fresh oregano, chopped
- ½ tablespoon fresh parsley, chopped
- Salt and black pepper, to taste
- 2 tablespoons olive oil, divided
- ½ cup fat-free Italian dressing
- Salt, to taste

Directions:
1. Preheat the Air fryer to 360-degree F and grease an Air fryer basket.
2. Mix the carrot slices and olive oil in a bowl and toss to coat well.
3. Arrange the carrot slices in the Air fryer basket and cook for about 12 minutes.
4. Dish out the carrot slices onto serving plates and sprinkle with herbs, salt and black pepper.
5. Transfer into the Air fryer basket and cook for 2 more minutes.
6. Dish out and serve hot.
- **Nutrition Info:** Calories: 93, Fat: 7.2g, Carbohydrates: 7.3g, Sugar: 3.8g, Protein: 0.7g, Sodium: 252mg

177.Bbq Pork Ribs

Servings: 2 To 3
Cooking Time: 5 Hrs 30 Minutes
Ingredients:
- 1 lb pork ribs
- 1 tsp soy sauce
- Salt and black pepper to taste
- 1 tsp oregano
- 1 tbsp + 1 tbsp maple syrup
- 3 tbsp barbecue sauce
- 2 cloves garlic, minced
- 1 tbsp cayenne pepper
- 1 tsp sesame oil

Directions:
1. Put the chops on a chopping board and use a knife to cut them into smaller pieces of desired sizes. Put them in a mixing bowl, add the soy sauce, salt, pepper, oregano, one tablespoon of maple syrup, barbecue sauce, garlic, cayenne pepper, and sesame oil. Mix well and place the pork in the fridge to marinate in the spices for 5 hours.
2. Preheat the Air Fryer to 350 F. Open the Air Fryer and place the ribs in the fryer basket.

Slide the fryer basket in and cook for 15 minutes. Open the Air fryer, turn the ribs using tongs, apply the remaining maple syrup with a brush, close the Air Fryer, and continue cooking for 10 minutes.
- **Nutrition Info:** 346 Calories; 11g Fat; 4g Carbs; 32g Protein; 1g Sugars; 1g Fiber

178.Spiced Salmon Kebabs

Servings: 3
Cooking Time: 15 Minutes
Ingredients:
- 2 tablespoons chopped fresh oregano
- 2 teaspoons sesame seeds
- 1 teaspoon ground cumin
- Salt and pepper to taste
- 1 ½ pounds salmon fillets
- 2 tablespoons olive oil
- 2 lemons, sliced into rounds

Directions:
1. Place the instant pot air fryer lid on and preheat the instant pot at 390 degrees F.
2. Place the grill pan accessory in the instant pot.
3. Create dry rub by combining the oregano, sesame seeds, cumin, salt, and pepper.
4. Rub the salmon fillets with the dry rub and brush with oil.
5. Place on the grill pan, close the air fryer lid and grill the salmon for 15 minutes.
6. Serve with lemon slices once cooked.
- **Nutrition Info:** Calories per serving 447 ; Carbs: 4.1g; Protein:47.6 g; Fat:26.6 g

179.Prawn Burgers

Servings: 2
Cooking Time: 6 Minutes
Ingredients:
- ½ cup prawns, peeled, deveined and finely chopped
- ½ cup breadcrumbs
- 2-3 tablespoons onion, finely chopped
- 3 cups fresh baby greens
- ½ teaspoon ginger, minced
- ½ teaspoon garlic, minced
- ½ teaspoon red chili powder
- ½ teaspoon ground cumin
- ¼ teaspoon ground turmeric
- Salt and ground black pepper, as required

Directions:
1. Preheat the Air fryer to 390 degree F and grease an Air fryer basket.
2. Mix the prawns, breadcrumbs, onion, ginger, garlic, and spices in a bowl.
3. Make small-sized patties from the mixture and transfer to the Air fryer basket.
4. Cook for about 6 minutes and dish out in a platter.

5. Serve immediately warm alongside the baby greens.
- **Nutrition Info:** Calories: 240, Fat: 2.7g, Carbohydrates: 37.4g, Sugar: 4g, Protein: 18g, Sodium: 371mg

180.Party Stuffed Pork Chops

Servings: 4
Cooking Time: 40 Minutes
Ingredients:
- 8 pork chops
- ¼ tsp pepper
- 4 cups stuffing mix
- ½ tsp salt
- 2 tbsp olive oil
- 4 garlic cloves, minced
- 2 tbsp sage leaves

Directions:
1. Preheat your air fryer to 350 f. cut a hole in pork chops and fill chops with stuffing mix. In a bowl, mix sage leaves, garlic cloves, oil, salt and pepper. Cover chops with marinade and let marinate for 10 minutes. Place the chops in your air fryer's cooking basket and cook for 25 minutes. Serve and enjoy!
- **Nutrition Info:** Calories: 364 Cal Total Fat: 13 g Saturated Fat: 4 g Cholesterol: 119 mg Sodium: 349 mg Total Carbs: 19 g Fiber: 3 g Sugar: 6 g Protein: 40 g

181.Steak With Cascabel-garlic Sauce

Servings: 4
Cooking Time: 20 Minutes
Ingredients:
- 2 teaspoons brown mustard
- 2 tablespoons mayonnaise
- 1 ½ pounds beef flank steak, trimmed and cubed
- 2 teaspoons minced cascabel
- ½ cup scallions, finely chopped
- 1/3 cup Crème fraîche
- 2 teaspoons cumin seeds
- 3 cloves garlic, pressed
- Pink peppercorns to taste, freshly cracked
- 1 teaspoon fine table salt
- 1/3 teaspoon black pepper, preferably freshly ground

Directions:
1. Firstly, fry the cumin seeds just about 1 minute or until they pop.
2. After that, season your beef flank steak with fine table salt, black pepper and the fried cumin seeds; arrange the seasoned beef cubes on the bottom of your baking dish that fits in the air fryer.
3. Throw in the minced cascabel, garlic, and scallions; air-fry approximately 8 minutes at 390 degrees F.

4. Once the beef cubes start to tender, add your favorite mayo, Crème fraîche, freshly cracked pink peppercorns and mustard; air-fry 7 minutes longer. Serve over hot wild rice.
- **Nutrition Info:** 329 Calories; 16g Fat; 8g Carbs; 37g Protein; 9g Sugars; 6g Fiber

182.Greek-style Monkfish With Vegetables

Servings: 2
Cooking Time: 20 Minutes
Ingredients:
- 2 teaspoons olive oil
- 1 cup celery, sliced
- 2 bell peppers, sliced
- 1 teaspoon dried thyme
- 1/2 teaspoon dried marjoram
- 1/2 teaspoon dried rosemary
- 2 monkfish fillets
- 1 tablespoon soy sauce
- 2 tablespoons lime juice
- Coarse salt and ground black pepper, to taste
- 1 teaspoon cayenne pepper
- 1/2 cup Kalamata olives, pitted and sliced

Directions:
1. In a nonstick skillet, heat the olive oil for 1 minute. Once hot, sauté the celery and peppers until tender, about 4 minutes. Sprinkle with thyme, marjoram, and rosemary and set aside.
2. Toss the fish fillets with the soy sauce, lime juice, salt, black pepper, and cayenne pepper. Place the fish fillets in a lightly greased cooking basket and bake at 390 degrees F for 8 minutes.
3. Turn them over, add the olives, and cook an additional 4 minutes. Serve with the sautéed vegetables on the side.
- **Nutrition Info:** 292 Calories; 11g Fat; 1g Carbs; 22g Protein; 9g Sugars; 6g Fiber

183.Salmon Steak Grilled With Cilantro Garlic Sauce

Servings: 2
Cooking Time: 15 Minutes
Ingredients:
- 2 salmon steaks
- Salt and pepper to taste
- 2 tablespoons vegetable oil
- 2 cloves of garlic, minced
- 1 cup cilantro leaves
- ½ cup Greek yogurt
- 1 teaspoon honey

Directions:
1. Place the instant pot air fryer lid on and preheat the instant pot at 390 degrees F.
2. Place the grill pan accessory in the instant pot.

3. Season the salmon steaks with salt and pepper. Brush with oil.
4. Place on the grill pan, close the air fryer lid and grill for 15 minutes and make sure to flip halfway through the cooking time.
5. In a food processor, mix the garlic, cilantro leaves, yogurt, and honey. Season with salt and pepper to taste. Pulse until smooth.
6. Serve the salmon steaks with the cilantro sauce.
- **Nutrition Info:** Calories: 485; Carbs: 6.3g; Protein: 47.6g; Fat: 29.9g

184.Italian Shrimp Scampi

Servings: 4
Cooking Time: 20 Minutes
Ingredients:
- 2 egg whites
- 1/2 cup coconut flour
- 1 cup Parmigiano-Reggiano, grated
- 1/2 teaspoon celery seeds
- 1/2 teaspoon porcini powder
- 1/2 teaspoon onion powder
- 1 teaspoon garlic powder
- 1/2 teaspoon dried rosemary
- 1/2 teaspoon sea salt
- 1/2 teaspoon ground black pepper
- 1 ½ pounds shrimp, deveined

Directions:
1. Whisk the egg with coconut flour and Parmigiano-Reggiano. Add in seasonings and mix to combine well.
2. Dip your shrimp in the batter. Roll until they are covered on all sides.
3. Cook in the preheated Air Fryer at 390 degrees F for 5 to 7 minutes or until golden brown. Work in batches. Serve with lemon wedges if desired.
- **Nutrition Info:** 300 Calories; 13g Fat; 5g Carbs; 47g Protein; 8g Sugars; 2g Fiber

185.Homemade Beef Stroganoff

Servings: 3
Cooking Time: 20 Minutes
Ingredients:
- 1 pound thin steak
- 4 tbsp butter
- 1 whole onion, chopped
- 1 cup sour cream
- 8 oz mushrooms, sliced
- 4 cups beef broth
- 16 oz egg noodles, cooked

Directions:
1. Preheat your Air Fryer to 400 F. Using a microwave proof bowl, melt butter in a microwave oven. In a mixing bowl, mix the melted butter, sliced mushrooms, cream, onion, and beef broth.
2. Pour the mixture over steak and set aside for 10 minutes. Place the marinated beef in your fryer's cooking basket, and cook for 10 minutes. Serve with cooked egg noodles and enjoy!
- **Nutrition Info:** 456 Calories; 37g Fat; 1g Carbs; 21g Protein; 5g Sugars; 6g Fiber

186.Sage Sausages Balls

Servings: 4
Cooking Time: 20 Minutes
Ingredients:
- 3 ½ oz sausages, sliced
- Salt and black pepper to taste
- 1 cup onion, chopped
- 3 tbsp breadcrumbs
- ½ tsp garlic puree
- 1 tsp sage

Directions:
1. Preheat your air fryer to 340 f. In a bowl, mix onions, sausage meat, sage, garlic puree, salt and pepper. Add breadcrumbs to a plate. Form balls using the mixture and roll them in breadcrumbs. Add onion balls in your air fryer's cooking basket and cook for 15 minutes. Serve and enjoy!
- **Nutrition Info:** Calories: 162 Cal Total Fat: 12.1 g Saturated Fat: 0 g Cholesterol: 25 mg Sodium: 324 mg Total Carbs: 7.3 g Fiber: 0 g Sugar: 0 g Protein: 6 g

187.Chicken Lasagna With Eggplants

Servings: 10
Cooking Time: 17 Minutes
Ingredients:
- 6 oz Cheddar cheese, shredded
- 7 oz Parmesan cheese, shredded
- 2 eggplants
- 1-pound ground chicken
- 1 teaspoon paprika
- 1 teaspoon salt
- ½ teaspoon cayenne pepper
- ½ cup heavy cream
- 2 teaspoon butter
- 4 oz chive stems, diced

Directions:
1. Take the air fryer basket tray and spread it with the butter.
2. Then peel the eggplants and slice them.
3. Separate the sliced eggplants into 3 parts.
4. Combine the ground chicken with the paprika, salt, cayenne pepper, and diced chives.
5. Mix the mixture up.
6. Separate the ground chicken mixture into 2 parts.
7. Make the layer of the first part of the sliced eggplant in the air fryer basket tray.

8. Then make the layer of the ground chicken mixture.
9. After this, sprinkle the ground chicken layer with the half of the shredded Cheddar cheese,
10. Then cover the cheese with the second part of the sliced eggplant.
11. The next step is to make the layer of the ground chicken and all shredded Cheddar cheese,
12. Cover the cheese layer with the last part of the sliced eggplants.
13. Then sprinkle the eggplants with shredded Parmesan cheese.
14. Pour the heavy cream and add butter.
15. Preheat the air fryer to 365 F.
16. Cook the lasagna for 17 minutes.
17. When the time is over – let the lasagna chill gently.
18. Serve it!
- **Nutrition Info:** calories 291, fat 17.6, fiber 4.6, carbs 7.8, protein 27.4

188.Stuffed Okra

Servings: 2
Cooking Time: 12 Minutes
Ingredients:
- 8 ounces large okra
- ¼ cup chickpea flour
- ¼ of onion, chopped
- 2 tablespoons coconut, grated freshly
- 1 teaspoon garam masala powder
- ½ teaspoon ground turmeric
- ½ teaspoon red chili powder
- ½ teaspoon ground cumin
- Salt, to taste

Directions:
1. Preheat the Air fryer to 390 ºF and grease an Air fryer basket.
2. Mix the flour, onion, grated coconut, and spices in a bowl and toss to coat well.
3. Stuff the flour mixture into okra and arrange into the Air fryer basket.
4. Cook for about 12 minutes and dish out in a serving plate.
- **Nutrition Info:** Calories: 166, Fat: 3.7g, Carbohydrates: 26.6g, Sugar: 5.3g, Protein: 7.6g, Sodium: 103mg

189.Cinnamon Pork Rinds

Servings: 2
Cooking Time: 20 Minutes
Ingredients:
- 2 oz. pork rinds
- ¼ cup powdered erythritol
- 2 tbsp. unsalted butter; melted.
- ½ tsp. ground cinnamon.

Directions:
1. Take a large bowl, toss pork rinds and butter. Sprinkle with cinnamon and erythritol, then toss to evenly coat.
2. Place pork rinds into the air fryer basket. Adjust the temperature to 400 Degrees F and set the timer for 5 minutes. Serve immediately.
- **Nutrition Info:** Calories: 264; Protein: 13g; Fiber: 4g; Fat: 28g; Carbs: 15g

190.Cheese Zucchini Boats

Servings: 2
Cooking Time: 20 Minutes
Ingredients:
- 2 medium zucchinis
- ¼ cup full-fat ricotta cheese
- ¼ cup shredded mozzarella cheese
- ¼ cup low-carb, no-sugar-added pasta sauce.
- 2 tbsp. grated vegetarian Parmesan cheese
- 1 tbsp. avocado oil
- ¼ tsp. garlic powder.
- ½ tsp. dried parsley.
- ¼ tsp. dried oregano.

Directions:
1. Cut off 1-inch from the top and bottom of each zucchini.
2. Slice zucchini in half lengthwise and use a spoon to scoop out a bit of the inside, making room for filling. Brush with oil and spoon 2 tbsp. pasta sauce into each shell
3. Take a medium bowl, mix ricotta, mozzarella, oregano, garlic powder and parsley
4. Spoon the mixture into each zucchini shell. Place stuffed zucchini shells into the air fryer basket.
5. Adjust the temperature to 350 Degrees F and set the timer for 20 minutes
6. To remove from the fryer basket, use tongs or a spatula and carefully lift out. Top with Parmesan. Serve immediately.
- **Nutrition Info:** Calories: 215; Protein: 15g; Fiber: 7g; Fat: 19g; Carbs: 3g

191.Curried Eggplant

Servings: 2
Cooking Time: 10 Minutes
Ingredients:
- 1 large eggplant, cut into ½-inch thick slices
- 1 garlic clove, minced
- ½ fresh red chili, chopped
- 1 tablespoon vegetable oil
- ¼ teaspoon curry powder
- Salt, to taste

Directions:
1. Preheat the Air fryer to 300 degree F and grease an Air fryer basket.

2. Mix all the ingredients in a bowl and toss to coat well.
3. Arrange the eggplant slices in the Air fryer basket and cook for about 10 minutes, tossing once in between.
4. Dish out onto serving plates and serve hot.
- **Nutrition Info:** Calories: 121, Fat: 7.3g, Carbohydrates: 14.2g, Sugar: 7g, Protein: 2.4g, Sodium: 83mg

192.Fish Cakes With Horseradish Sauce

Servings: 4
Cooking Time: 20 Minutes
Ingredients:
- Halibut Cakes:
- 1 pound halibut
- 2 tablespoons olive oil
- 1/2 teaspoon cayenne pepper
- 1/4 teaspoon black pepper
- Salt, to taste
- 2 tablespoons cilantro, chopped
- 1 shallot, chopped
- 2 garlic cloves, minced
- 1 cup Romano cheese, grated
- 1 egg, whisked
- 1 tablespoon Worcestershire sauce
- Mayo Sauce:
- 1 teaspoon horseradish, grated
- 1/2 cup mayonnaise

Directions:
1. Start by preheating your Air Fryer to 380 degrees F. Spritz the Air Fryer basket with cooking oil.
2. Mix all ingredients for the halibut cakes in a bowl; knead with your hands until everything is well incorporated.
3. Shape the mixture into equally sized patties. Transfer your patties to the Air Fryer basket. Cook the fish patties for 10 minutes, turning them over halfway through.
4. Mix the horseradish and mayonnaise. Serve the halibut cakes with the horseradish mayo.
- **Nutrition Info:** 532 Calories; 32g Fat; 3g Carbs; 28g Protein; 3g Sugars; 6g Fiber

193.Corned Beef With Carrots

Servings: 3
Cooking Time: 35 Minutes
Ingredients:
- 1 tbsp beef spice
- 1 whole onion, chopped
- 4 carrots, chopped
- 12 oz bottle beer
- 1½ cups chicken broth
- 4 pounds corned beef

Directions:
1. Preheat your air fryer to 380 f. Cover beef with beer and set aside for 20 minutes.

Place carrots, onion and beef in a pot and heat over high heat. Add in broth and bring to a boil. Drain boiled meat and veggies; set aside.
2. Top with beef spice. Place the meat and veggies in your air fryer's cooking basket and cook for 30 minutes.
- **Nutrition Info:** Calories: 464 Cal Total Fat: 17 g Saturated Fat: 6.8 g Cholesterol: 91.7 mg Sodium: 1904.2 mg Total Carbs: 48.9 g Fiber: 7.2 g Sugar: 5.8 g Protein: 30.6 g

194.Beef, Olives And Tomatoes

Servings: 4
Cooking Time: 35 Minutes
Ingredients:
- 2pounds beef stew meat, cubed
- 1cup black olives, pitted and halved
- 1cup cherry tomatoes, halved
- 1tablespoon smoked paprika
- 3tablespoons olive oil
- 1teaspoon coriander, ground
- Salt and black pepper to the taste

Directions:
1. In the air fryer's pan, mix the beef with the olives and the other ingredients, toss and cook at 390 degrees F for 35 minutes.
2. Divide between plates and serve.
- **Nutrition Info:** Calories 291, Fat 12, Fiber 9, Carbs 20, Protein 26

195.Green Beans And Lime Sauce

Servings: 4
Cooking Time: 20 Minutes
Ingredients:
- 1 lb. green beans, trimmed
- 2 tbsp. ghee; melted
- 1 tbsp. lime juice
- 1 tsp. chili powder
- A pinch of salt and black pepper

Directions:
1. Take a bowl and mix the ghee with the rest of the ingredients except the green beans and whisk really well.
2. Mix the green beans with the lime sauce, toss
3. Put them in your air fryer's basket and cook at 400°F for 8 minutes. Serve right away.
- **Nutrition Info:** Calories: 151; Fat: 4g; Fiber: 2g; Carbs: 4g; Protein: 6g

196.Air Fryer Veggie Quesdillas

Servings: 4
Cooking Time: 40 Minutes
Ingredients:
- 4 sprouted whole-grain flour tortillas (6-in.)
- 1 cup sliced red bell pepper
- 4 ounces reduced-fat Cheddar cheese, shredded

- 1 cup sliced zucchini
- 1 cup canned black beans, drained and rinsed (no salt)
- Cooking spray
- 2 ounces plain 2% reduced-fat Greek yogurt
- 1 teaspoon lime zest
- 1 Tbsp. fresh juice (from 1 lime)
- ¼ tsp. ground cumin
- 2 tablespoons chopped fresh cilantro
- 1/2 cup drained refrigerated pico de gallo

Directions:
1. Place tortillas on work surface, sprinkle 2 tablespoons shredded cheese over half of each tortilla and top with cheese on each tortilla with 1/4 cup each red pepper slices, zucchini slices, and black beans. Sprinkle evenly with remaining 1/2 cup cheese.
2. Fold tortillas over to form half-moon shaped quesadillas, lightly coat with cooking spray, and secure with toothpicks.
3. Lightly spray air fryer basket with cooking spray. Place 2 quesadillas in the basket, and cook at 400°F for 10 minutes until tortillas are golden brown and slightly crispy, cheese is melted, and vegetables are slightly softened. Turn quesadillas over halfway through cooking.
4. Repeat with remaining quesadillas.
5. Meanwhile, stir yogurt, lime juice, lime zest and cumin in a small bowl.
6. Cut each quesadilla into wedges and sprinkle with cilantro.
7. Serve with 1 tablespoon cumin cream and 2 tablespoons pico de gallo each.
- **Nutrition Info:** Calories 291 Fat 8g Saturated fat 4g Unsaturated fat 3g Protein 17g Carbohydrate 36g Fiber 8g Sugars 3g Sodium 518mg Calcium 30% DV Potassium 6% DV

197.Creole Beef Meatloaf

Servings: 6
Cooking Time: 15 Minutes
Ingredients:
- 1 lb. ground beef
- 1/2 tablespoon butter
- 1 red bell pepper diced
- 1/3 cup red onion diced
- 1/3 cup cilantro diced
- 1/3 cup zucchini diced
- 1 tablespoon creole seasoning
- 1/2 teaspoon turmeric
- 1/2 teaspoon cumin
- 1/2 teaspoon coriander
- 2 garlic cloves minced
- Salt and black pepper to taste

Directions:
1. Mix the beef minced with all the meatball ingredients in a bowl.

2. Make small meatballs out of this mixture and place them in the Air fryer basket.
3. Press "Power Button" of Air Fry Oven and turn the dial to select the "Air Fry" mode.
4. Press the Time button and again turn the dial to set the cooking time to 15 minutes.
5. Now push the Temp button and rotate the dial to set the temperature at 370 degrees F.
6. Once preheated, place the Air fryer basket in the oven and close its lid.
7. Slice and serve warm.
- **Nutrition Info:** Calories: 331 Cal Total Fat: 2.5 g Saturated Fat: 0.5 g Cholesterol: 35 mg Sodium: 595 mg Total Carbs: 69 g Fiber: 12.2 g Sugar: 12.5 g Protein: 26.7 g

198.Spicy Sesame-honey Chicken

Servings: 4
Cooking Time: 30 Minutes
Ingredients:
- 1 package of chicken thighs/wings
- 1 tablespoon sugar
- 1-1/3 tablespoons chili garlic sauce
- 1/4 cup soy sauce
- 1 tablespoon sesame oil
- 1 tablespoon ketchup
- 1 tablespoon honey
- 1 tablespoon soy sauce
- 1 teaspoon sugar or brown sugar
- 1 teaspoon cornstarch

Directions:
1. Create marinade by combining 1 tablespoon chili sauce, soy sauce, and sesame oil.
2. Toss chicken in marinade and refrigerate for at least 30 minutes, but up to a day.
3. Preheat toaster oven to 375°F. Place chicken on a baking sheet with a little space between each piece and bake for 30 minutes.
4. While the chicken bakes, create the sauce by combining all the leftover ingredients, including the 1/3 tablespoon of chili sauce.
5. Mix well and microwave in 30-second intervals until the sauce starts to thicken.
6. Toss chicken in sauce and serve.
- **Nutrition Info:** Calories: 401, Sodium: 1439 mg, Dietary Fiber: 0 g, Total Fat: 16.0 g, Total Carbs: 11.2 g, Protein: 50.6 g.

199.Beef Pieces With Tender Broccoli

Servings: 4
Cooking Time: 13 Minutes
Ingredients:
- 6 oz. broccoli
- 10 oz. beef brisket
- 4 oz chive stems
- 1 teaspoon paprika
- 1/3 cup water
- 1 teaspoon olive oil

- 1 teaspoon butter
- 1 tablespoon flax seeds
- ½ teaspoon chili flakes

Directions:
1. Cut the beef brisket into the medium/convenient pieces.
2. Sprinkle the beef pieces with the paprika and chili flakes.
3. Mix the meat up with the help of the hands.
4. Then preheat the air fryer to 360 F.
5. Spray the air fryer basket tray with the olive oil.
6. Put the beef pieces in the air fryer basket tray and cook the meat for 7 minutes.
7. Stir it once during the cooking.
8. Meanwhile, separate the broccoli into the florets.
9. When the time is over – add the broccoli florets in the air fryer basket tray.
10. Sprinkle the ingredients with the flax seeds and butter.
11. Add water.
12. Dice the chives and add them in the air fryer basket tray too.
13. Stir it gently using the wooden spatula.
14. Then cook the dish at 265 F for 6 minutes more.
15. When the broccoli is tender – the dish is cooked.
16. Serve the dish little bit chilled.
17. Enjoy!
- **Nutrition Info:** calories 187, fat 7.3, fiber 2.4, carbs 6.2, protein 23.4

200.Cocktail Franks In Blanket

Servings: 4
Cooking Time: 20 Minutes
Ingredients:
- 12 oz cocktail franks
- 8 oz can crescent rolls

Directions:
1. Use a paper towel to pat the cocktail franks to drain completely. Cut the dough in 1 by 5-inch rectangles using a knife. Gently roll the franks in the strips, making sure the ends are visible place in freezer for 5 minutes.
2. Preheat the fryer to 330 f. Take the franks out of the freezer and place them in the air fryer's basket and cook for 6-8 minutes. Increase the temperature to 390 f. Cook for another 3 minutes until a fine golden texture appears.
- **Nutrition Info:** Calories: 60 Cal Total Fat: 4.8 g Saturated Fat: 1.6 g Cholesterol: 2 mg Sodium: 136 mg Total Carbs: 2.4 g Fiber: 0.2 g Sugar: 0.1 g Protein: 1.6 g

201.Pepper Pork Chops

Servings: 2
Cooking Time: 6 Minutes
Ingredients:
- 2 pork chops
- 1 egg white
- ¾ cup xanthum gum
- ½ teaspoon sea salt
- ¼ teaspoon freshly ground black pepper
- 1 oil mister

Directions:
1. Preheat the Air fryer to 400 degree F and grease an Air fryer basket.
2. Whisk egg white with salt and black pepper in a bowl and dip the pork chops in it.
3. Cover the bowl and marinate for about 20 minutes.
4. Pour the xanthum gum over both sides of the chops and spray with oil mister.
5. Arrange the chops in the Air fryer basket and cook for about 6 minutes.
6. Dish out in a bowl and serve warm.
- **Nutrition Info:** Calories: 541, Fat: 34g, Carbohydrates: 3.4g, Sugar: 1g, Protein: 20.3g, Sodium: 547mg

202.Irish Whisky Steak

Servings: 6
Cooking Time: 20 Minutes
Ingredients:
- 2 pounds sirloin steaks
- 1 ½tablespoons tamari sauce
- 1/3 teaspoon cayenne pepper
- 1/3 teaspoon ground ginger
- 2 garlic cloves, thinly sliced
- 2 tablespoons Irish whiskey
- 2 tablespoons olive oil
- Fine sea salt, to taste

Directions:
1. Firstly, add all the ingredients, minus the olive oil and the steak, to a resealable plastic bag.
2. Throw in the steak and let it marinate for a couple of hours. After that, drizzle the sirloin steaks with 2 tablespoons olive oil.
3. Roast for approximately 22 minutesat 395 degrees F, turning it halfway through the time.
- **Nutrition Info:** 260 Calories; 17g Fat; 8g Carbs; 35g Protein; 2g Sugars; 1g Fiber

203.Filet Mignon With Chili Peanut Sauce

Servings: 4
Cooking Time: 20 Minutes
Ingredients:
- 2 pounds filet mignon, sliced into bite-sized strips
- 1 tablespoon oyster sauce
- 2 tablespoons sesame oil
- 2 tablespoons tamari sauce
- 1 tablespoon ginger-garlic paste

- 1 tablespoon mustard
- 1 teaspoon chili powder
- 1/4 cup peanut butter
- 2 tablespoons lime juice
- 1 teaspoon red pepper flakes
- 2 tablespoons water

Directions:
1. Place the beef strips, oyster sauce, sesame oil, tamari sauce, ginger-garlic paste, mustard, and chili powder in a large ceramic dish.
2. Cover and allow it to marinate for 2 hours in your refrigerator.
3. Cook in the preheated Air Fryer at 400 degrees F for 18 minutes, shaking the basket occasionally.
4. Mix the peanut butter with lime juice, red pepper flakes, and water. Spoon the sauce onto the air fried beef strips and serve warm.
- **Nutrition Info:** 420 Calories; 21g Fat; 5g Carbs; 50g Protein; 7g Sugars; 1g Fiber

204.Effortless Beef Schnitzel

Servings: 2
Cooking Time: 25 Minutes
Ingredients:
- 2 tbsp vegetable oil
- 2 oz breadcrumbs
- 1 whole egg, whisked
- 1 thin beef schnitzel, cut into strips
- 1 whole lemon

Directions:
1. Preheat your fryer to 356 F. In a bowl, add breadcrumbs and oil and stir well to get a loose mixture. Dip schnitzel in egg, then dip in breadcrumbs coat well. Place the prepared schnitzel your Air Fryer's cooking basket and cook for 12 minutes. Serve with a drizzle of lemon juice.
- **Nutrition Info:** 346 Calories; 11g Fat; 4g Carbs; 32g Protein; 1g Sugars; 1g Fiber

205.Broccoli And Tomato Sauce

Servings: 4
Cooking Time: 7 Minutes
Ingredients:
- 1 broccoli head, florets separated
- ¼ cup scallions; chopped
- ½ cup tomato sauce
- 1 tbsp. olive oil
- 1 tbsp. sweet paprika
- Salt and black pepper to taste.

Directions:
1. In a pan that fits the air fryer, combine the broccoli with the rest of the Ingredients: toss.
2. Put the pan in the fryer and cook at 380°F for 15 minutes

3. Divide between plates and serve.
- **Nutrition Info:** Calories: 163; Fat: 5g; Fiber: 2g; Carbs: 4g; Protein: 8g

206.Salsa Stuffed Eggplants

Servings: 2
Cooking Time: 25 Minutes
Ingredients:
- 1 large eggplant
- 8 cherry tomatoes, quartered
- ½ tablespoon fresh parsley
- 2 teaspoons olive oil, divided
- 2 teaspoons fresh lemon juice, divided
- 2 tablespoons tomato salsa
- Salt and black pepper, as required

Directions:
1. Preheat the Air fryer to 390 degree F and grease an Air fryer basket.
2. Arrange the eggplant into the Air fryer basket and cook for about 15 minutes.
3. Cut the eggplant in half lengthwise and drizzle evenly with one teaspoon of oil.
4. Set the Air fryer to 355 degree F and arrange the eggplant into the Air fryer basket, cut-side up.
5. Cook for another 10 minutes and dish out in a bowl.
6. Scoop out the flesh from the eggplant and transfer into a bowl.
7. Stir in the tomatoes, salsa, parsley, salt, black pepper, remaining oil, and lemon juice.
8. Squeeze lemon juice on the eggplant halves and stuff with the salsa mixture to serve.
- **Nutrition Info:** Calories: 192, Fat: 6.1g, Carbohydrates: 33.8g, Sugar: 20.4g, Protein: 6.9g, Sodium: 204mg

207.Healthy Mama Meatloaf

Servings: 8
Cooking Time: 40 Minutes
Ingredients:
- 1 tablespoon olive oil
- 1 green bell pepper, diced
- 1/2 cup diced sweet onion
- 1/2 teaspoon minced garlic
- 1-lb. ground beef
- 1 cup whole wheat bread crumbs
- 2 large eggs
- 3/4 cup shredded carrot
- 3/4 cup shredded zucchini
- salt and ground black pepper to taste
- 1/4 cup ketchup, or to taste

Directions:
1. Thoroughly mix ground beef with egg, onion, garlic, crumbs, and all the ingredients in a bowl.
2. Grease a meatloaf pan with oil or butter and spread the minced beef in the pan.

3. Press "Power Button" of Air Fry Oven and turn the dial to select the "Bake" mode.
4. Press the Time button and again turn the dial to set the cooking time to 40 minutes.
5. Now push the Temp button and rotate the dial to set the temperature at 375 degrees F.
6. Once preheated, place the beef baking pan in the oven and close its lid.
7. Slice and serve.
- **Nutrition Info:** Calories: 322 Cal Total Fat: 11.8 g Saturated Fat: 2.2 g Cholesterol: 56 mg Sodium: 321 mg Total Carbs: 14.6 g Fiber: 4.4 g Sugar: 8 g Protein: 17.3 g

208.Creamy Tuna Cakes

Servings: 4
Cooking Time: 15 Minutes
Ingredients:
- 2: 6-ouncescans tuna, drained
- 1½ tablespoon almond flour
- 1½ tablespoons mayonnaise
- 1 tablespoon fresh lemon juice
- 1 teaspoon dried dill
- 1 teaspoon garlic powder
- ½ teaspoon onion powder
- Pinch of salt and ground black pepper

Directions:
1. Preheat the Air fryer to 400-degree F and grease an Air fryer basket.
2. Mix the tuna, mayonnaise, almond flour, lemon juice, dill, and spices in a large bowl.
3. Make 4 equal-sized patties from the mixture and arrange in the Air fryer basket.
4. Cook for about 10 minutes and flip the sides.
5. Cook for 5 more minutes and dish out the tuna cakes in serving plates to serve warm.
- **Nutrition Info:** Calories: 200, Fat: 10.1g, Carbohydrates: 2.9g, Sugar: 0.8g, Protein: 23.4g, Sodium: 122mg

209.Salmon Casserole

Servings: 8
Cooking Time: 12 Minutes
Ingredients:
- 7 oz Cheddar cheese, shredded
- ½ cup cream
- 1-pound salmon fillet
- 1 tablespoon dried dill
- 1 teaspoon dried parsley
- 1 teaspoon salt
- 1 teaspoon ground coriander
- ½ teaspoon ground black pepper
- 2 green pepper, chopped
- 4 oz chive stems, diced
- 7 oz bok choy, chopped
- 1 tablespoon olive oil

Directions:

1. Sprinkle the salmon fillet with the dried dill, dried parsley, ground coriander, and ground black pepper.
2. Massage the salmon fillet gently and leave it for 5 minutes to make the fish soaks the spices.
3. Meanwhile, sprinkle the air fryer casserole tray with the olive oil inside.
4. After this, cut the salmon fillet into the cubes.
5. Separate the salmon cubes into 2 parts.
6. Then place the first part of the salmon cubes in the casserole tray.
7. Sprinkle the fish with the chopped bok choy, diced chives, and chopped green pepper.
8. After this, place the second part of the salmon cubes over the vegetables.
9. Then sprinkle the casserole with the shredded cheese and heavy cream.
10. Preheat the air fryer to 380 F.
11. Cook the salmon casserole for 12 minutes.
12. When the dish is cooked – it will have acrunchy light brown crust.
13. Serve it and enjoy!
- **Nutrition Info:** calories 216, fat 14.4, fiber 1.1, carbs 4.3, protein 18.2

210.Veggie Stuffed Bell Peppers

Servings: 6
Cooking Time: 25 Minutes
Ingredients:
- 6 large bell peppers, tops and seeds removed
- 1 carrot, peeled and finely chopped
- 1 potato, peeled and finely chopped
- ½ cup fresh peas, shelled
- 1/3 cup cheddar cheese, grated
- 2 garlic cloves, minced
- Salt and black pepper, to taste

Directions:
1. Preheat the Air fryer to 350 ºF and grease an Air fryer basket.
2. Mix vegetables, garlic, salt and black pepper in a bowl.
3. Stuff the vegetable mixture in each bell pepper and arrange in the Air fryer pan.
4. Cook for about 20 minutes and top with cheddar cheese.
5. Cook for about 5 more minutes and dish out to serve warm.
- **Nutrition Info:** Calories: 101, Fat: 2.5g, Carbohydrates: 17.1g, Sugar: 7.4g, Protein: 4.1g, Sodium: 51mg

211.Smoked Ham With Pears

Servings: 2
Cooking Time: 30 Minutes
Ingredients:
- 15 oz pears, halved

- 8 pound smoked ham
- 1 ½ cups brown sugar
- ¾ tbsp allspice
- 1 tbsp apple cider vinegar
- 1 tsp black pepper
- 1 tsp vanilla extract

Directions:
1. Preheat your air fryer to 330 f. In a bowl, mix pears, brown sugar, cider vinegar, vanilla extract, pepper, and allspice. Place the mixture in a frying pan and fry for 2-3 minutes. Pour the mixture over ham. Add the ham to the air fryer cooking basket and cook for 15 minutes. Serve ham with hot sauce, to enjoy!
- **Nutrition Info:** Calories: 550 Cal Total Fat: 29 g Saturated Fat: 0 g Cholesterol: 0 mg Sodium: 0 mg Total Carbs: 46 g Fiber: 0 g Sugar: 0 g Protein: 28 g

212.Almond Asparagus

Servings: 3
Cooking Time: 6 Minutes
Ingredients:
- 1 pound asparagus
- 1/3 cup almonds, sliced
- 2 tablespoons olive oil
- 2 tablespoons balsamic vinegar
- Salt and black pepper, to taste

Directions:
1. Preheat the Air fryer to 400 ºF and grease an Air fryer basket.
2. Mix asparagus, oil, vinegar, salt, and black pepper in a bowl and toss to coat well.
3. Arrange asparagus into the Air fryer basket and sprinkle with the almond slices.
4. Cook for about 6 minutes and dish out to serve hot.
- **Nutrition Info:** Calories: 173, Fat: 14.8g, Carbohydrates: 8.2g, Sugar: 3.3g, Protein: 5.6g, Sodium: 54mg

213.Oven-fried Herbed Chicken

Servings: 2
Cooking Time: 15 Minutes
Ingredients:
- 1/2 cup buttermilk
- 2 cloves garlic, minced
- 1-1/2 teaspoons salt
- 1 tablespoon oil
- 1/2 pound boneless, skinless chicken breasts
- 1 cup rolled oats
- 1/2 teaspoon red pepper flakes
- 1/2 cup grated parmesan cheese
- 1/4 cup fresh basil leaves or rosemary needles
- Olive oil spray

Directions:

1. Mix together buttermilk, oil, 1/2 teaspoon salt, and garlic in a shallow bowl.
2. Roll chicken in buttermilk and refrigerate in bowl overnight.
3. Preheat your toaster oven to 425°F.
4. Mix together the oats, red pepper, salt, parmesan, and basil, and mix roughly to break up oats.
5. Place the mixture on a plate.
6. Remove the chicken from the buttermilk mixture and let any excess drip off.
7. Roll the chicken in the oat mixture and transfer to a baking sheet lightly coated with olive oil spray.
8. Spray the chicken with oil spray and bake for 15 minutes.
- **Nutrition Info:** Calories: 651, Sodium: 713 mg, Dietary Fiber: 4.4 g, Total Fat: 31.2 g, Total Carbs: 34.1 g, Protein: 59.5 g.

214.Grilled Tasty Scallops

Servings: 2
Cooking Time: 10 Minutes
Ingredients:
- 1 pound sea scallops, cleaned and patted dry
- Salt and pepper to taste
- 3 dried chilies
- 2 tablespoon dried thyme
- 1 tablespoon dried oregano
- 1 tablespoon ground coriander
- 1 tablespoon ground fennel
- 2 teaspoons chipotle pepper

Directions:
1. Place the instant pot air fryer lid on and preheat the instant pot at 390 degrees F.
2. Place the grill pan accessory in the instant pot.
3. Mix all ingredients in a bowl.
4. Dump the scallops on the grill pan, close the air fryer lid and cook for 10 minutes.
- **Nutrition Info:** Calories:291 ; Carbs: 20.7g; Protein: 48.6g; Fat: 2.5g

215.Fennel & Tomato Chicken Paillard

Servings: 1
Cooking Time: 12 Minutes
Ingredients:
- 1/4 cup olive oil
- 1 boneless skinless chicken breast
- Salt and pepper
- 1 garlic clove, thinly sliced
- 1 small diced Roma tomato
- 1/2 fennel bulb, shaved
- 1/4 cup sliced mushrooms
- 2 tablespoons sliced black olives
- 1-1/2 teaspoons capers
- 2 sprigs fresh thyme
- 1 tablespoon chopped fresh parsley

Directions:
1. Start by pounding the chicken until it is about 1/2-inch thick.
2. Preheat the toaster oven to 400°F and brush the bottom of a baking pan with olive oil.
3. Sprinkle salt and pepper on both sides of the chicken and place it in the baking pan.
4. In a bowl, mix together all other ingredients, including the remaining olive oil.
5. Spoon mixture over chicken and bake for 12 minutes.
- **Nutrition Info:** Calories: 797, Sodium: 471 mg, Dietary Fiber: 6.0 g, Total Fat: 63.7 g, Total Carbs: 16.4 g, Protein: 45.8 g.

216.Garlic Parmesan Shrimp

Servings: 2
Cooking Time: 10 Minutes
Ingredients:
- 1 pound shrimp, deveined and peeled
- ½ cup parmesan cheese, grated
- ¼ cup cilantro, diced
- 1 tablespoon olive oil
- 1 teaspoon salt
- 1 teaspoon fresh cracked pepper
- 1 tablespoon lemon juice
- 6 garlic cloves, diced

Directions:
1. Preheat the Air fryer to 350 degree F and grease an Air fryer basket.
2. Drizzle shrimp with olive oil and lemon juice and season with garlic, salt and cracked pepper.
3. Cover the bowl with plastic wrap and refrigerate for about 3 hours.
4. Stir in the parmesan cheese and cilantro to the bowl and transfer to the Air fryer basket.
5. Cook for about 10 minutes and serve immediately.
- **Nutrition Info:** Calories: 602, Fat: 23.9g, Carbohydrates: 46.5g, Sugar: 2.9g, Protein: 11.3g, Sodium: 886mg

217.Broccoli Stuffed Peppers

Servings: 2
Cooking Time: 40 Minutes
Ingredients:
- 4 eggs
- 1/2 cup cheddar cheese, grated
- 2 bell peppers, cut in half and remove seeds 1/2 tsp garlic powder
- 1 tsp dried thyme
- 1/4 cup feta cheese, crumbled 1/2 cup broccoli, cooked
- 1/4 tsp pepper 1/2 tsp salt

Directions:
1. Preheat the air fryer to 325 F.
2. Stuff feta and broccoli into the bell peppers halved.
3. Beat egg in a bowl with seasoning and pour egg mixture into the pepper halved over feta and broccoli.
4. Place bell pepper halved into the air fryer basket and cook for 35-40 minutes.
5. Top with grated cheddar cheese and cook until cheese melted.
6. Serve and enjoy.
- **Nutrition Info:** Calories 340 Fat 22 g Carbohydrates 12 g Sugar 8.2 g Protein 22 g Cholesterol 374 mg

218.Amazing Bacon And Potato Platter

Servings: 4
Cooking Time: 40 Minutes
Ingredients:
- 4 potatoes, halved
- 6 garlic cloves, squashed
- 4 streaky cut rashers bacon
- 2 sprigs rosemary
- 1 tbsp olive oil

Directions:
1. Preheat your air fryer to 392 f. In a mixing bowl, mix garlic, bacon, potatoes and rosemary; toss in oil. Place the mixture in your air fryer's cooking basket and roast for 25-30 minutes. Serve and enjoy!
- **Nutrition Info:** Calories: 336 Cal Total Fat: 18.5 g Saturated Fat: 0 g Cholesterol: 82 mg Sodium: 876 mg Total Carbs: 69.9 g Fiber: 0 g Sugar: 0 g Protein: 0 g

219.One-pan Shrimp And Chorizo Mix Grill

Servings: 4
Cooking Time: 15 Minutes
Ingredients:
- 1 ½ pounds large shrimps, peeled and deveined
- Salt and pepper to taste
- 6 links fresh chorizo sausage
- 2 bunches asparagus spears, trimmed
- Lime wedges

Directions:
1. Place the instant pot air fryer lid on and preheat the instant pot at 390 degrees F.
2. Place the grill pan accessory in the instant pot.
3. Season the shrimps with salt and pepper to taste. Set aside.
4. Place the chorizo on the grill pan and the sausage.
5. Place the asparagus on top.
6. Close the air fryer lid and grill for 15 minutes.
7. Serve with lime wedges.
- **Nutrition Info:** Calories:124 ; Carbs: 9.4g; Protein: 8.2g; Fat: 7.1g

220.Breaded Shrimp With Lemon

Servings: 3
Cooking Time: 14 Minutes
Ingredients:
- ½ cup plain flour
- 2 egg whites
- 1 cup breadcrumbs
- 1 pound large shrimp, peeled and deveined
- Salt and ground black pepper, as required
- ¼ teaspoon lemon zest
- ¼ teaspoon cayenne pepper
- ¼ teaspoon red pepper flakes, crushed
- 2 tablespoons vegetable oil

Directions:
1. Preheat the Air fryer to 400 degree F and grease an Air fryer basket.
2. Mix flour, salt, and black pepper in a shallow bowl.
3. Whisk the egg whites in a second bowl and mix the breadcrumbs, lime zest and spices in a third bowl.
4. Coat each shrimp with the flour, dip into egg whites and finally, dredge in the breadcrumbs.
5. Drizzle the shrimp evenly with olive oil and arrange half of the coated shrimps into the Air fryer basket.
6. Cook for about 7 minutes and dish out the coated shrimps onto serving plates.
7. Repeat with the remaining mixture and serve hot.
- **Nutrition Info:** Calories: 432, Fat: 11.3g, Carbohydrates: 44.8g, Sugar: 2.5g, Protein: 37.7g, Sodium: 526mg

221.Venetian Liver

Servings: 6
Cooking Time: 15-30;
Ingredients:
- 500g veal liver
- 2 white onions
- 100g of water
- 2 tbsp vinegar
- Salt and pepper to taste

Directions:
1. Chop the onion and put it inside the pan with the water. Set the air fryer to 1800C and cook for 20 minutes.
2. Add the liver cut into small pieces and vinegar, close the lid, and cook for an additional 10 minutes.
3. Add salt and pepper.
- **Nutrition Info:** Calories 131, Fat 14.19 g, Carbohydrates 16.40 g, Sugars 5.15 g, Protein 25.39 g, Cholesterol 350.41 mg

222.Tasty Sausage Bacon Rolls

Servings: 4
Cooking Time: 1 Hour 44 Minutes
Ingredients:
- Sausage:
- 8 bacon strips
- 8 pork sausages
- Relish:
- 8 large tomatoes
- 1 clove garlic, peeled
- 1 small onion, peeled
- 3 tbsp chopped parsley
- A pinch of salt
- A pinch of pepper
- 2 tbsp sugar
- 1 tsp smoked paprika
- 1 tbsp white wine vinegar

Directions:
1. Start with the relish; add the tomatoes, garlic, and onion in a food processor. Blitz them for 10 seconds until the mixture is pulpy. Pour the pulp into a saucepan, add the vinegar, salt, pepper, and place it over medium heat.
2. Bring to simmer for 10 minutes; add the paprika and sugar. Stir with a spoon and simmer for 10 minutes until pulpy and thick. Turn off the heat, transfer the relish to a bowl and chill it for an hour. In 30 minutes after putting the relish in the refrigerator, move on to the sausages. Wrap each sausage with a bacon strip neatly and stick in a bamboo skewer at the end of the sausage to secure the bacon ends.
3. Open the Air Fryer, place 3 to 4 wrapped sausages in the fryer basket and cook for 12 minutes at 350 F. Ensure that the bacon is golden and crispy before removing them. Repeat the cooking process for the remaining wrapped sausages. Remove the relish from the refrigerator. Serve the sausages and relish with turnip mash.
- **Nutrition Info:** 346 Calories; 11g Fat; 4g Carbs; 32g Protein; 1g Sugars; 1g Fiber

223.Garlic Lamb Shank

Servings: 5
Cooking Time: 24 Minutes
Ingredients:
- 17 oz. lamb shanks
- 2 tablespoon garlic, peeled
- 1 teaspoon kosher salt
- 1 tablespoon dried parsley
- 4 oz chive stems, chopped
- ½ cup chicken stock
- 1 teaspoon butter
- 1 teaspoon dried rosemary
- 1 teaspoon nutmeg
- ½ teaspoon ground black pepper

Directions:
1. Chop the garlic roughly.

2. Make the cuts in the lamb shank and fill the cuts with the chopped garlic.
3. Then sprinkle the lamb shank with the kosher salt, dried parsley, dried rosemary, nutmeg, and ground black pepper.
4. Stir the spices on the lamb shank gently.
5. Then put the butter and chicken stock in the air fryer basket tray.
6. Preheat the air fryer to 380 F.
7. Put the chives in the air fryer basket tray.
8. Add the lamb shank and cook the meat for 24 minutes.
9. When the lamb shank is cooked – transfer it to the serving plate and sprinkle with the remaining liquid from the cooked meat.
10. Enjoy!

- **Nutrition Info:** calories 205, fat 8.2, fiber 0.8, carbs 3.8, protein 27.2

224.Pesto & White Wine Salmon

Servings: 4
Cooking Time: 10 Minutes
Ingredients:

- 1-1/4 pounds salmon filet
- 2 tablespoons white wine
- 2 tablespoons pesto
- 1 lemon

Directions:

1. Cut the salmon into 4 pieces and place on a greased baking sheet.
2. Slice the lemon into quarters and squeeze 1 quarter over each piece of salmon.
3. Drizzle wine over salmon and set aside to marinate while preheating the toaster oven on broil.
4. Spread pesto over each piece of salmon.
5. Broil for at least 10 minutes, or until the fish is cooked to desired doneness and the pesto is browned.

- **Nutrition Info:** Calories: 236, Sodium: 111 mg, Dietary Fiber: 0.9 g, Total Fat: 12.1 g, Total Carbs: 3.3 g, Protein: 28.6 g.

225.Morning Ham And Cheese Sandwich

Servings: 4
Cooking Time: 15 Minutes
Ingredients:

- 8 slices whole wheat bread
- 4 slices lean pork ham
- 4 slices cheese
- 8 slices tomato

Directions:

1. Preheat your air fryer to 360 f. Lay four slices of bread on a flat surface. Spread the slices with cheese, tomato, turkey and ham. Cover with the remaining slices to form sandwiches. Add the sandwiches to the air fryer cooking basket and cook for 10 minutes.

- **Nutrition Info:** Calories: 361 Cal Total Fat: 16.7 g Saturated Fat: 0 g Cholesterol: 0 mg Sodium: 1320 mg Total Carbs: 32.5 g Fiber: 2.3 g Sugar: 5.13 g Protein: 19.3 g

226.Hot Pork Skewers

Servings: 3 To 4
Cooking Time: 1 Hour 20 Minutes
Ingredients:

- 1 lb pork steak, cut in cubes
- ¼ cup soy sauce
- 2 tsp smoked paprika
- 1 tsp powdered chili
- 1 tsp garlic salt
- 1 tsp red chili flakes
- 1 tbsp white wine vinegar
- 3 tbsp steak sauce
- Skewing:
- 1 green pepper, cut in cubes
- 1 red pepper, cut in cubes
- 1 yellow squash, seeded and cut in cubes
- 1 green squash, seeded and cut in cubes
- Salt and black pepper to taste to season

Directions:

1. In a mixing bowl, add the pork cubes, soy sauce, smoked paprika, powdered chili, garlic salt, red chili flakes, white wine vinegar, and steak sauce. Mix them using a ladle. Refrigerate to marinate them for 1 hour.
2. After one hour, remove the marinated pork from the fridge and preheat the Air Fryer to 370 F.
3. On each skewer, stick the pork cubes and vegetables in the order that you prefer. Have fun doing this. Once the pork cubes and vegetables are finished, arrange the skewers in the fryer basket and grill them for 8 minutes. You can do them in batches. Once ready, remove them onto the serving platter and serve with salad.

- **Nutrition Info:** 456 Calories; 37g Fat; 1g Carbs; 21g Protein; 5g Sugars; 6g Fiber

227.Okra With Green Beans

Servings: 2
Cooking Time: 20 Minutes
Ingredients:

- ½, 10-ouncesbag frozen cut okra
- ½, 10-ouncesbag frozen cut green beans
- ¼ cup nutritional yeast
- 3 tablespoons balsamic vinegar
- Salt and black pepper, to taste

Directions:

1. Preheat the Air fryer to 400 ºF and grease an Air fryer basket.
2. Mix the okra, green beans, nutritional yeast, vinegar, salt, and black pepper in a bowl and toss to coat well.

3. Arrange the okra mixture into the Air fryer basket and cook for about 20 minutes.
4. Dish out in a serving dish and serve hot.
- **Nutrition Info:** Calories: 126, Fat: 1.3g, Carbohydrates: 19.7g, Sugar: 2.1g, Protein: 11.9g, Sodium: 100mg

228.Lobster Lasagna Maine Style

Servings: 6
Cooking Time: 50 Minutes
Ingredients:
- 1/2 (15 ounces) container ricotta cheese
- 1 egg
- 1 cup shredded Cheddar cheese
- 1/2 cup shredded mozzarella cheese
- 1/2 cup grated Parmesan cheese
- 1/2 medium onion, minced
- 1-1/2 teaspoons minced garlic
- 1 tablespoon chopped fresh parsley
- 1/2 teaspoon freshly ground black pepper
- 1 (16 ounces) jar Alfredo pasta sauce
- 8 no-boil lasagna noodles
- 1 pound cooked and cubed lobster meat
- 5-ounce package baby spinach leaves

Directions:

1. Mix well half of Parmesan, half of the mozzarella, half of cheddar, egg, and ricotta cheese in a medium bowl. Stir in pepper, parsley, garlic, and onion.
2. Place the instant pot air fryer lid on, lightly grease baking pan of the instant pot with cooking spray.
3. On the bottom of the pan, spread ½ of the Alfredo sauce, top with a single layer of lasagna noodles. Followed by 1/3 of lobster meat, 1/3 of ricotta cheese mixture, 1/3 of spinach. Repeat layering process until all ingredients are used up.
4. Sprinkle remaining cheese on top. Shake pan to settle lasagna and burst bubbles. Cover pan with foil and place the baking pan in the instant pot.
5. Close the air fryer lid and cook at 360 ºF for 30 minutes
6. Remove foil and cook for 10 minutes at 390 ºF until tops are lightly browned.
7. Let it stand for 10 minutes.
8. Serve and enjoy.
- **Nutrition Info:** Calories: 558; Carbs: 20.4g; Protein: 36.8g; Fat: 36.5g

229.Korean-style Chicken Wings

Servings: 4
Cooking Time: 20 Minutes
Ingredients:
- 1 pound chicken wings
- 8 oz flour
- 8 oz breadcrumbs
- 3 beaten eggs
- 4 tbsp canola oil
- Salt and black pepper to taste
- 2 tbsp sesame seeds
- 2 tbsp Korean red pepper paste
- 1 tbsp apple cider vinegar
- 2 tbsp honey
- 1 tbsp soy sauce
- Sesame seeds, to serve

Directions:
1. Separate the chicken wings into winglets and drumettes. In a bowl, mix salt, olive oil, and pepper. Coat the chicken with flour followed by eggs and breadcrumbs. Place in the basket and fit in the baking tray. Oil with cooking spray and cook for 15 minutes on Air Fry mode at 350 F.
2. Mix red pepper paste, apple cider vinegar, soy sauce, honey, and ¼ cup of water in a saucepan and bring to a boil over medium heat. Simmer until the sauce thickens, about 3-4 minutes. Pour the sauce over the chicken pieces. Garnish with sesame seeds and serve.

230.Stuffed Pork Loin

Servings: 8
Cooking Time: 35 Minutes
Ingredients:
- 3 tbsp. butter
- 2 onions, sliced thin
- ½ cup beef broth
- 3 lb. pork loin, center cut
- 2 tbsp. extra virgin olive oil
- 1 tsp salt
- 1/4 tsp pepper
- 1 tsp Italian seasoning
- 2 cups gruyere cheese, grated
- Nonstick cooking spray

Directions:
1. Melt butter in a large skillet over med-high heat. Add onions and broth and cook until onions are brown and tender, about 15 minutes. Transfer to bowl and keep warm.
2. Butterfly the pork making sure you do not cut all the way through. Open up the tenderloin, cover with plastic wrap and pound to 1/3-inch thick.
3. In a small bowl, combine salt, pepper, and Italian seasoning. Rub both sides of pork with mixture.
4. Spread half the cooked onions on one side of pork and top with half the cheese. Tightly roll up pork and tie with butcher string.
5. Heat oil in skillet. Add the tenderloin and brown on all sides.
6. Set the oven to convection bake on 425°F for 35 minutes.
7. Lightly spray the baking pan with cooking spray and place pork on it. After the oven has preheated for 5 minutes, place the baking pan in position 1 and cook 30 minutes. Basting occasionally with juice from the pan.
8. Top pork with remaining onions and cheese. Increase heat to broil and cook another 5 minutes, or until cheese is melted and golden brown. Let rest 5 minutes before slicing and serving.
- **Nutrition Info:** Calories 448, Total Fat 24g, Saturated Fat 11g, Total Carbs 3g, Net Carbs 0g, Protein 55g, Sugar 1g, Fiber 0g, Sodium 715mg, Potassium 795mg, Phosphorus 665mg

231.Crunchy Parmesan Pork Chops

Servings: 4
Cooking Time: 10 Minutes
Ingredients:
- 4 pork chops, boneless
- 2 tbsp olive oil
- 1/4 tsp pepper
- 1/2 tsp garlic powder
- 1 tsp dried parsley
- 1/4 tsp smoked paprika
- 2 tbsp breadcrumbs
- 1/4 cup parmesan cheese, grated

Directions:
1. Fit the oven with the rack in position
2. In a shallow dish, mix breadcrumbs, paprika, parmesan cheese, garlic powder, parsley, and pepper.
3. Brush pork chops with oil and coat with breadcrumb mixture.
4. Place coated pork chops into the baking pan.
5. Set to bake at 450 F for 15 minutes. After 5 minutes place the baking pan in the preheated oven.
6. Serve and enjoy.
- **Nutrition Info:** Calories 350 Fat 28.3 g Carbohydrates 3.1 g Sugar 0.3 g Protein 20.4 g Cholesterol 73 mg

232.Garlic Kangaroo

Servings:x
Cooking Time:x

Ingredients:

- 1 lb. boneless kangaroo
- 2 cup dry breadcrumbs
- 2 tsp. oregano
- 2 tsp. red chili flakes
- 2 tsp. garlic paste
- 1 ½ tbsp. ginger-garlic paste
- 4 tbsp. lemon juice
- 2 tsp. salt
- 1 tsp. red chili powder
- 6 tbsp. corn flour
- 4 eggs

Directions:

1. Mix all the ingredients for the marinade and put the kangaroo Oregano Fingers inside and let it rest overnight. Mix the breadcrumbs, oregano and red chili flakes well and place the marinated Oregano Fingers on this mixture. Cover it with plastic wrap and leave it till right before you serve to cook. Pre heat the oven at 160 degrees Fahrenheit for 5 minutes.
2. Place the Oregano Fingers in the fry basket and close it. Let them cook at the same temperature for another 15 minutes or so. Toss the Oregano Fingers well so that they are cooked uniformly. Drizzle the garlic paste and serve.

233.Teriyaki Chicken Thighs With Lemony Snow Peas

Servings:4
Cooking Time: 34 Minutes
Ingredients:

- ¼ cup chicken broth
- ½ teaspoon grated fresh ginger
- ⅛ teaspoon red pepper flakes
- 1½ tablespoons soy sauce
- 4 (5-ounce / 142-g) bone-in chicken thighs, trimmed
- 1 tablespoon mirin
- ½ teaspoon cornstarch
- 1 tablespoon sugar
- 6 ounces (170 g) snow peas, strings removed
- ⅛ teaspoon lemon zest
- 1 garlic clove, minced
- ¼ teaspoon salt
- Ground black pepper, to taste
- ½ teaspoon lemon juice

Directions:

1. Combine the broth, ginger, pepper flakes, and soy sauce in a large bowl. Stir to mix well.
2. Pierce 10 to 15 holes into the chicken skin. Put the chicken in the broth mixture and toss to coat well. Let sit for 10 minutes to marinate.
3. Transfer the marinated chicken on a plate and pat dry with paper towels.
4. Scoop 2 tablespoons of marinade in a microwave-safe bowl and combine with mirin, cornstarch and sugar. Stir to mix well. Microwave for 1 minute or until frothy and has a thick consistency. Set aside.
5. Arrange the chicken in the air fryer basket, skin side up.
6. Put the air fryer basket on the baking pan and slide into Rack Position 2, select Air Fry, set temperature to 400ºF (205ºC) and set time to 25 minutes.
7. Flip the chicken halfway through.
8. When cooking is complete, brush the chicken skin with marinade mixture. Air fry the chicken for 5 more minutes or until glazed.
9. Remove the chicken from the oven. Allow the chicken to cool for 10 minutes.
10. Meanwhile, combine the snow peas, lemon zest, garlic, salt, and ground black pepper in a small bowl. Toss to coat well.
11. Transfer the snow peas in the basket.
12. Put the air fryer basket on the baking pan and slide into Rack Position 2, select Air Fry, set temperature to 400ºF (205ºC) and set time to 3 minutes.
13. When cooking is complete, the peas should be soft.
14. Remove the peas from the oven and toss with lemon juice.
15. Serve the chicken with lemony snow peas.

234.Macadamia Nuts Crusted Pork Rack

Servings:2
Cooking Time: 35 Minutes
Ingredients:

- 1 clove garlic, minced
- 2 tablespoons olive oil
- 1 pound (454 g) rack of pork
- 1 cup chopped macadamia nuts
- 1 tablespoon bread crumbs
- 1 tablespoon rosemary, chopped
- 1 egg
- Salt and ground black pepper, to taste

Directions:

1. Combine the garlic and olive oil in a small bowl. Stir to mix well.
2. On a clean work surface, rub the pork rack with the garlic oil and sprinkle with salt and black pepper on both sides.
3. Combine the macadamia nuts, bread crumbs, and rosemary in a shallow dish. Whisk the egg in a large bowl.
4. Dredge the pork in the egg, then roll the pork over the macadamia nut mixture to coat well. Shake the excess off.
5. Arrange the pork in the basket.

6. Put the air fryer basket on the baking pan and slide into Rack Position 2, select Air Fry, set temperature to 350ºF (180ºC) and set time to 30 minutes.
7. After 30 minutes, remove from the oven. Flip the pork rack. Return to the oven and increase temperature to 390ºF (199ºC) and set time to 5 minutes. Keep cooking.
8. When cooking is complete, the pork should be browned.
9. Serve immediately.

235.Tangy Chicken Drumsticks With Cauliflower

Servings:4
Cooking Time: 30 Minutes
Ingredients:
- 1 lb chicken drumsticks
- ½ tsp oregano
- ¼ cup oats
- ¼ cup milk
- 1 cup cauliflower florets, steamed
- 1 egg
- 1 tbsp cayenne pepper powder
- Salt and black pepper to taste

Directions:
1. Preheat on AirFry function to 350 F. Season the drumsticks with salt and pepper and rub them with the milk. Place all the other ingredients, except for the egg in a food processor.
2. Process until smooth. Dip each drumstick in the egg first, and then in the oat mixture. Arrange them on a greased baking tray. Press Start and cook in the oven for 20 minutes. Serve warm.

236.Mango Chicken With Avocado

Servings:2
Cooking Time: 20 Minutes + Marinating Time
Ingredients:
- 2 chicken breasts, cubed
- 1 mango, cubed
- 1 avocado, pitted and sliced
- 1 chili pepper, chopped
- 5 tbsp balsamic vinegar
- 2 tbsp olive oil
- 2 garlic cloves, minced
- ¼ tsp dried oregano
- 1 tbsp fresh parsley, chopped
- ¼ tsp mustard powder

Directions:
1. In a blender, add mango, chili pepper, mustard powder, garlic, oregano, olive oil, and balsamic vinegar and pulse until smooth. Pour the liquid over chicken and let marinate for 3 hours.
2. Preheat on AirFry function to 350 F. Transfer the chicken to the basket and press

Start.Cook for 14-16 minutes. Top with avocado and parsley and serve.

237.Lamb Marinade Cutlet With Capsicum

Servings:x
Cooking Time:x
Ingredients:
- 2 cups sliced lamb
- 1 big capsicum (Cut this capsicum into big cubes)
- 2 cup fresh green coriander
- ½ cup mint leaves
- 4 tsp. fennel
- 2 tbsp. ginger-garlic paste
- 1 small onion
- 6-7 flakes garlic (optional)
- Salt to taste
- 1 onion (Cut it into quarters. Now separate the layers carefully.)
- 5 tbsp. gram flour
- A pinch of salt to taste
- 3 tbsp. lemon juice

Directions:
1. You will first need to make the sauce. Add the ingredients to a blender and make a thick paste. Slit the pieces of lamb and stuff half the paste into the cavity obtained. Take the remaining paste and add it to the gram flour and salt. Toss the pieces of lamb in this mixture and set aside. Apply a little bit of the mixture on the capsicum and onion.
2. Place these on a stick along with the lamb pieces. Pre heat the oven at 290 Fahrenheit for around 5 minutes. Open the basket. Arrange the satay sticks properly. Close the basket.
3. Keep the sticks with the lamb at 180 degrees for around half an hour while the sticks with the vegetables are to be kept at the same temperature for only 7 minutes.
4. Turn the sticks in between so that one side does not get burnt and also to provide a uniform cook.

238.Corn Flour Lamb Fries With Red Chili

Servings:x
Cooking Time:x
Ingredients:
- 2 tsp. salt
- 1 tsp. pepper powder
- 1 lb. boneless lamb cut into Oregano Fingers
- 2 cup dry breadcrumbs
- 2 tsp. oregano
- 2 tsp. red chili flakes
- 1 ½ tbsp. ginger-garlic paste
- 4 tbsp. lemon juice
- 1 tsp. red chili powder
- 6 tbsp. corn flour
- 4 eggs

Directions:
1. Mix all the ingredients for the marinade and put the lamb Oregano Fingers inside and let it rest overnight.
2. Mix the breadcrumbs, oregano and red chili flakes well and place the
3. marinated Oregano Fingers on this mixture. Cover it with plastic wrap and leave it till right before you serve to cook.
4. Pre heat the oven at 160 degrees Fahrenheit for 5 minutes. Place the Oregano Fingers in the fry basket and close it. Let them cook at the same temperature for another 15 minutes or so. Toss the Oregano Fingers well so that they are cooked uniformly.

239.Cheesy Chicken Casserole

Servings: 4
Cooking Time: 20 Minutes
Ingredients:
- 1 lb cooked chicken, shredded
- 1/2 cup salsa
- 4 oz cream cheese, softened
- 4 cups cauliflower florets
- 1/4 cup Greek yogurt
- 1 cup cheddar cheese, shredded
- 1/8 tsp pepper
- 1/2 tsp kosher salt

Directions:
1. Fit the oven with the rack in position
2. Add cauliflower into the boiling water and cook until tender. Drain well.
3. In a mixing bowl, mix cauliflower, salsa, cream cheese, chicken, yogurt, pepper, and salt.
4. Pour cauliflower mixture into the greased casserole dish and top with shredded cheddar cheese.
5. Set to bake at 375 F for 25 minutes. After 5 minutes place the casserole dish in the preheated oven.
6. Serve and enjoy.
- **Nutrition Info:** Calories 427 Fat 23.1 g Carbohydrates 9 g Sugar 4.1 g Protein 45.8 g Cholesterol 149 mg

240.Chicken Casserole With Coconut

Servings:4
Cooking Time: 20 Minutes
Ingredients:
- 2 large eggs
- 1 tsp garlic powder
- Salt and black pepper to taste
- ¾ cup breadcrumbs
- ¾ cup shredded coconut
- 1 lb chicken tenders

Directions:

1. Preheat on AirFry function to 400 F. In a wide dish, whisk eggs with garlic powder, pepper, and salt. In another bowl, mix the breadcrumbs and coconut.
2. Dip the chicken tenders in eggs, then in the coconut mix; shake off any excess. Place the prepared chicken tenders in the basket and press Start. Cook for 12-14 minutes until golden.

241.Easy Pesto Chicken

Servings: 4
Cooking Time: 35 Minutes
Ingredients:
- 4 chicken breasts, sliced into 8 pieces
- 8 oz mozzarella cheese, shredded
- 1/4 cup pesto
- 1/4 tsp pepper
- 1/2 tsp salt

Directions:
1. Fit the oven with the rack in position
2. Season chicken with pepper and salt and place in a greased baking dish.
3. Spread pesto and cheese on top of chicken.
4. Set to bake at 350 F for 40 minutes. After 5 minutes place the baking dish in the preheated oven.
5. Serve and enjoy.
- **Nutrition Info:** Calories 505 Fat 27.3 g Carbohydrates 3.1 g Sugar 1 g Protein 59.8 g Cholesterol 164 mg

242.Mayo Chicken Breasts With Basil & Cheese

Servings:4
Cooking Time: 20 Minutes
Ingredients:
- 4 chicken breasts, cubed
- 1 tsp garlic powder
- 1 cup mayonnaise
- Salt and black pepper to taste
- ½ cup cream cheese, softened
- Chopped basil for garnish

Directions:
1. In a bowl, mix cream cheese, mayonnaise, garlic powder, and salt. Add in the chicken and toss to coat. Place the chicken in the basket and Press Start. Cook for 15 minutes at 380 F on AirFry function. Serve garnished with roughly chopped fresh basil.

243.Smoky Paprika Pork And Vegetable Kabobs

Servings:4
Cooking Time: 15 Minutes
Ingredients:
- 1 pound (454 g) pork tenderloin, cubed
- 1 teaspoon smoked paprika
- Salt and ground black pepper, to taste

- 1 green bell pepper, cut into chunks
- 1 zucchini, cut into chunks
- 1 red onion, sliced
- 1 tablespoon oregano
- Cooking spray
- Special Equipment:
- Small bamboo skewers, soaked in water for 20 minutes to keep them from burning while cooking

Directions:
1. Spritz the air fryer basket with cooking spray.
2. Add the pork to a bowl and season with the smoked paprika, salt and black pepper. Thread the seasoned pork cubes and vegetables alternately onto the soaked skewers. Arrange the skewers in the pan.
3. Put the air fryer basket on the baking pan and slide into Rack Position 2, select Air Fry, set temperature to 350ºF (180ºC) and set time to 15 minutes.
4. After 7 minutes, remove from the oven. Flip the pork skewers. Return to the oven and continue cooking.
5. When cooking is complete, the pork should be browned and vegetables are tender.
6. Transfer the skewers to the serving dishes and sprinkle with oregano. Serve hot.

244.Stuffed Pork Chops

Servings: 4
Cooking Time: 35 Minutes
Ingredients:
- 4 pork chops, boneless and thick-cut
- 2 tbsp olives, chopped
- 3 tbsp sun-dried tomatoes, chopped
- 1/2 cup goat cheese, crumbled
- 3 garlic cloves, minced
- 2 tbsp fresh parsley, chopped

Directions:
1. Fit the oven with the rack in position
2. In a bowl, combine together cheese, garlic, parsley, olives, and sun-dried tomatoes.
3. Stuff cheese mixture all the pork chops.
4. Season pork chops with pepper and salt and place in baking pan.
5. Set to bake at 375 F for 40 minutes. After 5 minutes place the baking pan in the preheated oven.
6. Serve and enjoy.
- **Nutrition Info:** Calories 295 Fat 22.6 g Carbohydrates 1.6 g Sugar 0.4 g Protein 20.2 g Cholesterol 75 mg

245.Lettuce-wrapped Turkey And Mushroom Meatballs

Servings:6
Cooking Time: 15 Minutes
Ingredients:

- Sauce:
- 2 tablespoons tamari
- 2 tablespoons tomato sauce
- 1 tablespoon lime juice
- ¼ teaspoon peeled and grated fresh ginger
- 1 clove garlic, smashed to a paste
- ½ cup chicken broth
- $^1/_3$ cup sugar
- 2 tablespoons toasted sesame oil
- Cooking spray
- Meatballs:
- 2 pounds (907 g) ground turkey
- ¾ cup finely chopped button mushrooms
- 2 large eggs, beaten
- 1½ teaspoons tamari
- ¼ cup finely chopped green onions, plus more for garnish
- 2 teaspoons peeled and grated fresh ginger
- 1 clove garlic, smashed
- 2 teaspoons toasted sesame oil
- 2 tablespoons sugar
- For Serving:
- Lettuce leaves, for serving
- Sliced red chiles, for garnish (optional)
- Toasted sesame seeds, for garnish (optional)

Directions:
1. Spritz the air fryer basket with cooking spray.
2. Combine the ingredients for the sauce in a small bowl. Stir to mix well. Set aside.
3. Combine the ingredients for the meatballs in a large bowl. Stir to mix well, then shape the mixture in twelve 1½-inch meatballs.
4. Arrange the meatballs in the basket, then baste with the sauce.
5. Put the air fryer basket on the baking pan and slide into Rack Position 2, select Air Fry, set temperature to 350ºF (180ºC) and set time to 15 minutes.
6. Flip the balls halfway through.
7. When cooking is complete, the meatballs should be golden brown.
8. Unfold the lettuce leaves on a large serving plate, then transfer the cooked meatballs on the leaves. Spread the red chiles and sesame seeds over the balls, then serve.

246.Pork Tandoor

Servings:x
Cooking Time:x
Ingredients:
- 2 cup fresh green coriander
- ½ cup mint leaves
- 4 tsp. fennel
- 2 tbsp. ginger-garlic paste
- 1 small onion
- 2 cups sliced pork belly

- 1 big capsicum (Cut this capsicum into big cubes)
- 1 onion (Cut it into quarters. Now separate the layers carefully.)
- 5 tbsp. gram flour
- A pinch of salt to taste
- 6-7 flakes garlic (optional)
- Salt to taste
- 3 tbsp. lemon juice

Directions:
1. You will first need to make the sauce. Add the ingredients to a blender and make a thick paste. Slit the pieces of pork and stuff half the paste into the cavity obtained. Take the remaining paste and add it to the gram flour and salt. Toss the pieces of Pork in this mixture and set aside. Apply a little bit of the mixture on the capsicum and onion.
2. Place these on a stick along with the pork pieces. Pre heat the oven at 290 Fahrenheit for around 5 minutes. Open the basket. Arrange the satay sticks properly.
3. Close the basket. Keep the sticks with the pork at 180 degrees for around half an hour while the sticks with the vegetables are to be kept at the same temperature for only 7 minutes. Turn the sticks in between so that one side does not get burnt and also to provide a uniform cook.

247.Garlic Venison With Red Chili Flakes

Servings:x
Cooking Time:x
Ingredients:
- 1 lb. boneless venison cut into Oregano Fingers
- 2 cup dry breadcrumbs
- 6 tbsp. corn flour
- 4 eggs
- 2 tsp. oregano
- 2 tsp. red chili flakes
- 2 tsp. garlic paste
- 1 ½ tbsp. ginger-garlic paste
- 4 tbsp. lemon juice
- 2 tsp. salt
- 1 tsp. red chili powder

Directions:
1. Mix all the ingredients for the marinade and put the venison Oregano Fingers inside and let it rest overnight.
2. Mix the breadcrumbs, oregano and red chili flakes well and place the marinated Oregano Fingers on this mixture. Cover it with plastic wrap and leave it till right before you serve to cook.
3. Pre heat the oven at 160 degrees Fahrenheit for 5 minutes. Place the Oregano Fingers in the fry basket and close it. Let them cook at the same temperature for another 15 minutes or so. Toss the Oregano Fingers well so that they are cooked uniformly. Drizzle the garlic paste and serve.

248.Popcorn Turkey

Servings: 4
Cooking Time: 10 Minutes
Ingredients:
- Nonstick cooking spray
- 1 cup flour
- 2 eggs
- ½ cup milk
- 2 tbsp. Cajun seasoning
- 2 cups bread crumbs
- 1 large turkey breast, cut in 1-inch pieces

Directions:
1. Place the baking pan in position 2 of the oven. Lightly spray the fryer basket with cooking spray.
2. In a large bowl, whisk together flour, eggs, milk, and seasoning.
3. Place bread crumbs in a shallow dish.
4. Add the turkey to the batter and stir to coat. Roll each piece of turkey in the bread crumbs and place them in the fryer basket, these may need to be cooked in batches. Spray them lightly with cooking spray.
5. Place the basket in the oven and set to air fry on 375°F for 10 minutes. Cook turkey nuggets until crisp and golden brown, turning over halfway through cooking time. Serve with your favorite dipping sauce.

- **Nutrition Info:** Calories 655, Total Fat 11g, Saturated Fat 3g, Total Carbs 64g, Net Carbs 61g, Protein 78g, Sugar 5g, Fiber 3g, Sodium 690mg, Potassium 855mg, Phosphorus 744mg

249.Thai Curry Beef Meatballs

Servings:4
Cooking Time: 15 Minutes
Ingredients:
- 1 pound (454 g) ground beef
- 1 tablespoon sesame oil
- 2 teaspoons chopped lemongrass
- 1 teaspoon red Thai curry paste
- 1 teaspoon Thai seasoning blend
- Juice and zest of ½ lime
- Cooking spray

Directions:
1. Spritz the air fryer basket with cooking spray.
2. In a medium bowl, combine all the ingredients until well blended.
3. Shape the meat mixture into 24 meatballs and arrange them in the pan.
4. Put the air fryer basket on the baking pan and slide into Rack Position 2, select Air Fry,

set temperature to 380ºF (193ºC) and set
time to 15 minutes.
5. Flip the meatballs halfway through.
6. When cooking is complete, the meatballs
should be browned.
7. Transfer the meatballs to plates. Let cool for
5 minutes before serving.

250.Turkey Meatballs

Servings: 4
Cooking Time: 25 Minutes
Ingredients:
- 1 lb ground chicken
- 2 garlic cloves, minced
- 1/2 cup parmesan cheese, grated
- 1/2 cup breadcrumbs
- 1 egg, lightly beaten
- 2 tbsp cilantro, chopped
- 1 tbsp olive oil
- 1/2 tsp red pepper flakes
- 1/4 cup shallots, chopped
- Pepper
- Salt

Directions:
1. Fit the oven with the rack in position
2. Add all ingredients into the large bowl and
mix until well combined.
3. Make small balls from the meat mixture and
place them into the baking pan.
4. Set to bake at 400 F for 30 minutes. After 5
minutes place the baking pan in the
preheated oven.
5. Serve and enjoy.
- **Nutrition Info:** Calories 361 Fat 16.2 g
Carbohydrates 12.6 g Sugar 1 g Protein 40 g
Cholesterol 150 mg

251.Cajun Burger Patties

Servings: 2
Cooking Time: 10 Minutes
Ingredients:
- 1 egg, lightly beaten
- 1/2 lb ground pork
- 1/2 cup breadcrumbs
- 1 tbsp Cajun seasoning
- Pepper
- Salt

Directions:
1. Fit the oven with the rack in position 2.
2. Line the air fryer basket with parchment
paper.
3. Add all ingredients into the large bowl and
mix until well combined.
4. Make two equal shapes of patties from meat
mixture and place in the air fryer basket
then place an air fryer basket in the baking
pan.
5. Place a baking pan on the oven rack. Set to
air fry at 360 F for 10 minutes.

6. Serve and enjoy.
- **Nutrition Info:** Calories 300 Fat 7.6 g
Carbohydrates 19.6 g Sugar 1.8 g Protein
36.1 g Cholesterol 165 mg

252.Easy Cocktail Franks Rolls

Servings:4
Cooking Time: 20 Minutes
Ingredients:
- 12 oz cocktail franks
- 8 oz can crescent rolls

Directions:
1. Cut the dough in 1 by 5-inch rectangles with
a knife. Gently roll the franks in the strips,
making sure the ends are visible Place in
freezer for 5 minutes.
2. Preheat oven to 330 F on AirFry function.
Take the franks out of the freezer and place
them in the frying basket. Press Start and
cook for 8-10 minutes. Increase
temperature to 390 F, and cook for another
3 minutes until a fine golden texture
appears.

253.Cheesy Bacon Chicken

Servings: 4
Cooking Time: 30 Minutes
Ingredients:
- 4 chicken breasts, sliced in half
- 1 cup cheddar cheese, shredded
- 8 bacon slices, cooked & chopped
- 6 oz cream cheese
- Pepper
- Salt

Directions:
1. Fit the oven with the rack in position
2. Place season chicken with pepper and salt
and place it into the greased baking dish.
3. Add cream cheese and bacon on top of
chicken.
4. Sprinkle shredded cheddar cheese on top of
chicken.
5. Set to bake at 400 F for 35 minutes. After 5
minutes place the baking dish in the
preheated oven.
6. Serve and enjoy.
- **Nutrition Info:** Calories 745 Fat 50.9 g
Carbohydrates 2.1 g Sugar 0.2 g Protein
66.6 g Cholesterol 248 mg

254.Meatloaf(2)

Servings: 6
Cooking Time: 55 Minutes
Ingredients:
- 2 lbs ground beef
- 1/2 cup sunflower seed flour
- 1/2 cup salsa, low-fodmap
- 2 eggs, lightly beaten
- 1 tsp oregano

- 1 tsp paprika
- 1 tsp cumin
- 1/4 cup fresh cilantro, chopped
- 1/4 cup green onion, chopped
- 1 bell pepper, diced & sautéed
- 1/2 tsp salt

Directions:
1. Fit the oven with the rack in position
2. Add all ingredients into the mixing bowl and mix until well combined.
3. Pour mixture into the greased loaf pan.
4. Set to bake at 375 F for 60 minutes. After 5 minutes place the loaf pan in the preheated oven.
5. Slice and serve.

- **Nutrition Info:** Calories 306 Fat 10.4 g Carbohydrates 3.1 g Sugar 0.9 g Protein 47.3 g Cholesterol 162 mg

255.Flavorful Lemon Pepper Chicken

Servings: 4
Cooking Time: 25 Minutes
Ingredients:
- 4 chicken breasts, boneless & skinless
- 3 tbsp fresh lemon juice
- 2 tsp ground black pepper
- 5 tbsp olive oil
- 1/2 tsp sea salt

Directions:
1. Fit the oven with the rack in position
2. Heat 2 tablespoons of oil in a pan over medium-high heat. Brown chicken in a pan.
3. In a small bowl, mix lemon juice, remaining oil, pepper, and salt.
4. Place browned chicken into the baking dish. Pour lemon juice mixture over chicken.
5. Set to bake at 425 F for 30 minutes. After 5 minutes place the baking dish in the preheated oven.
6. Serve and enjoy.

- **Nutrition Info:** Calories 433 Fat 28.4 g Carbohydrates 0.9 g Sugar 0.3 g Protein 42.4 g Cholesterol 130 mg

256.Buffalo Chicken Tenders

Servings: 5
Cooking Time: 25 Minutes
Ingredients:
- Nonstick cooking spray
- 2/3 cup panko bread crumbs
- ½ tsp cayenne pepper
- ½ tsp paprika
- ½ tsp garlic powder
- ½ tsp salt
- 3 chicken breasts, boneless, skinless & cut in 10 strips
- ½ cup butter, melted
- ½ cup hot sauce

Directions:

1. Line a baking sheet with foil and spray with cooking spray.
2. In a shallow dish combine, bread crumbs and seasonings.
3. Dip chicken in crumb mixture to coat all sides. Lay on prepared pan and refrigerate 1 hour.
4. In a small bowl, whisk together butter and hot sauce.
5. Place baking pan in position 2 of the oven. Lightly spray the fryer basket with cooking spray.
6. Dip each piece of chicken in the butter mixture and place in basket. Place the basket on the baking pan.
7. Set oven to air fry on 400°F for 25 minutes. Cook until outside is crispy and golden brown and chicken is no longer pink. Turn chicken over halfway through cooking time. Serve immediately.

- **Nutrition Info:** Calories 371, Total Fat 23g, Saturated Fat 12g, Total Carbs 10g, Net Carbs 9g, Protein 31g, Sugar 1g, Fiber 1g, Sodium 733mg, Potassium 505mg, Phosphorus 310mg

257.Air Fryer Chicken Parmesan

Servings: 4
Cooking Time: 9 Minutes
Ingredients:
- ½ C. keto marinara
- 6 tbsp. mozzarella cheese
- 1 tbsp. melted ghee
- 2 tbsp. grated parmesan cheese
- 6 tbsp. gluten-free seasoned breadcrumbs
- 1   8-ounce chicken breasts

Directions:
1. Preparing the Ingredients. Ensure air fryer oven is preheated to 360 degrees. Spray the basket with olive oil.
2. Mix parmesan cheese and breadcrumbs together. Melt ghee.
3. Brush melted ghee onto the chicken and dip into breadcrumb mixture.
4. Place coated chicken in the air fryer oven and top with olive oil.
5. Air Frying. Set temperature to 360°F, and set time to 6 minutes. Cook 2 breasts for 6 minutes and top each breast with a tablespoon of sauce and 1½ tablespoons of mozzarella cheese. Cook another 3 minutes to melt cheese.
6. Keep cooked pieces warm as you repeat the process with remaining breasts.

- **Nutrition Info:** CALORIES: 251; FAT: 10G; PROTEIN:31G; SUGAR:0G

258.Fruity Chicken Breasts With Bbq Sauce

Servings: 2
Cooking Time: 20 Minutes
Ingredients:
- 2 chicken breasts, cubed
- 2 green bell peppers, sliced
- ½ onion, sliced
- 1 can drain pineapple chunks
- ½ cup barbecue sauce

Directions:
1. Preheat on Bake function to 370 F. Thread the green bell peppers, chicken cubes, onions, and pineapple chunks on the skewers. Brush with barbecue sauce and cook in your for 20 minutes until slightly crispy. Serve.

259.Meat And Rice Stuffed Bell Peppers

Servings:4
Cooking Time: 18 Minutes
Ingredients:
- ¾ pound (340 g) lean ground beef
- 4 ounces (113 g) lean ground pork
- ¼ cup onion, minced
- 1 (15-ounce / 425-g) can crushed tomatoes
- 1 teaspoon Worcestershire sauce
- 1 teaspoon barbecue seasoning
- 1 teaspoon honey
- ½ teaspoon dried basil
- ½ cup cooked brown rice
- ½ teaspoon garlic powder
- ½ teaspoon oregano
- ½ teaspoon salt
- 2 small bell peppers, cut in half, stems removed, deseeded
- Cooking spray

Directions:
1. Spritz the baking pan with cooking spray.
2. Arrange the beef, pork, and onion in the baking pan.
3. Slide the baking pan into Rack Position 1, select Convection Bake, set temperature to 360ºF (182ºC) and set time to 8 minutes.
4. Break the ground meat into chunks halfway through the cooking.
5. When cooking is complete, the ground meat should be lightly browned.
6. Meanwhile, combine the tomatoes, Worcestershire sauce, barbecue seasoning, honey, and basil in a saucepan. Stir to mix well.
7. Transfer the cooked meat mixture to a large bowl and add the cooked rice, garlic powder, oregano, salt, and ¼ cup of the tomato mixture. Stir to mix well.
8. Stuff the pepper halves with the mixture, then arrange the pepper halves in the basket.
9. Put the air fryer basket on the baking pan and slide into Rack Position 2, select Air Fry, set time to 10 minutes.
10. When cooking is complete, the peppers should be lightly charred.
11. Serve the stuffed peppers with the remaining tomato sauce on top.

260.Roasted Pork Tenderloin

Servings: 4
Cooking Time: 1 Hour
Ingredients:
- 1 (3-pound) pork tenderloin
- 2 tablespoons extra-virgin olive oil
- 2 garlic cloves, minced
- 1 teaspoon dried basil
- 1 teaspoon dried oregano
- 1 teaspoon dried thyme
- Salt
- Pepper

Directions:
1. Preparing the Ingredients. Drizzle the pork tenderloin with the olive oil.
2. Rub the garlic, basil, oregano, thyme, and salt and pepper to taste all over the tenderloin.
3. Air Frying. Place the tenderloin in the air fryer oven. Cook for 45 minutes.
4. Use a meat thermometer to test for doneness
5. Open the air fryer oven and flip the pork tenderloin. Cook for an additional 15 minutes.
6. Remove the cooked pork from the air fryer oven and allow it to rest for 10 minutes before cutting.
- **Nutrition Info:** CALORIES: 283; FAT: 10G; PROTEIN:48

261.Amazing Bacon & Potato Platter

Servings: 4
Cooking Time: 40 Minutes
Ingredients:
- 4 potatoes, halved
- 6 garlic cloves, squashed
- 4 streaky cut rashers bacon
- 1 tbsp olive oil

Directions:
1. In a mixing bowl, mix garlic, bacon, potatoes, and olive oil; toss to coat. Place the mixture in the basket and fit in the baking tray; roast for 25-30 minutes at 400 F on Air Fry, shaking once.

262.Mustardy Chicken

Servings: 4
Cooking Time: 20 Minutes
Ingredients:
- 1 tsp garlic powder

- 4 chicken breasts, sliced
- 1 tbsp fresh thyme, chopped
- ½ cup dry white wine
- Salt and black pepper to taste
- ½ cup Dijon mustard
- 2 cups breadcrumbs
- 1 tbsp lemon zest
- 2 tbsp olive oil

Directions:

1. In a bowl, mix garlic, breadcrumbs, olive oil, lemon zest, salt, and pepper. In another bowl, mix mustard and wine.
2. Dip the chicken slices in the wine mixture and then coat in the crumb mixture. Place the prepared chicken in the greased basket and fit in the baking tray; cook for 15 minutes at 350 F on Air Fry function, shaking once until golden brown. Serve.

263.Garlic Chicken

Servings: 6
Cooking Time: 40 Minutes
Ingredients:

- 2 lbs chicken thighs, skinless and boneless
- 10 garlic cloves, sliced
- 2 tbsp olive oil
- 2 tbsp fresh parsley, chopped
- 1 fresh lemon juice
- Pepper
- Salt

Directions:

1. Fit the oven with the rack in position
2. Place chicken in baking pan and season with pepper and salt.
3. Sprinkle parsley and garlic over the chicken. Drizzle with oil and lemon juice.
4. Set to bake at 450 F for 45 minutes. After 5 minutes place the baking pan in the preheated oven.
5. Serve and enjoy.
- **Nutrition Info:** Calories 337 Fat 16 g Carbohydrates 1.9 g Sugar 0.2 g Protein 44.2 g Cholesterol 135 mg

264.Goat Cheese Meatballs

Servings: 8
Cooking Time: 12 Minutes
Ingredients:

- 1 lb ground beef
- 1 lb ground pork
- 2 eggs, lightly beaten
- 1/4 cup fresh parsley, chopped
- 1 tbsp garlic, minced
- 1 onion, chopped
- 1 tbsp Worcestershire sauce
- 1/2 cup goat cheese, crumbled
- 1/2 cup breadcrumbs
- Pepper
- Salt

Directions:

1. Fit the oven with the rack in position 2.
2. Line the air fryer basket with parchment paper.
3. Add all ingredients into a large bowl and mix until well combined.
4. Make small balls from meat mixture and place in the air fryer basket then place an air fryer basket in the baking pan.
5. Place a baking pan on the oven rack. Set to air fry at 400 F for 12 minutes.
6. Serve and enjoy.
- **Nutrition Info:** Calories 253 Fat 8.1 g Carbohydrates 7.2 g Sugar 1.6 g Protein 35.6 g Cholesterol 136 mg

265.Honey Chicken Drumsticks

Servings:2
Cooking Time: 20 Minutes + Marinating Time
Ingredients:

- 2 chicken drumsticks, skin removed
- 2 tbsp olive oil
- 2 tbsp honey
- ½ tbsp garlic puree

Directions:

1. Mix all the ingredients in a bowl. Allow to marinate for 30 minutes. Place the chicken in the basket and press Start. Cook for 15 minutes at 400 F on AirFry function. Serve warm.

266.Lechon Kawali

Servings:4
Cooking Time: 30 Minutes
Ingredients:

- 1 pound (454 g) pork belly, cut into three thick chunks
- 6 garlic cloves
- 2 bay leaves
- 2 tablespoons soy sauce
- 1 teaspoon kosher salt
- 1 teaspoon ground black pepper
- 3 cups water
- Cooking spray

Directions:

1. Put all the ingredients in a pressure cooker, then put the lid on and cook on high for 15 minutes.
2. Natural release the pressure and release any remaining pressure, transfer the tender pork belly on a clean work surface. Allow to cool under room temperature until you can handle.
3. Generously Spritz the air fryer basket with cooking spray.
4. Cut each chunk into two slices, then put the pork slices in the pan.
5. Put the air fryer basket on the baking pan and slide into Rack Position 2, select Air Fry,

set temperature to 400ºF (205ºC) and set time to 15 minutes.
6. After 7 minutes, remove from the oven. Flip the pork. Return to the oven and continue cooking.
7. When cooking is complete, the pork fat should be crispy.
8. Serve immediately.

267.Garlic Infused Roast Beef

Servings: 10
Cooking Time: 75 Minutes
Ingredients:
- 3 lb. beef roast, room temperature
- 4 cloves garlic, cut in thin slivers
- Olive oil spray,
- 1 tsp salt
- 1 tsp pepper
- 2 tsp rosemary

Directions:
1. Trim off the fat from the roast. Use a sharp knife to pierce the roast in intervals, ½-inch deep. Insert garlic sliver in holes, pushing into the meat.
2. Lightly spray the beef with oil and season with salt, pepper, and rosemary.
3. Place the baking pan in position 1 of the oven. Set to convection bake on 325°F for 60 minutes.
4. Spray the fryer basket with oil and place roast in it. Once the oven has preheated for 5 minutes, place the basket on the pan. Cook 60 minutes, or until beef reaches desired doneness.
5. Remove from oven and let rest 10 minutes. Slice thinly and serve.
- **Nutrition Info:** Calories 265, Total Fat 13g, Saturated Fat 5g, Total Carbs 1g, Net Carbs 1g, Protein 36g, Sugar 0g, Fiber 0g, Sodium 342mg, Potassium 478mg, Phosphorus 288mg

268.Cheesy Baked Burger Patties

Servings: 6
Cooking Time: 15 Minutes
Ingredients:
- 2 lbs ground beef
- 1 tsp onion powder
- 1 tsp garlic powder
- 1/2 cup mozzarella cheese, shredded
- 1/2 cup cheddar cheese, shredded
- Pepper
- Salt

Directions:
1. Fit the oven with the rack in position
2. Add all ingredients into the large bowl and mix until well combined.
3. Make patties from the meat mixture and place it into the baking pan.

4. Set to bake at 400 F for 20 minutes. After 5 minutes place the baking pan in the preheated oven.
5. Serve and enjoy.
- **Nutrition Info:** Calories 329 Fat 13 g Carbohydrates 0.9 g Sugar 0.3 g Protein 49 g Cholesterol 146 mg

269.Sumptuous Beef And Pork Sausage Meatloaf

Servings:4
Cooking Time: 25 Minutes
Ingredients:
- ¾ pound (340 g) ground chuck
- 4 ounces (113 g) ground pork sausage
- 2 eggs, beaten
- 1 cup Parmesan cheese, grated
- 1 cup chopped shallot
- 3 tablespoons plain milk
- 1 tablespoon oyster sauce
- 1 tablespoon fresh parsley
- 1 teaspoon garlic paste
- 1 teaspoon chopped porcini mushrooms
- ½ teaspoon cumin powder
- Seasoned salt and crushed red pepper flakes, to taste

Directions:
1. In a large bowl, combine all the ingredients until well blended.
2. Place the meat mixture in the baking pan. Use a spatula to press the mixture to fill the pan.
3. Slide the baking pan into Rack Position 1, select Convection Bake, set temperature to 360ºF (182ºC) and set time to 25 minutes.
4. When cooking is complete, the meatloaf should be well browned.
5. Let the meatloaf rest for 5 minutes. Transfer to a serving dish and slice. Serve warm.

270.Teriyaki Pork Ribs With Tomato Sauce

Servings: 3
Cooking Time: 20 Minutes + Marinating Time
Ingredients:
- 1 pound pork ribs
- Salt and black pepper to taste
- 1 tbsp sugar
- 1 tsp ginger juice
- 1 tsp five-spice powder
- 1 tbsp teriyaki sauce
- 1 tbsp soy sauce
- 1 garlic clove, minced
- 2 tbsp honey
- 1 tbsp tomato sauce
- 1 tbsp olive oil

Directions:

1. In a bowl, mix pepper, sugar, five-spice powder, salt, ginger juice, and teriyaki sauce. Add pork ribs to the marinade and let sit for 2 hours.
2. Add ribs to the greased basket and fit in the baking tray; cook for 8 minutes on Air Fry function at 350 F. In a separate bowl, mix soy sauce, garlic, honey, 1 tbsp of water, and tomato sauce.
3. In a pan over medium heat, heat olive oil and fry garlic for 30 seconds. Add fried pork ribs and pour in the sauce. Stir-fry for a few minutes and serve.

271.Dry-rubbed Flat Iron Steak

Servings:x
Cooking Time:x
Ingredients:
- 1 tsp coarse salt
- 1 tsp paprika
- 1 tsp cumin
- 1 tsp garlic powder
- 1 tsp onion powder
- ½ tsp coriander
- ½ tsp thyme
- ¼ tsp black pepper
- 4 (6-oz) flat iron steaks
- 2 Tbsp olive oil

Directions:
1. Combine first eight ingredients in a small bowl.
2. Rub the seasonings onto the steaks and drizzle with 2 Tbsp olive oil.
3. Heat oven over medium heat.
4. Place steaks into oven and sear for 3 minutes on each side. Cook
5. for an additional 3 minutes for medium-rare.
6. Let meat rest for 10 minutes before slicing.

272.Poultry Fried Baked Pastry

Servings:x
Cooking Time:x
Ingredients:
- 1 or 2 green chilies that are finely chopped or mashed
- ½ tsp. cumin
- 1 tsp. coarsely crushed coriander
- 1 dry red chili broken into pieces
- A small amount of salt (to taste)
- 2 tbsp. unsalted butter
- 1 ½ cup all-purpose flour
- A pinch of salt to taste
- Water to knead the dough
- 1 lb. mixed minced poultry (squab, chicken, duck, pheasant, turkey)
- ¼ cup boiled peas
- 1 tsp. powdered ginger
- ½ tsp. dried mango powder

- ½ tsp. red chili power.
- 1-2 tbsp. coriander.

Directions:
1. You will first need to make the outer covering. In a large bowl, add the flour, butter and enough water to knead it into dough that is stiff. Transfer this to a container and leave it to rest for five minutes. Place a pan on medium flame and add the oil. Roast the mustard seeds and once roasted, add the coriander seeds and the chopped dry red chilies. Add all the dry ingredients for the filling and mix the ingredients well. Add a little water and continue to stir the ingredients. Make small balls out of the dough and roll them out.
2. Cut the rolled-out dough into halves and apply a little water on the edges to help you fold the halves into a cone. Add the filling to the cone and close up the samosa. Pre-heat the oven for around 5 to 6 minutes at 300 Fahrenheit. Place all the samosas in the fry basket and close the basket properly. Keep the oven at 200 degrees for another 20 to 25 minutes.
3. Around the halfway point, open the basket and turn the samosas over for uniform cooking. After this, fry at 250 degrees for around 10 minutes in order to give them the desired golden-brown color. Serve hot. Recommended sides are tamarind or mint sauce.

273.Chicken With Potatoes And Corn

Servings:4
Cooking Time: 25 Minutes
Ingredients:
- 4 bone-in, skin-on chicken thighs
- 2 teaspoons kosher salt, divided
- 1 cup Bisquick baking mix
- ½ cup butter, melted, divided
- 1 pound (454 g) small red potatoes, quartered
- 3 ears corn, shucked and cut into rounds 1- to 1½-inches thick
- $^1/_3$ cup heavy whipping cream
- ½ teaspoon freshly ground black pepper

Directions:
1. Sprinkle the chicken on all sides with 1 teaspoon of kosher salt. Place the baking mix in a shallow dish. Brush the thighs on all sides with ¼ cup of butter, then dredge them in the baking mix, coating them all on sides. Place the chicken in the center of the baking pan.
2. Place the potatoes in a large bowl with 2 tablespoons of butter and toss to coat. Place them on one side of the chicken on the pan.
3. Place the corn in a medium bowl and drizzle with the remaining butter. Sprinkle with ¼

teaspoon of kosher salt and toss to coat. Place on the pan on the other side of the chicken.
4. Slide the baking pan into Rack Position 2, select Roast, set temperature to 375ºF (190ºC), and set time to 25 minutes.
5. After 20 minutes, remove from the oven and put the potatoes back to the bowl. Return the pan to oven and continue cooking.
6. As the chicken continues cooking, add the cream, black pepper, and remaining kosher salt to the potatoes. Lightly mash the potatoes with a potato masher.
7. When cooking is complete, the corn should be tender and the chicken cooked through, reading 165ºF (74ºC) on a meat thermometer. Remove from the oven. Serve the chicken with the smashed potatoes and corn on the side.

274.Char Siu

Servings:4
Cooking Time: 15 Minutes
Ingredients:
- ¼ cup honey
- 1 teaspoon Chinese five-spice powder
- 1 tablespoon Shaoxing wine (rice cooking wine)
- 1 tablespoon hoisin sauce
- 2 teaspoons minced garlic
- 2 teaspoons minced fresh ginger
- 2 tablespoons soy sauce
- 1 tablespoon sugar
- 1 pound (454 g) fatty pork shoulder, cut into long, 1-inch-thick pieces
- Cooking spray

Directions:
1. Combine all the ingredients, except for the pork should, in a microwave-safe bowl. Stir to mix well. Microwave until the honey has dissolved. Stir periodically.
2. Pierce the pork pieces generously with a fork, then put the pork in a large bowl. Pour in half of the honey mixture. Set the remaining sauce aside until ready to serve.
3. Press the pork pieces into the mixture to coat and wrap the bowl in plastic and refrigerate to marinate for at least 8 hours.
4. Spritz the air fryer basket with cooking spray.
5. Discard the marinade and transfer the pork pieces in the basket.
6. Put the air fryer basket on the baking pan and slide into Rack Position 2, select Air Fry, set temperature to 400ºF (205ºC) and set time to 15 minutes.
7. Flip the pork halfway through.
8. When cooking is complete, the pork should be well browned.

9. Meanwhile, microwave the remaining marinade on high for a minute or until it has a thick consistency. Stir periodically.
10. Remove the pork from the oven and allow to cool for 10 minutes before serving with the thickened marinade.

275.Pesto & Spinach Beef Rolls

Servings:4
Cooking Time: 30 Minutes
Ingredients:
- 2 lb beef steak, thinly sliced
- Salt and black pepper to taste
- 3 tbsp pesto
- ½ cup mozzarella cheese, shredded
- 1 cup spinach, chopped
- 1 bell pepper, deseeded and sliced

Directions:
1. Preheat oven to 400 F on Bake function. Place the beef slices between 2 baking paper sheets and flatten them with a rolling pin to about a fifth of an inch thick. Lay the slices on a clean surface and spread them with the pesto. Top with mozzarella, spinach, and bell pepper.
2. Roll up the slices and secure using a toothpick. Season with salt and pepper. Place the slices in the greased basket and Bake for 15 minutes. Serve immediately!

276.Chicken Burger Patties

Servings: 4
Cooking Time: 25 Minutes
Ingredients:
- 1 lb ground chicken
- 1 egg, lightly beaten
- 1 cup cheddar cheese, shredded
- 1 cup carrot, grated
- 1 cup cauliflower, grated
- 1/8 tsp red pepper flakes
- 2 garlic cloves, minced
- 1/2 cup onion, minced
- 3/4 cup breadcrumbs
- Pepper
- Salt

Directions:
1. Fit the oven with the rack in position
2. Add all ingredients into the bowl and mix until well combined.
3. Make small patties and place them in a parchment-lined baking pan.
4. Set to bake at 400 F for 30 minutes. After 5 minutes place the baking pan in the preheated oven.
5. Serve and enjoy.
- **Nutrition Info:** Calories 451 Fat 20 g Carbohydrates 20.9 g Sugar 4.1 g Protein 44.9 g Cholesterol 172 mg

277.Italian Veggie Chicken

Servings: 4
Cooking Time: 30 Minutes

Ingredients:

- 4 chicken breasts
- 1 cup mozzarella cheese, shredded
- 6 bacon slices, cooked & chopped
- 8 oz can artichoke hearts, sliced
- 1 cup cherry tomatoes, cut in half
- 1 zucchini, sliced
- 1 tbsp dried basil
- 1/4 tsp salt

Directions:

1. Fit the oven with the rack in position
2. Place chicken breasts into the casserole dish and sprinkle with basil and salt.
3. Spread artichoke hearts, cherry tomatoes, and zucchini on top of chicken.
4. Sprinkle shredded cheese and bacon on top of vegetables.
5. Set to bake at 375 F for 35 minutes. After 5 minutes place the casserole dish in the preheated oven.
6. Serve and enjoy.
- **Nutrition Info:** Calories 484 Fat 24.2 g Carbohydrates 6.9 g Sugar 2.5 g Protein 56.8 g Cholesterol 165 mg

278.Easy Creamy Chicken

Servings: 4
Cooking Time: 55 Minutes
Ingredients:

- 4 chicken breasts
- 1 tsp garlic powder
- 1 tsp dried basil
- 1 tsp dried oregano
- 3/4 cup parmesan cheese, grated
- 1 cup sour cream
- 1 cup mozzarella cheese, shredded
- 1/2 tsp pepper
- 1/2 tsp salt

Directions:

1. Fit the oven with the rack in position
2. Season chicken with pepper and salt and place into the greased baking dish.
3. Mix together sour cream, mozzarella cheese, parmesan cheese, oregano, basil, garlic powder, and salt and pour over chicken.
4. Set to bake at 375 F for 60 minutes. After 5 minutes place the baking dish in the preheated oven.
5. Serve and enjoy.
- **Nutrition Info:** Calories 479 Fat 27.8 g Carbohydrates 4.2 g Sugar 0.3 g Protein 51.7 g Cholesterol 171 mg

279.Flank Steak Fajitas

Servings:x
Cooking Time:x
Ingredients:

- 3 cloves garlic
- ½ cup soy sauce
- ½ cup honey
- 3 sprigs rosemary
- Salt and pepper, to taste
- 2 limes, juiced
- 3 bell peppers of various colors, washed, seeded and sliced
- 2 medium onions, peeled and sliced into rings
- 10 Portobello mushrooms, washed and sliced
- 4 flour tortillas

Directions:

1. Combine garlic, soy sauce, honey, rosemary, salt, pepper and lime juice in a Ziploc bag. Add steak and marinate for 1-2 hours in the refrigerator.
2. Remove meat from marinade and shake off excess liquid.
3. Place oven on the grill and heat until smoking. At this point, you can sear the meat in the pot or directly on the grill. If you cook meat directly on the grill, sear for 3-4 minutes on each side.
4. While meat cooks on the grill, add 1 Tbsp oil to the oven a add peppers, onions, mushrooms, salt and pepper. Allow vegetables to sear. Stir frequently for about 6 minutes.
5. Meat and vegetables should be ready about the same time. Transfer both to a platter and place tortillas in oven to toast, about 30 seconds. Allow meat to rest. Slice against the grain and serve along with vegetables.

280.Chinese-style Broccoli & Beef Steak

Servings:4
Cooking Time: 25 Minutes
Ingredients:

- ¾ lb circular beef steak, cut into strips
- 1 lb broccoli, cut into florets
- ⅓ cup oyster sauce
- 2 tbsp sesame oil
- ⅓ cup sherry
- 1 tsp soy sauce
- 1 tsp white sugar
- 1 tsp cornstarch
- 1 tbsp olive oil
- 1 garlic clove, minced

Directions:

1. In a bowl, mix cornstarch, sherry, oyster sauce, sesame oil, soy sauce, sugar, garlic, ginger and add in the beef steaks; toss to coat. Marinate for 45 minutes.
2. Preheat oven to 390 F on AirFry function. Place the steaks in the frying basket and cook for 20 minutes. Serve warm with green salad.

281.Paprika Chicken Breasts With Ham & Cheese

Servings:4
Cooking Time: 35 Minutes
Ingredients:

- 4 chicken breasts
- 4 ham slices

- 4 Swiss cheese slices
- 3 tbsp all-purpose flour
- 4 tbsp butter
- 1 tbsp paprika
- 1 tbsp chicken bouillon granules
- ½ cup dry white wine
- 1 cup heavy whipping cream
- 1 tbsp cornstarch

Directions:
1. Preheat on AirFry function to 380 F. Pound the chicken breasts and put a slice of ham on each of the chicken breasts. Fold the edges over the filling and secure with toothpicks.
2. In a bowl, combine paprika and flour and coat in the chicken. Press Start and fry the chicken for 14-16 minutes.
3. Melt the butter in a skillet and add the bouillon and wine. Stir to combine and reduce the heat to low. Remove the chicken from the oven and place in the skillet. Let simmer for 5 minutes.

282.Air Fryer Juicy Pork Chops

Servings: 2
Cooking Time: 12 Minutes
Ingredients:
- 2 pork chops
- 2 tbsp brown sugar
- 1 tbsp olive oil
- 1/4 tsp garlic powder
- 1/2 tsp onion powder
- 1 tsp ground mustard
- 1 tbsp paprika
- Pepper
- Salt

Directions:
1. Fit the oven with the rack in position 2.
2. Add all dry ingredients into the small bowl and mix well.
3. Brush pork chops with oil and rub with spice mixture.
4. Place pork chops in the air fryer basket then place an air fryer basket in the baking pan.
5. Place a baking pan on the oven rack. Set to air fry at 400 F for 12 minutes.
6. Serve and enjoy.
- **Nutrition Info:** Calories 371 Fat 27.8 g Carbohydrates 12.1 g Sugar 9.5 g Protein 19 g Cholesterol 69 mg

283.Chicken Parm

Servings: 4
Cooking Time: 35 Minutes
Ingredients:
- Nonstick cooking spray
- ½ cup flour
- 2 eggs
- 2/3 cup panko bread crumbs
- 2/3 cup Italian seasoned bread crumbs
- 1/3 + ¼ cup parmesan cheese, divided
- 2 tbsp. fresh parsley, chopped

- ½ tsp salt
- ¼ tsp pepper
- 4 chicken breast halves, skinless & boneless
- 24 oz. marinara sauce
- 1 cup mozzarella cheese, grated

Directions:
1. Place the baking pan in position 2 of the oven. Lightly spray the fryer basket with cooking spray.
2. Place flour in a shallow dish.
3. In a separate shallow dish, beat the eggs.
4. In a third shallow dish, combine both bread crumbs, 1/3 cup parmesan cheese, 2 tablespoons parsley, salt, and pepper.
5. Place chicken between two sheets of plastic wrap and pound to ½-inch thick.
6. Dip chicken first in flour, then eggs, and bread crumb mixture to coat. Place in basket and place the basket on the baking pan.
7. Set oven to air fry on 375°F for 10 minutes. Turn chicken over halfway through cooking time.
8. Remove chicken and baking pan from the oven. Place the rack in position 1. Set oven to bake on 425°F for 30 minutes.
9. Pour 1 ½ cups marinara in the bottom of 8x11-inch baking dish. Place chicken over sauce and add another 2 tablespoons marinara to tops of chicken. Top chicken with mozzarella and parmesan cheese.
10. Once oven preheats for 5 minutes, place the dish in the oven and bake 20-25 minutes until bubbly and cheese is golden brown. Serve.
- **Nutrition Info:** Calories 529, Total Fat 13g, Saturated Fat 5g, Total Carbs 52g, Net Carbs 47g, Protein 51g, Sugar 9g, Fiber 5g, Sodium 1437mg, Potassium 1083mg, Phosphorus 709mg

284.Chicken Ciabatta Sandwiches

Servings:4
Cooking Time: 13 Minutes
Ingredients:
- 2 (8-ounce / 227-g) boneless, skinless chicken breasts
- 1 teaspoon kosher salt, divided
- 1 cup all-purpose flour
- 1 teaspoon Italian seasoning
- 2 large eggs
- 2 tablespoons plain yogurt
- 2 cups panko bread crumbs
- $1^1/_3$ cups grated Parmesan cheese, divided
- 2 tablespoons olive oil
- 4 ciabatta rolls, split in half
- ½ cup marinara sauce
- ½ cup shredded Mozzarella cheese

Directions:
1. Lay the chicken breasts on a cutting board and cut each one in half parallel to the board so you have 4 fairly even, flat fillets. Place a piece of plastic wrap over the

chicken pieces and use a rolling pin to gently pound them to an even thickness, about ½-inch thick. Season the chicken on both sides with ½ teaspoon of kosher salt.

2. Place the flour on a plate and add the remaining kosher salt and the Italian seasoning. Mix with a fork to distribute evenly. In a wide bowl, whisk together the eggs with the yogurt. In a small bowl combine the panko, 1 cup of Parmesan cheese, and olive oil. Place this in a shallow bowl.

3. Lightly dredge both sides of the chicken pieces in the seasoned flour, and then dip them in the egg wash to coat completely, letting the excess drip off. Finally, dredge the chicken in the bread crumbs. Carefully place the breaded chicken pieces in the basket.

4. Put the air fryer basket on the baking pan and slide into Rack Position 2, select Air Fry, set temperature to 375ºF (190ºC), and set time to 10 minutes.

5. After 5 minutes, remove from the oven. Carefully turn the chicken over. Return to the oven and continue cooking. When cooking is complete, remove from the oven.

6. Unfold the rolls on the basket and spread each half with 1 tablespoon of marinara sauce. Place a chicken breast piece on the bottoms of the buns and sprinkle the remaining Parmesan cheese over the chicken pieces. Divide the Mozzarella among the top halves of the buns.

7. Select Convection Broil, set temperature to High, and set time to 3 minutes.

8. Check the sandwiches halfway through. When cooking is complete, the Mozzarella cheese should be melted and bubbly.

9. Remove from the oven and close the sandwiches and serve.

285.Lush Salisbury Steak With Mushroom Gravy

Servings:2

Cooking Time: 33 Minutes

Ingredients:
- For the Mushroom Gravy:
- ¾ cup sliced button mushrooms
- ¼ cup thinly sliced onions
- ¼ cup unsalted butter, melted
- ½ teaspoon fine sea salt
- ¼ cup beef broth
- For the Steaks:
- ½ pound (227 g) ground beef (85% lean)
- 1 tablespoon dry mustard
- 2 tablespoons tomato paste
- ¼ teaspoon garlic powder
- ½ teaspoon onion powder
- ½ teaspoon fine sea salt
- ¼ teaspoon ground black pepper
- Chopped fresh thyme leaves, for garnish

Directions:
1. Toss the mushrooms and onions with butter in the baking pan to coat well, then sprinkle with salt.

2. Slide the baking pan into Rack Position 1, select Convection Bake, set temperature to 390ºF (199ºC) and set time to 8 minutes.

3. Stir the mixture halfway through the cooking.

4. When cooking is complete, the mushrooms should be tender.

5. Pour the broth in the baking pan and set time to 10 more minutes to make the gravy.

6. Meanwhile, combine all the ingredients for the steaks, except for the thyme leaves, in a large bowl. Stir to mix well. Shape the mixture into two oval steaks.

7. Arrange the steaks over the gravy and set time to 15 minutes. When cooking is complete, the patties should be browned. Flip the steaks halfway through.

8. Transfer the steaks onto a plate and pour the gravy over. Sprinkle with fresh thyme and serve immediately.

FISH & SEAFOOD RECIPES

286.Seafood Platter

Servings:x
Cooking Time:x
Ingredients:
- 1 large plate with assorted prepared seafood
- 3 tbsp. vinegar or lemon juice
- 2 or 3 tsp. paprika
- 1 tsp. black pepper
- 1 tsp. salt
- 3 tsp. ginger-garlic paste
- 1 cup yogurt
- 4 tsp. tandoori masala
- 2 tbsp. dry fenugreek leaves
- 1 tsp. black salt
- 1 tsp. chat masala
- 1 tsp. garam masala powder
- 1 tsp. red chili powder
- 1 tsp. salt
- 3 drops of red color

Directions:
1. Make the first marinade and soak the seafood in it for four hours. While this is happening, make the second marinade and soak the seafood in it overnight to let the flavors blend.
2. Pre heat the oven at 160 degrees Fahrenheit for 5 minutes. Place the Oregano Fingers in the fry basket and close it. Let them cook at the same temperature for another 15 minutes or so. Toss the Oregano Fingers well so that they are cooked uniformly. Serve them with mint sauce.

287.Rosemary Buttered Prawns

Servings: 2
Cooking Time: 15 Minutes + Marinating Time
Ingredients:
- 8 large prawns
- 1 rosemary sprig, chopped
- ½ tbsp melted butter
- Salt and black pepper to taste

Directions:
1. Combine butter, rosemary, salt, and pepper in a bowl. Add in the prawns and mix to coat. Cover the bowl and refrigerate for 1 hour.
2. Preheat on Air Fry function to 350 F Remove the prawns from the fridge and place them in the basket. Fit in the baking tray and cook for 10 minutes, flipping once. Serve.

288.Salmon Fritters

Servings:x
Cooking Time:x
Ingredients:
- 2 tbsp. garam masala
- 1 lb. fileted Salmon
- 3 tsp ginger finely chopped
- 1-2 tbsp. fresh coriander leaves
- 2 or 3 green chilies finely chopped
- 1 ½ tbsp. lemon juice
- Salt and pepper to taste

Directions:
1. Mix the ingredients in a clean bowl.
2. Mold this mixture into round and flat French Cuisine Galettes.
3. Wet the French Cuisine Galettes slightly with water.
4. Pre heat the oven at 160 degrees Fahrenheit for 5 minutes. Place the French Cuisine Galettes in the fry basket and let them cook for another 25 minutes at the same temperature. Keep rolling them over to get a uniform cook. Serve either with mint sauce or ketchup.

289.Baked Halibut Steaks With Parsley

Servings: 4
Cooking Time: 10 Minutes
Ingredients:
- 1 pound (454 g) halibut steaks
- ¼ cup vegetable oil
- 2½ tablespoons Worcester sauce
- 2 tablespoons honey
- 2 tablespoons vermouth
- 1 tablespoon freshly squeezed lemon juice
- 1 tablespoon fresh parsley leaves, coarsely chopped
- Salt and pepper, to taste
- 1 teaspoon dried basil

Directions:
1. Put all the ingredients in a large mixing dish and gently stir until the fish is coated evenly. Transfer the fish to the baking pan.
2. Slide the baking pan into Rack Position 1, select Convection Bake, set temperature to 375ºF (190ºC), and set time to 10 minutes.
3. Flip the fish halfway through cooking time.
4. When cooking is complete, the fish should reach an internal temperature of at least 145ºF (63ºC) on a meat thermometer. Remove from the oven and let the fish cool for 5 minutes before serving.

290.Honey Glazed Salmon

Servings: 4
Cooking Time: 8 Minutes
Ingredients:
- 4 salmon fillets
- 2 tsp soy sauce
- 1 tbsp honey
- Pepper
- Salt

Directions:
1. Fit the oven with the rack in position 2.
2. Brush salmon with soy sauce and season with pepper and salt.
3. Place salmon in the air fryer basket then place an air fryer basket in the baking pan.
4. Place a baking pan on the oven rack. Set to air fry at 375 F for 8 minutes.
5. Brush salmon with honey and serve.
- **Nutrition Info:** Calories 253 Fat 11 g Carbohydrates 4.6 g Sugar 4.4 g Protein 34.7 g Cholesterol 78 mg

291.Simple Salmon Patties

Servings: 2
Cooking Time: 7 Minutes
Ingredients:
- 8 oz salmon fillet, minced
- 1 egg, lightly beaten
- 1/4 tsp garlic powder
- 1/4 tsp onion powder
- 1/8 tsp paprika
- 2 tbsp breadcrumbs
- Pepper
- Salt

Directions:
1. Fit the oven with the rack in position 2.
2. Add all ingredients into the bowl and mix until well combined.
3. Make patties from mixture and place in the air fryer basket then place an air fryer basket in the baking pan.
4. Place a baking pan on the oven rack. Set to air fry at 390 F for 7 minutes.
5. Serve and enjoy.
- **Nutrition Info:** Calories 211 Fat 9.6 g Carbohydrates 5.6 g Sugar 0.8 g Protein 25.8 g Cholesterol 132 mg

292.Healthy Haddock

Servings: 2
Cooking Time: 25 Minutes
Ingredients:
- 1 lb haddock fillets
- 1/4 cup parsley, chopped
- 1 lemon juice
- 1/4 cup brown sugar
- 1/4 cup onion, diced
- 1 tsp ginger, grated
- 3/4 cup soy sauce
- Pepper
- Salt

Directions:
1. Fit the oven with the rack in position
2. Add fish fillets and remaining ingredients into the large bowl and coat well and place in the refrigerator for 1 hour.
3. Place marinated fish fillets into the baking dish.

4. Set to bake at 325 F for 30 minutes. After 5 minutes place the baking dish in the preheated oven.
5. Serve and enjoy.
- **Nutrition Info:** Calories 391 Fat 2.5 g Carbohydrates 28 g Sugar 20.4 g Protein 61.7 g Cholesterol 168 mg

293.Prawn French Cuisine Galette

Servings:x
Cooking Time:x
Ingredients:
- 2 tbsp. garam masala
- 1 lb. minced prawn
- 3 tsp ginger finely chopped
- 1-2 tbsp. fresh coriander leaves
- 2 or 3 green chilies finely chopped
- 1 ½ tbsp. lemon juice
- Salt and pepper to taste

Directions:
1. Mix the ingredients in a clean bowl.
2. Mold this mixture into round and flat French Cuisine Galettes.
3. Wet the French Cuisine Galettes slightly with water.
4. Pre heat the oven at 160 degrees Fahrenheit for 5 minutes. Place the French Cuisine Galettes in the fry basket and let them cook for another 25 minutes at the same temperature. Keep rolling them over to get a uniform cook. Serve either with mint sauce or ketchup.

294.Easy Blackened Shrimp

Servings: 6
Cooking Time: 10 Minutes
Ingredients:
- 1 lb shrimp, deveined
- 1 tbsp olive oil
- 1/4 tsp pepper
- 2 tsp blackened seasoning
- 1/4 tsp salt

Directions:
1. Fit the oven with the rack in position
2. Toss shrimp with oil, pepper, blackened seasoning, and salt.
3. Transfer shrimp into the baking pan.
4. Set to bake at 400 F for 15 minutes. After 5 minutes place the baking pan in the preheated oven.
5. Serve and enjoy.
- **Nutrition Info:** Calories 167 Fat 4.3 g Carbohydrates 10.5 g Sugar 0 g Protein 20.6 g Cholesterol 159 mg

295.Baked Buttery Shrimp

Servings: 4
Cooking Time: 15 Minutes
Ingredients:

- 1 lb shrimp, peel & deveined
- 2 tsp garlic powder
- 2 tsp dry mustard
- 2 tsp cumin
- 2 tsp paprika
- 2 tsp black pepper
- 4 tsp cayenne pepper
- 1/2 cup butter, melted
- 2 tsp onion powder
- 1 tsp dried oregano
- 1 tsp dried thyme
- 3 tsp salt

Directions:
1. Fit the oven with the rack in position
2. Add shrimp, butter, and remaining ingredients into the mixing bowl and toss well.
3. Transfer shrimp mixture into the baking pan.
4. Set to bake at 400 F for 20 minutes. After 5 minutes place the baking pan in the preheated oven.
5. Serve and enjoy.
- **Nutrition Info:** Calories 372 Fat 26.2 g Carbohydrates 7.5 g Sugar 1.3 g Protein 27.6 g Cholesterol 300 mg

296.Seafood Pizza

Servings:x
Cooking Time:x
Ingredients:
- One pizza base
- Grated pizza cheese (mozzarella cheese preferably) for topping
- Some pizza topping sauce
- Use cooking oil for brushing and topping purposes
- ingredients for topping:
- 2 onions chopped
- 2 cups mixed seafood
- 2 capsicums chopped
- 2 tomatoes that have been deseeded and chopped
- 1 tbsp. (optional) mushrooms/corns
- 2 tsp. pizza seasoning
- Some cottage cheese that has been cut into small cubes (optional)

Directions:
1. Put the pizza base in a pre-heated oven for around 5 minutes. (Pre heated to 340 Fahrenheit). Take out the base. Pour some pizza sauce on top of the base at the center. Using a spoon spread the sauce over the base making sure that you leave some gap around the circumference. Grate some mozzarella cheese and sprinkle it over the sauce layer. Take all the vegetables and the seafood and mix them in a bowl. Add some oil and seasoning.

2. Also add some salt and pepper according to taste. Mix them properly. Put this topping over the layer of cheese on the pizza. Now sprinkle some more grated cheese and pizza seasoning on top of this layer. Pre heat the oven at 250 Fahrenheit for around 5 minutes.
3. Open the fry basket and place the pizza inside. Close the basket and keep the fryer at 170 degrees for another 10 minutes. If you feel that it is undercooked you may put it at the same temperature for another 2 minutes or so.

297.Delightful Catfish Fillets

Servings: 4
Cooking Time: 25 Minutes
Ingredients:
- 4 catfish fillets
- ¼ cup seasoned fish fry
- 1 tbsp olive oil
- 1 tbsp parsley, chopped

Directions:
1. Add seasoned fish fry and catfish fillets in a large Ziploc bag and massage well to coat. Place the fillets in your Air Fryer basket and fit in the baking tray; cook for 10 minutes at 360 F on Air Fry function. Flip the fish and cook for 2-3 more minutes. Top with parsley and serve.

298.Maryland Crab Cakes

Servings: 6
Cooking Time: 10 Minutes
Ingredients:
- Nonstick cooking spray
- 2 eggs
- 1 cup Panko bread crumbs
- 1 stalk celery, chopped
- 3 tbsp. mayonnaise
- 1 tsp Worcestershire sauce
- ¼ cup mozzarella cheese, grated
- 1 tsp Italian seasoning
- 1 tbsp. fresh parsley, chopped
- 1 tsp pepper
- ¾ lb. lump crabmeat, drained

Directions:
1. Place baking pan in position 2 of the oven. Lightly spray the fryer basket with cooking spray.
2. In a large bowl, combine all ingredients except crab meat, mix well.
3. Fold in crab carefully so it retains some chunks. Form mixture into 12 patties.
4. Place patties in a single layer in the fryer basket. Place the basket on the baking pan.
5. Set oven to air fryer on 350°F for 10 minutes. Cook until golden brown, turning

over halfway through cooking time. Serve immediately.

- **Nutrition Info:** Calories 172, Total Fat 8g, Saturated Fat 2g, Total Carbs 14g, Net Carbs 13g, Protein 16g, Sugar 1g, Fiber 1g, Sodium 527mg, Potassium 290mg, Phosphorus 201mg

299.Tropical Shrimp Skewers

Servings: 4
Cooking Time: 5 Minutes
Ingredients:

- 1 tbsp. lime juice
- 1 tbsp. honey
- ¼ tsp red pepper flakes
- ¼ tsp pepper
- ¼ tsp ginger
- Nonstick cooking spray
- 1 lb. medium shrimp, peel, devein & leave tails on
- 2 cups peaches, drain & chop
- ½ green bell pepper, chopped fine
- ¼ cup scallions, chopped

Directions:

1. Soak 8 small wooden skewers in water for 15 minutes.
2. In a small bowl, whisk together lime juice, honey and spices. Transfer 2 tablespoons of the mixture to a medium bowl.
3. Place the baking pan in position 2 of the oven. Lightly spray fryer basket with cooking spray. Set oven to broil on 400°F for 10 minutes.
4. Thread 5 shrimp on each skewer and brush both sides with marinade. Place in basket and after 5 minutes, place on the baking pan. Cook 4-5 minutes or until shrimp turn pink.
5. Add peaches, bell pepper, and scallions to reserved honey mixture, mix well. Divide salsa evenly between serving plates and top with 2 skewers each. Serve immediately.

- **Nutrition Info:** Calories 181, Total Fat 1g, Saturated Fat 0g, Total Carbs 27g, Net Carbs 25g, Protein 16g, Sugar 21g, Fiber 2g, Sodium 650mg, Potassium 288mg, Phosphorus 297mg

300.Parmesan-crusted Hake With Garlic Sauce

Servings:3
Cooking Time: 10 Minutes
Ingredients:

- Fish:
- 6 tablespoons mayonnaise
- 1 tablespoon fresh lime juice
- 1 teaspoon Dijon mustard
- 1 cup grated Parmesan cheese
- Salt, to taste

- ¼ teaspoon ground black pepper, or more to taste
- 3 hake fillets, patted dry
- Nonstick cooking spray
- Garlic Sauce:
- ¼ cup plain Greek yogurt
- 2 tablespoons olive oil
- 2 cloves garlic, minced
- ½ teaspoon minced tarragon leaves

Directions:

1. Mix the mayo, lime juice, and mustard in a shallow bowl and whisk to combine. In another shallow bowl, stir together the grated Parmesan cheese, salt, and pepper.
2. Dredge each fillet in the mayo mixture, then roll them in the cheese mixture until they are evenly coated on both sides.
3. Spray the air fryer basket with nonstick cooking spray. Place the fillets in the pan.
4. Put the air fryer basket on the baking pan and slide into Rack Position 2, select Air Fry, set temperature to 395ºF (202ºC), and set time to 10 minutes.
5. Flip the fillets halfway through the cooking time.
6. Meanwhile, in a small bowl, whisk all the ingredients for the sauce until well incorporated.
7. When cooking is complete, the fish should flake apart with a fork. Remove the fillets from the oven and serve warm alongside the sauce.

301.Parmesan Salmon & Asparagus

Servings: 4
Cooking Time: 20 Minutes
Ingredients:

- 4 salmon fillets
- 1 cup parmesan cheese, shredded
- 1 tbsp garlic, minced
- 3 tbsp olive oil
- 1 lb asparagus, ends trimmed
- 1/4 tsp pepper
- 1/4 tsp salt

Directions:

1. Fit the oven with the rack in position
2. Place fish fillets and asparagus in a parchment-lined baking pan.
3. Brush fish fillets with olive oil. Season with pepper and salt.
4. Sprinkle with garlic and shredded parmesan cheese on top.
5. Set to bake at 400 F for 25 minutes. After 5 minutes place the baking pan in the preheated oven.
6. Serve and enjoy.

- **Nutrition Info:** Calories 424 Fat 26.5 g Carbohydrates 6 g Sugar 2.2 g Protein 44.4 g Cholesterol 95 mg

302.Fired Shrimp With Mayonnaise Sauce

Servings:4
Cooking Time: 7 Minutes
Ingredients:
- Shrimp
- 12 jumbo shrimp
- ½ teaspoon garlic salt
- ¼ teaspoon freshly cracked mixed peppercorns
- Sauce:
- 4 tablespoons mayonnaise
- 1 teaspoon grated lemon rind
- 1 teaspoon Dijon mustard
- 1 teaspoon chipotle powder
- ½ teaspoon cumin powder

Directions:
1. In a medium bowl, season the shrimp with garlic salt and cracked mixed peppercorns.
2. Place the shrimp in the air fryer basket.
3. Put the air fryer basket on the baking pan and slide into Rack Position 2, select Air Fry, set temperature to 395ºF (202ºC), and set time to 7 minutes.
4. After 5 minutes, remove from the oven and flip the shrimp. Return to the oven and continue cooking for 2 minutes more, or until they are pink and no longer opaque.
5. Meanwhile, stir together all the ingredients for the sauce in a small bowl until well mixed.
6. When cooking is complete, remove the shrimp from the oven and serve alongside the sauce.

303.Garlic-butter Shrimp With Vegetables

Servings:4
Cooking Time: 15 Minutes
Ingredients:
- 1 pound (454 g) small red potatoes, halved
- 2 ears corn, shucked and cut into rounds, 1 to 1½ inches thick
- 2 tablespoons Old Bay or similar seasoning
- ½ cup unsalted butter, melted
- 1 (12- to 13-ounce / 340- to 369-g) package kielbasa or other smoked sausages
- 3 garlic cloves, minced
- 1 pound (454 g) medium shrimp, peeled and deveined

Directions:
1. Place the potatoes and corn in a large bowl.
2. Stir together the butter and Old Bay seasoning in a small bowl. Drizzle half the butter mixture over the potatoes and corn, tossing to coat. Spread out the vegetables in the baking pan.
3. Slide the baking pan into Rack Position 2, select Roast, set temperature to 350ºF (180ºC), and set time to 15 minutes.
4. Meanwhile, cut the sausages into 2-inch lengths, then cut each piece in half lengthwise. Put the sausages and shrimp in a medium bowl and set aside.
5. Add the garlic to the bowl of remaining butter mixture and stir well.
6. After 10 minutes, remove the pan and pour the vegetables into the large bowl. Drizzle with the garlic butter and toss until well coated. Arrange the vegetables, sausages, and shrimp in the pan.
7. Return to the oven and continue cooking. After 5 minutes, check the shrimp for doneness. The shrimp should be pink and opaque. If they are not quite cooked through, roast for an additional 1 minute.
8. When done, remove from the oven and serve on a plate.

304.Shrimp Momo's Recipe

Servings:x
Cooking Time:x
Ingredients:
- 1 ½ cup all-purpose flour
- ½ tsp. salt
- 5 tbsp. water
- For filling:
- 2 cups minced shrimp
- 2 tbsp. oil
- 2 tsp. ginger-garlic paste
- 2 tsp. soya sauce
- 2 tsp. vinegar

Directions:
1. Squeeze the dough and cover it with plastic wrap and set aside. Next, cook the ingredients for the filling and try to ensure that the shrimp is covered well with the sauce. Roll the dough and cut it into a square. Place the filling in the center.
2. Now, wrap the dough to cover the filling and pinch the edges together. Pre heat the oven at 200° F for 5 minutes. Place the wontons in the fry basket and close it. Let them cook at the same temperature for another 20 minutes. Recommended sides are chili sauce or ketchup.

305.Mediterranean Sole

Servings: 6
Cooking Time: 20 Minutes
Ingredients:
- Nonstick cooking spray
- 2 tbsp. olive oil
- 8 scallions, sliced thin
- 2 cloves garlic, diced fine
- 4 tomatoes, chopped
- ½ cup dry white wine
- 2 tbsp. fresh parsley, chopped fine
- 1 tsp oregano

- 1 tsp pepper
- 2 lbs. sole, cut in 6 pieces
- 4 oz. feta cheese, crumbled

Directions:

1. Place the rack in position 1 of the oven. Spray an 8x11-inch baking dish with cooking spray.
2. Heat the oil in a medium skillet over medium heat. Add scallions and garlic and cook until tender, stirring frequently.
3. Add the tomatoes, wine, parsley, oregano, and pepper. Stir to mix. Simmer for 5 minutes, or until sauce thickens. Remove from heat.
4. Pour half the sauce on the bottom of the prepared dish. Lay fish on top then pour remaining sauce over the top. Sprinkle with feta.
5. Set the oven to bake on 400°F for 25 minutes. After 5 minutes, place the baking dish on the rack and cook 15-18 minutes or until fish flakes easily with a fork. Serve immediately.

- **Nutrition Info:** Calories 220, Total Fat 12g, Saturated Fat 4g, Total Carbs 6g, Net Carbs 4g, Protein 22g, Sugar 4g, Fiber 2g, Sodium 631mg, Potassium 540mg, Phosphorus 478mg

306.Lobster Grandma's Easy To Cook Wontons

Servings:x
Cooking Time:x
Ingredients:

- 1 ½ cup all-purpose flour
- ½ tsp. salt
- 5 tbsp. water
- For filling:
- 2 cups minced lobster
- 2 tbsp. oil
- 2 tsp. ginger-garlic paste
- 2 tsp. soya sauce
- 2 tsp. vinegar

Directions:

1. Squeeze the dough and cover it with plastic wrap and set aside. Next, cook the ingredients for the filling and try to ensure that the lobster is covered well with the sauce.
2. Roll the dough and place the filling in the center. Now, wrap the dough to cover the filling and pinch the edges together.
3. Pre heat the oven at 200° F for 5 minutes. Place the wontons in the fry basket and close it. Let them cook at the same temperature for another 20 minutes. Recommended sides are chili sauce or ketchup.

307.Prawn Momo's Recipe

Servings:x
Cooking Time:x
Ingredients:

- 1 ½ cup all-purpose flour
- ½ tsp. salt
- 5 tbsp. water
- For filling:
- 2 cups minced prawn
- 2 tbsp. oil
- 2 tsp. ginger-garlic paste
- 2 tsp. soya sauce
- 2 tsp. vinegar

Directions:

1. Squeeze the dough and cover it with plastic wrap and set aside. Next, cook the ingredients for the filling and try to ensure that the prawn is covered well with the sauce. Roll the dough and cut it into a square.
2. Place the filling in the center. Now, wrap the dough to cover the filling and pinch the edges together. Pre heat the oven at 200° F for 5 minutes. Place the wontons in the fry basket and close it. Let them cook at the same temperature for another 20 minutes. Recommended sides are chili sauce or ketchup.

308.Grilled Soy Salmon Fillets

Servings: 4
Cooking Time: 8 Minutes
Ingredients:

- 4 salmon fillets
- 1/4 teaspoon ground black pepper
- 1/2 teaspoon cayenne pepper
- 1/2 teaspoon salt
- 1 teaspoon onion powder
- 1 tablespoon fresh lemon juice
- 1/2 cup soy sauce
- 1/2 cup water
- 1 tablespoon honey
- 2 tablespoons extra-virgin olive oil

Directions:

1. Preparing the Ingredients. Firstly, pat the salmon fillets dry using kitchen towels. Season the salmon with black pepper, cayenne pepper, salt, and onion powder.
2. To make the marinade, combine together the lemon juice, soy sauce, water, honey, and olive oil. Marinate the salmon for at least 2 hours in your refrigerator.
3. Arrange the fish fillets on a grill basket in your air fryer oven.
4. Air Frying. Bake at 330 degrees for 8 to 9 minutes, or until salmon fillets are easily flaked with a fork.
5. Work with batches and serve warm.

309.Oyster Club Sandwich

Servings:x
Cooking Time:x
Ingredients:
- 2 slices of white bread
- 1 tbsp. softened butter
- ½ lb. shelled oyster
- 1 small capsicum
- For Barbeque Sauce:
- ¼ tbsp. Worcestershire sauce
- ½ tsp. olive oil
- ½ flake garlic crushed
- ¼ cup chopped onion
- ¼ tsp. mustard powder
- 1 tbsp. tomato ketchup
- ½ tbsp. sugar
- ¼ tbsp. red chili sauce
- ½ cup water.
- A pinch of salt and black pepper to taste

Directions:
1. Take the slices of bread and remove the edges. Now cut the slices horizontally. Cook the ingredients for the sauce and wait till it thickens. Now, add the oyster to the sauce and stir till it obtains the flavors.
2. Roast the capsicum and peel the skin off. Cut the capsicum into slices. Mix the ingredients together and apply it to the bread slices. Pre-heat the oven for 5 minutes at 300 Fahrenheit. Open the basket of the Fryer and place the prepared Classic Sandwiches in it such that no two Classic Sandwiches are touching each other. Now keep the fryer at 250 degrees for around 15 minutes.
3. Turn the Classic Sandwiches in between the cooking process to cook both slices. Serve the Classic Sandwiches with tomato ketchup or mint sauce.

310.Panko Catfish Nuggets

Servings:4
Cooking Time: 7 To 8 Minutes
Ingredients:
- 2 medium catfish fillets, cut into chunks (approximately 1 × 2 inch)
- Salt and pepper, to taste
- 2 eggs
- 2 tablespoons skim milk
- ½ cup cornstarch
- 1 cup panko bread crumbs
- Cooking spray

Directions:
1. In a medium bowl, season the fish chunks with salt and pepper to taste.
2. In a small bowl, beat together the eggs with milk until well combined.
3. Place the cornstarch and bread crumbs into separate shallow dishes.
4. Dredge the fish chunks one at a time in the cornstarch, coating well on both sides, then dip in the egg mixture, shaking off any excess, finally press well into the bread crumbs. Spritz the fish chunks with cooking spray.
5. Arrange the fish chunks in the air fryer basket in a single layer.
6. Put the air fryer basket on the baking pan and slide into Rack Position 2, select Air Fry, set temperature to 390ºF (199ºC), and set time to 8 minutes.
7. Flip the fish chunks halfway through the cooking time.
8. When cooking is complete, they should be no longer translucent in the center and golden brown. Remove the fish chunks from the oven to a plate. Serve warm.

311.Pecan-crusted Catfish Fillets

Servings:4
Cooking Time: 12 Minutes
Ingredients:
- ½ cup pecan meal
- 1 teaspoon fine sea salt
- ¼ teaspoon ground black pepper
- 4 (4-ounce / 113-g) catfish fillets
- Avocado oil spray
- For Garnish (Optional):
- Fresh oregano
- Pecan halves

Directions:
1. Spray the air fryer basket with avocado oil spray.
2. Combine the pecan meal, sea salt, and black pepper in a large bowl. Dredge each catfish fillet in the meal mixture, turning until well coated. Spritz the fillets with avocado oil spray, then transfer to the basket.
3. Put the air fryer basket on the baking pan and slide into Rack Position 2, select Air Fry, set temperature to 375ºF (190ºC), and set time to 12 minutes.
4. Flip the fillets halfway through the cooking time.
5. When cooking is complete, the fish should be cooked through and no longer translucent. Remove from the oven and sprinkle the oregano sprigs and pecan halves on top for garnish, if desired. Serve immediately.

312.Lemon Pepper White Fish Fillets

Servings: 2
Cooking Time: 12 Minutes
Ingredients:
- 12 oz white fish fillets
- 1/2 tsp lemon pepper seasoning
- Pepper

- Salt

Directions:
1. Fit the oven with the rack in position 2.
2. Spray fish fillets with cooking spray and season with lemon pepper seasoning, pepper, and salt.
3. Place fish fillets in the air fryer basket then place an air fryer basket in the baking pan.
4. Place a baking pan on the oven rack. Set to air fry at 360 F for 12 minutes.
5. Serve and enjoy.
- **Nutrition Info:** Calories 294 Fat 12.8 g Carbohydrates 0.4 g Sugar 0 g Protein 41.7 g Cholesterol 131 mg

313.Delicious Fried Seafood

Servings: 4
Cooking Time: 15 Minutes
Ingredients:
- 1 lb fresh scallops, mussels, fish fillets, prawns, shrimp
- 2 eggs, lightly beaten
- Salt and black pepper to taste
- 1 cup breadcrumbs mixed with zest of 1 lemon

Directions:
1. Dip each piece of the seafood into the eggs and season with salt and pepper. Coat in the crumbs and spray with oil. Arrange into the frying basket and fit in the baking tray; cook for 10 minutes at 400 F on Air Fry function, turning once halfway through. Serve.

314.Spicy Lemon Garlic Tilapia

Servings: 2
Cooking Time: 15 Minutes
Ingredients:
- 4 tilapia fillets
- 1 lemon, cut into slices
- 1/2 tsp pepper
- 1/2 tsp chili powder
- 1 tsp garlic, minced
- 3 tbsp butter, melted
- 1 tbsp fresh lemon juice
- Salt

Directions:
1. Fit the oven with the rack in position
2. Place fish fillets into the baking dish.
3. Arrange lemon slices on top of fish fillets.
4. Mix together the remaining ingredients and pour over fish fillets.
5. Set to bake at 350 F for 20 minutes. After 5 minutes place the baking dish in the preheated oven.
6. Serve and enjoy.
- **Nutrition Info:** Calories 354 Fat 19.6 g Carbohydrates 4 g Sugar 1 g Protein 42.8 g Cholesterol 156 mg

315.Air Fried Cod Fillets

Servings:4
Cooking Time: 12 Minutes
Ingredients:
- 4 cod fillets
- ¼ teaspoon fine sea salt
- 1 teaspoon cayenne pepper
- ¼ teaspoon ground black pepper, or more to taste
- ½ cup fresh Italian parsley, coarsely chopped
- ½ cup non-dairy milk
- 4 garlic cloves, minced
- 1 Italian pepper, chopped
- 1 teaspoon dried basil
- ½ teaspoon dried oregano
- Cooking spray

Directions:
1. Lightly spritz the air fryer basket with cooking spray.
2. Season the fillets with salt, cayenne pepper, and black pepper.
3. Pulse the remaining ingredients in a food processor, then transfer the mixture to a shallow bowl. Coat the fillets with the mixture. Place the fillets in the basket.
4. Put the air fryer basket on the baking pan and slide into Rack Position 2, select Air Fry, set temperature to 375ºF (190ºC), and set time to 12 minutes.
5. When cooking is complete, the fish will be flaky. Remove from the oven and serve on a plate.

316.Flavorful Herb Salmon

Servings: 4
Cooking Time: 15 Minutes
Ingredients:
- 1 lb salmon fillets
- 1/2 tbsp dried rosemary
- 1 tbsp olive oil
- 1/4 tsp dried basil
- 1 tbsp dried chives
- 1/4 tsp dried thyme
- Pepper
- Salt

Directions:
1. Fit the oven with the rack in position 2.
2. Place salmon skin side down in air fryer basket then place an air fryer basket in baking pan.
3. Mix olive oil, thyme, basil, chives, and rosemary in a small bowl.
4. Brush salmon with oil mixture.
5. Place a baking pan on the oven rack. Set to air fry at 400 F for 15 minutes.
6. Serve and enjoy.

- **Nutrition Info:** Calories 182 Fat 10.6 g Carbohydrates 0.4 g Sugar 0 g Protein 22.1 g Cholesterol 50 mg

317.Scallops And Spring Veggies

Servings: 4
Cooking Time: 8 Minutes
Ingredients:
- ½ pound asparagus ends trimmed, cut into 2-inch pieces
- 1 cup sugar snap peas
- 1 pound sea scallops
- 1 tablespoon lemon juice
- 2 teaspoons olive oil
- ½ teaspoon dried thyme
- Pinch salt
- Freshly ground black pepper

Directions:
1. Preparing the Ingredients. Place the asparagus and sugar snap peas in the Oven rack/basket. Place the Rack on the middle-shelf of the air fryer oven.
2. Air Frying. Cook for 2 to 3 minutes or until the vegetables are just starting to get tender.
3. Meanwhile, check the scallops for a small muscle attached to the side, and pull it off and discard.
4. In a medium bowl, toss the scallops with the lemon juice, olive oil, thyme, salt, and pepper. Place into the Oven rack/basket on top of the vegetables. Place the Rack on the middle-shelf of the air fryer oven.
5. Air Frying. Steam for 5 to 7 minutes. Until the scallops are just firm, and the vegetables are tender. Serve immediately.
- **Nutrition Info:** CALORIES: 162; CARBS:10G; FAT: 4G; PROTEIN:22G; FIBER:3G

318.Old Bay Crab Cakes

Servings: 4
Cooking Time: 20 Minutes
Ingredients:
- 2 slices dried bread, crusts removed
- Small amount of milk
- 1 tablespoon mayonnaise
- 1 tablespoon Worcestershire sauce
- 1 tablespoon baking powder
- 1 tablespoon parsley flakes
- 1 teaspoon Old Bay® Seasoning
- 1/4 teaspoon salt
- 1 egg
- 1 pound lump crabmeat

Directions:
1. Preparing the Ingredients. Crush your bread over a large bowl until it is broken down into small pieces. Add milk and stir until bread crumbs are moistened. Mix in mayo and Worcestershire sauce. Add remaining

ingredients and mix well. Shape into 4 patties.
2. Air Frying. Cook at 360 degrees for 20 minutes, flip half way through.
- **Nutrition Info:** CALORIES: 165; CARBS:5.8; FAT: 4.5G; PROTEIN:24G; FIBER:0G

319.Cheesy Tuna Patties

Servings:4
Cooking Time: 17 To 18 Minutes
Ingredients:
- Tuna Patties:
- 1 pound (454 g) canned tuna, drained
- 1 egg, whisked
- 2 tablespoons shallots, minced
- 1 garlic clove, minced
- 1 cup grated Romano cheese
- Sea salt and ground black pepper, to taste
- 1 tablespoon sesame oil
- Cheese Sauce:
- 1 tablespoon butter
- 1 cup beer
- 2 tablespoons grated Colby cheese

Directions:
1. Mix together the canned tuna, whisked egg, shallots, garlic, cheese, salt, and pepper in a large bowl and stir to incorporate.
2. Divide the tuna mixture into four equal portions and form each portion into a patty with your hands. Refrigerate the patties for 2 hours.
3. When ready, brush both sides of each patty with sesame oil, then place in the baking pan.
4. Slide the baking pan into Rack Position 1, select Convection Bake, set temperature to 360ºF (182ºC), and set time to 14 minutes.
5. Flip the patties halfway through the cooking time.
6. Meanwhile, melt the butter in a saucepan over medium heat.
7. Pour in the beer and whisk constantly, or until it begins to bubble. Add the grated Colby cheese and mix well. Continue cooking for 3 to 4 minutes, or until the cheese melts. Remove from the heat.
8. When cooking is complete, the patties should be lightly browned and cooked through. Remove the patties from the oven to a plate. Drizzle them with the cheese sauce and serve immediately.

320.Soy And Ginger Shrimp

Servings: 4
Cooking Time: 10 Minutes
Ingredients:
- 2 tablespoons olive oil
- 2 tablespoons scallions, finely chopped
- 2 cloves garlic, chopped

- 1 teaspoon fresh ginger, grated
- 1 tablespoon dry white wine
- 1 tablespoon balsamic vinegar
- 1/4 cup soy sauce
- 1 tablespoon sugar
- 1 pound shrimp
- Salt and ground black pepper, to taste

Directions:

1. Preparing the Ingredients. To make the marinade, warm the oil in a saucepan; cook all ingredients, except the shrimp, salt, and black pepper. Now, let it cool.
2. Marinate the shrimp, covered, at least an hour, in the refrigerator.
3. Air Frying. After that, bake the shrimp at 350 degrees F for 8 to 10 minutes (depending on the size), turning once or twice. Season prepared shrimp with salt and black pepper and serve right away.

321.Tilapia Meunière With Vegetables

Servings:4
Cooking Time: 20 Minutes
Ingredients:

- 10 ounces (283 g) Yukon Gold potatoes, sliced ¼-inch thick
- 5 tablespoons unsalted butter, melted, divided
- 1 teaspoon kosher salt, divided
- 4 (8-ounce / 227-g) tilapia fillets
- ½ pound (227 g) green beans, trimmed
- Juice of 1 lemon
- 2 tablespoons chopped fresh parsley, for garnish

Directions:

1. In a large bowl, drizzle the potatoes with 2 tablespoons of melted butter and ¼ teaspoon of kosher salt. Transfer the potatoes to the baking pan.
2. Slide the baking pan into Rack Position 2, select Roast, set temperature to 375ºF (190ºC), and set time to 20 minutes.
3. Meanwhile, season both sides of the fillets with ½ teaspoon of kosher salt. Put the green beans in the medium bowl and sprinkle with the remaining ¼ teaspoon of kosher salt and 1 tablespoon of butter, tossing to coat.
4. After 10 minutes, remove from the oven and push the potatoes to one side. Put the fillets in the middle of the pan and add the green beans on the other side. Drizzle the remaining 2 tablespoons of butter over the fillets. Return the pan to the oven and continue cooking, or until the fish flakes easily with a fork and the green beans are crisp-tender.
5. When cooked, remove from the oven. Drizzle the lemon juice over the fillets and sprinkle the parsley on top for garnish. Serve hot.

322.Lemon Butter Shrimp

Servings: 4
Cooking Time: 12 Minutes
Ingredients:

- 1 1/4 lbs shrimp, peeled & deveined
- 2 tbsp fresh parsley, chopped
- 2 tbsp fresh lemon juice
- 1 tbsp garlic, minced
- 1/4 cup butter
- Pepper
- Salt

Directions:

1. Fit the oven with the rack in position
2. Add shrimp into the baking dish.
3. Melt butter in a pan over low heat. Add garlic and sauté for 30 seconds. Stir in lemon juice.
4. Pour melted butter mixture over shrimp. Season with pepper and salt.
5. Set to bake at 350 F for 17 minutes. After 5 minutes place the baking dish in the preheated oven.
6. Garnish with parsley and serve.
- **Nutrition Info:** Calories 276 Fat 14 g Carbohydrates 3.2 g Sugar 0.2 g Protein 32.7 g Cholesterol 329 mg

323.Herbed Salmon With Asparagus

Servings: 2
Cooking Time: 12 Minutes
Ingredients:

- 2 teaspoons olive oil, plus additional for drizzling
- 2 (5-ounce / 142-g) salmon fillets, with skin
- Salt and freshly ground black pepper, to taste
- 1 bunch asparagus, trimmed
- 1 teaspoon dried tarragon
- 1 teaspoon dried chives
- Fresh lemon wedges, for serving

Directions:

1. Rub the olive oil all over the salmon fillets. Sprinkle with salt and pepper to taste.
2. Put the asparagus on the foil-lined baking pan and place the salmon fillets on top, skin-side down.
3. Slide the baking pan into Rack Position 1, select Convection Bake, set temperature to 350ºF (180ºC), and set time to 12 minutes.
4. When cooked, the fillets should register 145ºF (63ºC) on an instant-read thermometer. Remove from the oven and cut the salmon fillets in half crosswise, then use a metal spatula to lift flesh from skin and transfer to a serving plate. Discard the

skin and drizzle the salmon fillets with
additional olive oil. Scatter with the herbs.
5. Serve the salmon fillets with asparagus
   spears and lemon wedges on the side.

324.Spinach & Tuna Balls With Ricotta

Servings:4
Cooking Time: 20 Minutes
Ingredients:
- 14 oz store-bought crescent dough
- ½ cup spinach, steamed
- 1 cup ricotta cheese, crumbled
- ¼ tsp garlic powder
- 1 tsp fresh oregano, chopped
- ½ cup canned tuna, drained

Directions:
1. Preheat on AirFry function to 350 F. Roll
   the dough onto a lightly floured flat surface.
   Combine the ricotta cheese, spinach, tuna,
   oregano, salt, and garlic powder together in
   a bowl.
2. Cut the dough into 4 equal pieces. Divide
   the mixture between the dough pieces.
   Make sure to place the filling in the center.
   Fold the dough and secure with a fork. Place
   onto a lined baking dish and press Start.
   Cook for 12 minutes until lightly browned.
   Serve.

325.Lobster Spicy Lemon Kebab

Servings:x
Cooking Time:x
Ingredients:
- 1 lb. lobster (Shelled and cubed)
- 3 onions chopped
- 5 green chilies-roughly chopped
- 1 ½ tbsp. ginger paste
- 1 ½ tsp garlic paste
- 1 ½ tsp salt
- 3 tsp lemon juice
- 2 tsp garam masala
- 4 tbsp. chopped coriander
- 3 tbsp. cream
- 2 tbsp. coriander powder
- 4 tbsp. fresh mint chopped
- 3 tbsp. chopped capsicum
- 3 eggs
- 2 ½ tbsp. white sesame seeds

Directions:
1. Take all the ingredients mentioned under
   the first heading and mix them in a bowl.
   Grind them thoroughly to make a smooth
   paste.
2. Take the eggs in a different bowl and beat
   them. Add a pinch of salt and leave them
   aside.
3. Take a flat plate and in it mix the sesame
   seeds and breadcrumbs.

4. Dip the lobster cubes in the egg and salt
   mixture and then in the mixture of
5. breadcrumbs and sesame seeds. Leave
   these kebabs in the fridge for an hour or so
   to set.
6. Pre heat the oven at 160 degrees
   Fahrenheit for around 5 minutes. Place the
   kebabs in the basket and let them cook for
   another 25 minutes at the same
   temperature. Turn the kebabs over in
   between the cooking process to get a
   uniform cook. Serve the kebabs with mint
   sauce.

326.Goat Cheese Shrimp

Servings:2
Cooking Time: 8 Minutes
Ingredients:
- 1 pound (454 g) shrimp, deveined
- 1½ tablespoons olive oil
- 1½ tablespoons balsamic vinegar
- 1 tablespoon coconut aminos
- ½ tablespoon fresh parsley, roughly
  chopped
- Sea salt flakes, to taste
- 1 teaspoon Dijon mustard
- ½ teaspoon smoked cayenne pepper
- ½ teaspoon garlic powder
- Salt and ground black peppercorns, to taste
- 1 cup shredded goat cheese

Directions:
1. Except for the cheese, stir together all the
   ingredients in a large bowl until the shrimp
   are evenly coated.
2. Place the shrimp in the air fryer basket.
3. Put the air fryer basket on the baking pan
   and slide into Rack Position 2, select Roast,
   set temperature to 385ºF (196ºC), and set
   time to 8 minutes.
4. When cooking is complete, the shrimp
   should be pink and cooked through.
   Remove from the oven and serve with the
   shredded goat cheese sprinkled on top.

327.Party Cod Nuggets

Servings:4
Cooking Time: 25 Minutes
Ingredients:
- 1 ¼ lb cod fillets, cut into 4 chunks each
- ½ cup flour
- 1 egg
- 1 cup cornflakes
- 1 tbsp olive oil
- Salt and black pepper to taste

Directions:
1. Place the oil and cornflakes in a food
   processor and process until crumbed.
   Season the fish chunks with salt and pepper.
   In a bowl, beat the egg with 1 tbsp of water.

2. Dredge the chunks in flour first, then dip in the egg, and finally coat with cornflakes. Arrange on a lined sheet and press Start. Cook on AirFry function at 350 F for 15 minutes until crispy. Serve.

328.Marinated Salmon

Servings: 2
Cooking Time: 10 Minutes
Ingredients:

- 2 salmon fillets, skinless and boneless
- For marinade:
- 2 tbsp scallions, minced
- 1 tbsp ginger, grated
- 2 garlic cloves, minced
- 2 tbsp mirin
- 2 tbsp soy sauce
- 1 tbsp olive oil

Directions:

1. Fit the oven with the rack in position 2.
2. Add all marinade ingredients into the zip-lock bag and mix well.
3. Add salmon in the bag. The sealed bag shakes well and places it in the fridge for 30 minutes.
4. Arrange marinated salmon fillets in an air fryer basket then place an air fryer basket in the baking pan.
5. Place a baking pan on the oven rack. Set to air fry at 360 F for 10 minutes.
6. Serve and enjoy.
- **Nutrition Info:** Calories 345 Fat 18.2 g Carbohydrates 11.6 g Sugar 4.5 g Protein 36.1 g Cholesterol 78 mg

329.Shrimp And Cherry Tomato Kebabs

Servings:4
Cooking Time: 5 Minutes
Ingredients:

- 1½ pounds (680 g) jumbo shrimp, cleaned, shelled and deveined
- 1 pound (454 g) cherry tomatoes
- 2 tablespoons butter, melted
- 1 tablespoons Sriracha sauce
- Sea salt and ground black pepper, to taste
- 1 teaspoon dried parsley flakes
- ½ teaspoon dried basil
- ½ teaspoon dried oregano
- ½ teaspoon mustard seeds
- ½ teaspoon marjoram
- Special Equipment:
- 4 to 6 wooden skewers, soaked in water for 30 minutes

Directions:

1. Put all the ingredients in a large bowl and toss to coat well.
2. Make the kebabs: Thread, alternating jumbo shrimp and cherry tomatoes, onto the wooden skewers. Place the kebabs in the air fryer basket.
3. Put the air fryer basket on the baking pan and slide into Rack Position 2, select Air Fry, set temperature to 400ºF (205ºC), and set time to 5 minutes.
4. When cooking is complete, the shrimp should be pink and the cherry tomatoes should be softened. Remove from the oven. Let the shrimp and cherry tomato kebabs cool for 5 minutes and serve hot.

330.Roasted Salmon With Asparagus

Servings:4
Cooking Time: 15 Minutes
Ingredients:

- 4 (6-ounce / 170 g) salmon fillets, patted dry
- 1 teaspoon kosher salt, divided
- 1 tablespoon honey
- 2 tablespoons unsalted butter, melted
- 2 teaspoons Dijon mustard
- 2 pounds (907 g) asparagus, trimmed
- Lemon wedges, for serving

Directions:

1. Season both sides of the salmon fillets with ½ teaspoon of kosher salt.
2. Whisk together the honey, 1 tablespoon of butter, and mustard in a small bowl. Set aside.
3. Arrange the asparagus in the baking pan. Drizzle the remaining 1 tablespoon of butter all over and season with the remaining ½ teaspoon of salt, tossing to coat. Move the asparagus to the outside of the pan.
4. Put the salmon fillets in the pan, skin-side down. Brush the fillets generously with the honey mixture.
5. Slide the baking pan into Rack Position 2, select Roast, set temperature to 375ºF (190ºC), and set time to 15 minutes.
6. Toss the asparagus once halfway through the cooking time.
7. When done, transfer the salmon fillets and asparagus to a plate. Serve warm with a squeeze of lemon juice.

331.Lemony Tuna

Servings: 4
Cooking Time: 10 Minutes
Ingredients:

- 2 (6-ounce) cans water packed plain tuna
- 2 teaspoons Dijon mustard
- ½ cup breadcrumbs
- 1 tablespoon fresh lime juice
- 2 tablespoons fresh parsley, chopped
- 1 egg
- Chefman of hot sauce

- 3 tablespoons canola oil
- Salt and freshly ground black pepper, to taste

Directions:
1. Preparing the Ingredients. Drain most of the liquid from the canned tuna.
2. In a bowl, add the fish, mustard, crumbs, citrus juice, parsley, and hot sauce and mix till well combined. Add a little canola oil if it seems too dry. Add egg, salt and stir to combine. Make the patties from tuna mixture. Refrigerate the tuna patties for about 2 hours.
3. Air Frying. Preheat the air fryer oven to 355 degrees F. Cook for about 10-12 minutes.

332.Herbed Salmon With Roasted Asparagus

Servings:2
Cooking Time: 12 Minutes
Ingredients:
- 2 teaspoons olive oil, plus additional for drizzling
- 2 (5-ounce / 142-g) salmon fillets, with skin
- Salt and freshly ground black pepper, to taste
- 1 bunch asparagus, trimmed
- 1 teaspoon dried tarragon
- 1 teaspoon dried chives
- Fresh lemon wedges, for serving

Directions:
1. Rub the olive oil all over the salmon fillets. Sprinkle with salt and pepper to taste.
2. Put the asparagus on the foil-lined baking pan and place the salmon fillets on top, skin-side down.
3. Slide the baking pan into Rack Position 2, select Roast, set temperature to 425ºF (220ºC), and set time to 12 minutes.
4. When cooked, the fillets should register 145ºF (63ºC) on an instant-read thermometer. Remove from the oven and cut the salmon fillets in half crosswise, then use a metal spatula to lift flesh from skin and transfer to a serving plate. Discard the skin and drizzle the salmon fillets with additional olive oil. Scatter with the herbs.
5. Serve the salmon fillets with roasted asparagus spears and lemon wedges on the side.

333.Breaded Fish Fillets

Servings:4
Cooking Time: 7 Minutes
Ingredients:
- 1 pound (454 g) fish fillets
- 1 tablespoon coarse brown mustard
- 1 teaspoon Worcestershire sauce
- ½ teaspoon hot sauce

- Salt, to taste
- Cooking spray
- Crumb Coating:
- ¾ cup panko bread crumbs
- ¼ cup stone-ground cornmeal
- ¼ teaspoon salt

Directions:
1. On your cutting board, cut the fish fillets crosswise into slices, about 1 inch wide.
2. In a small bowl, stir together the mustard, Worcestershire sauce, and hot sauce to make a paste and rub this paste on all sides of the fillets. Season with salt to taste.
3. In a shallow bowl, thoroughly combine all the ingredients for the crumb coating and spread them on a sheet of wax paper.
4. Roll the fish fillets in the crumb mixture until thickly coated. Spritz all sides of the fish with cooking spray, then arrange them in the air fryer basket in a single layer.
5. Put the air fryer basket on the baking pan and slide into Rack Position 2, select Air Fry, set temperature to 400ºF (205ºC), and set time to 7 minutes.
6. When cooking is complete, the fish should flake apart with a fork. Remove from the oven and serve warm.

334.Dill Salmon Patties

Servings: 2
Cooking Time: 10 Minutes
Ingredients:
- 14 oz can salmon, drained and discard bones
- 1 tsp dill, chopped
- 1 egg, lightly beaten
- 1/4 tsp garlic powder
- 1/2 cup breadcrumbs
- 1/4 cup onion, diced
- Pepper
- Salt

Directions:
1. Fit the oven with the rack in position 2.
2. Add all ingredients into the large bowl and mix well.
3. Make equal shapes of patties from mixture and place in the air fryer basket then place the air fryer basket in the baking pan.
4. Place a baking pan on the oven rack. Set to air fry at 370 F for 10 minutes.
5. Serve and enjoy.
- **Nutrition Info:** Calories 422 Fat 15.7 g Carbohydrates 21.5 g Sugar 2.5 g Protein 46 g Cholesterol 191 mg

335.Spicy Halibut

Servings: 4
Cooking Time: 12 Minutes
Ingredients:

- 1 lb halibut fillets
- 1/2 tsp chili powder
- 1/2 tsp smoked paprika
- 1/4 cup olive oil
- 1/4 tsp garlic powder
- Pepper
- Salt

Directions:
1. Fit the oven with the rack in position
2. Place halibut fillets in a baking dish.
3. In a small bowl, mix oil, garlic powder, paprika, pepper, chili powder, and salt.
4. Brush fish fillets with oil mixture.
5. Set to bake at 425 F for 17 minutes. After 5 minutes place the baking dish in the preheated oven.
6. Serve and enjoy.
- **Nutrition Info:** Calories 236 Fat 15.3 g Carbohydrates 0.5 g Sugar 0.1 g Protein 24 g Cholesterol 36 mg

336.Old Bay Shrimp

Servings:4
Cooking Time: 10 Minutes
Ingredients:
- 1 lb jumbo shrimp
- Salt to taste
- ¼ tsp old bay seasoning
- ⅓ tsp smoked paprika
- ¼ tsp chili powder
- 1 tbsp olive oil

Directions:
1. Preheat on AirFry function to 390 F. In a bowl, add the shrimp, paprika, oil, salt, old bay seasoning, and chili powder; mix well. Place the shrimp in the oven and cook for 5 minutes.

337.Parsley Catfish Fillets

Servings:4
Cooking Time: 25 Minutes
Ingredients:
- 4 catfish fillets, rinsed and dried
- ¼ cup seasoned fish fry
- 1 tbsp olive oil
- 1 tbsp fresh parsley, chopped

Directions:
1. Add seasoned fish fry and fillets in a large Ziploc bag; massage well to coat. Place the fillets in the basket and cook for 14-16 minutes at 360 F on AirFry function. Top with parsley.

338.Air Fried Haddock Filets

Servings: 8
Cooking Time: 20 Minutes
Ingredients:
- Nonstick cooking spray
- 2 egg whites
- ½ tsp dill
- ½ tsp pepper
- 1 cup cornflakes, crushed
- 2 lbs. haddock fillets, cut in 8 pieces

Directions:
1. Place baking pan in position 2 of the oven. Lightly spray fryer basket with cooking spray.
2. In a shallow bowl, whisk together egg whites, dill, and pepper.
3. Place crushed cornflakes in a separate shallow dish.
4. Dip fish in egg mixture, then cornflakes, coating completely. Place in fryer basket.
5. Place basket on the baking pan and set oven to air fryer on 400°F. Cook 18-20 minutes, turning over halfway through, until fish flakes easily with a fork. Serve.
- **Nutrition Info:** Calories 193, Total Fat 1g, Saturated Fat 0g, Total Carbs 7g, Net Carbs 7g, Protein 39g, Sugar 1g, Fiber 0g, Sodium 568mg, Potassium 692mg, Phosphorus 524mg

339.Delicious Shrimp Casserole

Servings: 10
Cooking Time: 30 Minutes
Ingredients:
- 1 lb shrimp, peeled & tail off
- 2 tsp onion powder
- 2 tsp old bay seasoning
- 2 cups cheddar cheese, shredded
- 10.5 oz can cream of mushroom soup
- 12 oz long-grain rice
- 1 tsp salt

Directions:
1. Fit the oven with the rack in position
2. Cook rice according to the packet instructions.
3. Add shrimp into the boiling water and cook for 4 minutes or until cooked. Drain shrimp.
4. In a bowl, mix rice, shrimp, and remaining ingredients and pour into the greased 13*9-inch casserole dish.
5. Set to bake at 350 F for 35 minutes. After 5 minutes place the casserole dish in the preheated oven.
6. Serve and enjoy.
- **Nutrition Info:** Calories 286 Fat 9 g Carbohydrates 31 g Sugar 1 g Protein 18.8 g Cholesterol 120 mg

340.Browned Shrimp Patties

Servings:4
Cooking Time: 12 Minutes
Ingredients:
- ½ pound (227 g) raw shrimp, shelled, deveined, and chopped finely
- 2 cups cooked sushi rice

- ¼ cup chopped red bell pepper
- ¼ cup chopped celery
- ¼ cup chopped green onion
- 2 teaspoons Worcestershire sauce
- ½ teaspoon salt
- ½ teaspoon garlic powder
- ½ teaspoon Old Bay seasoning
- ½ cup plain bread crumbs
- Cooking spray

Directions:
1. Put all the ingredients except the bread crumbs and oil in a large bowl and stir to incorporate.
2. Scoop out the shrimp mixture and shape into 8 equal-sized patties with your hands, no more than ½-inch thick. Roll the patties in the bread crumbs on a plate and spray both sides with cooking spray. Place the patties in the air fryer basket.
3. Put the air fryer basket on the baking pan and slide into Rack Position 2, select Air Fry, set temperature to 390ºF (199ºC), and set time to 12 minutes.
4. Flip the patties halfway through the cooking time.
5. When cooking is complete, the outside should be crispy brown. Divide the patties among four plates and serve warm.

341.Shrimp With Smoked Paprika & Cayenne Pepper

Servings: 3
Cooking Time: 10 Minutes
Ingredients:
- 6 oz tiger shrimp, 12 to 16 pieces
- 1 tbsp olive oil
- ½ a tbsp old bay seasoning
- ¼ a tbsp cayenne pepper
- ¼ a tbsp smoked paprika
- A pinch of sea salt

Directions:
1. Preheat on Air Fry function to 380 F. Mix olive oil, old bay seasoning, cayenne pepper, smoked paprika, and sea salt in a large bowl. Add in the shrimp and toss to coat. Place the shrimp in the frying basket and fit in the baking tray; cook for 6-7 minutes, sahing once. Serve.

342.Miso White Fish Fillets

Servings: 2
Cooking Time: 10 Minutes
Ingredients:
- 2 cod fish fillets
- 2 tbsp brown sugar
- 2 tbsp miso
- 1 tbsp garlic, chopped

Directions:
1. Fit the oven with the rack in position 2.
2. Add all ingredients to the zip-lock bag and marinate fish in the refrigerator overnight.
3. Place marinated fish fillets in the air fryer basket then place an air fryer basket in the baking pan.
4. Place a baking pan on the oven rack. Set to air fry at 350 F for 10 minutes.
5. Serve and enjoy.
- **Nutrition Info:** Calories 9 Fat 0.1 g Carbohydrates 0.5 g Sugar 0.3 g Protein 1.5 g Cholesterol 3 mg

343.Aloo Patties

Servings:x
Cooking Time:x
Ingredients:

- 1 tbsp. fresh coriander leaves
- ¼ tsp. red chili powder
- ¼ tsp. cumin powder
- 1 cup mashed potato
- A pinch of salt to taste
- ¼ tsp. ginger finely chopped
- 1 green chili finely chopped
- 1 tsp. lemon juice

Directions:

1. Mix the ingredients together and ensure that the flavors are right. You will now make round patties with the mixture and roll them out well.
2. Pre heat the oven at 250 Fahrenheit for 5 minutes. Open the basket of the Fryer and arrange the patties in the basket. Close it carefully. Keep the fryer at 150 degrees for around 10 or 12 minutes. In between the cooking process, turn the patties over to get a uniform cook. Serve hot with mint sauce.

344.Potato Club Barbeque Sandwich

Servings:x
Cooking Time:x
Ingredients:

- ½ flake garlic crushed
- ¼ cup chopped onion
- ¼ tbsp. red chili sauce
- 2 slices of white bread
- 1 tbsp. softened butter
- 1 cup boiled potato
- 1 small capsicum
- ¼ tbsp. Worcestershire sauce
- ½ tsp. olive oil

Directions:

1. Take the slices of bread and remove the edges. Now cut the slices horizontally.
2. Cook the ingredients for the sauce and wait till it thickens. Now, add the potato to the sauce and stir till it obtains the flavors. Roast the capsicum and peel the skin off. Cut the capsicum into slices. Mix the ingredients together and apply it to the bread slices.
3. Pre-heat the oven for 5 minutes at 300 Fahrenheit. Open the basket of the Fryer and place the prepared Classic Sandwiches in it such that no two Classic Sandwiches are touching each other. Now keep the fryer at 250 degrees for around 15 minutes. Turn the Classic Sandwiches in between the cooking process to cook both slices. Serve the Classic Sandwiches with tomato ketchup or mint sauce.

345.Cheddar & Tempeh Stuffed Mushrooms

Servings: 3 To 4
Cooking Time: 20 Minutes
Ingredients:

- 14 mushroom caps
- 1 clove garlic, minced
- Salt and pepper to taste
- 4 slices tempeh, chopped
- ¼ cup grated Cheddar cheese
- 1 tbsp olive oil
- 1 tbsp chopped parsley

Directions:

1. Preheat on Air Fry function to 390 F. In a bowl, add olive oil, tempeh, cheddar cheese, parsley, salt, pepper, and garlic. Mix well with a spoon. Fill the mushroom caps with the tempeh mixture.
2. Place the stuffed mushrooms in the basket and fit in the baking tray; cook for 8 minutes. Once golden and crispy, plate them and serve with green salad.

346.Spicy Sweet Potato Friespotato Fries

Servings: 4
Cooking Time: 37 Minutes
Ingredients:

- 2 tbsp. sweet potato fry seasoning mix
- 2 tbsp. olive oil
- 2 sweet potatoes
- Seasoning Mix:
- 2 tbsp. salt
- 1 tbsp. cayenne pepper
- 1 tbsp. dried oregano
- 1 tbsp. fennel
- 2 tbsp. coriander

Directions:

1. Preparing the Ingredients. Slice both ends off sweet potatoes and peel. Slice lengthwise in half and again crosswise to make four pieces from each potato.
2. Slice each potato piece into 2-3 slices, then slice into fries.
3. Grind together all of seasoning mix ingredients and mix in the salt.
4. Ensure the air fryer oven is preheated to 350 degrees.
5. Toss potato pieces in olive oil, sprinkling with seasoning mix and tossing well to coat thoroughly.
6. Air Frying. Add fries to air fryer rack/basket. Set temperature to 350°F, and set time to 27 minutes. Select START/STOP to begin.

7. Take out the basket and turn fries. Turn off air fryer oven and let cook 10-12 minutes till fries are golden.

- **Nutrition Info:** CALORIES: 89; FAT: 14G; PROTEIN: 8Gs; SUGAR:3

347.Cottage Cheese Fried Baked Pastry

Servings:x
Cooking Time:x
Ingredients:
- 1 or 2 green chilies that are finely chopped or mashed
- ½ tsp. cumin
- 1 tsp. coarsely crushed coriander
- 1 dry red chili broken into pieces
- A small amount of salt (to taste)
- ½ tsp. dried mango powder
- ½ tsp. red chili power
- 1-2 tbsp. coriander
- 2 tbsp. unsalted butter
- 1 ½ cup all-purpose flour
- A pinch of salt to taste
- Water
- 2 cups mashed cottage cheese
- ¼ cup boiled peas
- 1 tsp. powdered ginger

Directions:
1. Mix the dough for the outer covering and make it stiff and smooth. Leave it to rest in a container while making the filling.
2. Cook the ingredients in a pan and stir them well to make a thick paste. Roll the paste out.
3. Roll the dough into balls and flatten them. Cut them in halves and add the filling. Use water to help you fold the edges to create the shape of a cone.
4. Pre-heat the oven for around 5 to 6 minutes at 300 Fahrenheit. Place all the samosas in the fry basket and close the basket properly. Keep the oven at 200 degrees for another 20 to 25 minutes. Around the halfway point, open the basket and turn the samosas over for uniform cooking. After this, fry at 250 degrees for around 10 minutes in order to give them the desired golden-brown color. Serve hot. Recommended sides are tamarind or mint sauce.

348.Honey Chili Potatoes

Servings:x
Cooking Time:x
Ingredients:
- 1 capsicum, cut into thin and long pieces (lengthwise).
- 2 tbsp. olive oil
- 2 onions. Cut them into halves.
- 1 ½ tbsp. sweet chili sauce
- 1 ½ tsp. ginger garlic paste
- ½ tbsp. red chili sauce.
- 2 tbsp. tomato ketchup
- 3 big potatoes (Cut into strips or cubes)
- 2 ½ tsp. ginger-garlic paste
- ¼ tsp. salt
- 1 tsp. red chili sauce
- ¼ tsp. red chili powder/black pepper
- A few drops of edible orange food coloring
- 2 tsp. soya sauce
- 2 tsp. vinegar
- A pinch of black pepper powder
- 1-2 tsp. red chili flakes

Directions:
1. Create the mix for the potato Oregano Fingers and coat the chicken well with it.
2. Pre heat the oven at 250 Fahrenheit for 5 minutes or so. Open the basket of the Fryer. Place the Oregano Fingers inside the basket. Now let the fryer stay at 290 Fahrenheit for another 20 minutes. Keep tossing the Oregano Fingers periodically through the cook to get a uniform cook.
3. Add the ingredients to the sauce and cook it with the vegetables till it thickens. Add the Oregano Fingers to the sauce and cook till the flavors have blended.

349.Butter Burgers

Servings: 4
Cooking Time: 30 Minutes
Ingredients:
- Nonstick cooking spray
- ½ cup black beans, rinsed & drained
- 12 oz. mushrooms, sliced
- 1 ½ cup brown rice, cooked
- ½ cup oats
- 1 tsp salt
- ½ tsp pepper
- 1 tsp garlic powder
- 1 tsp onion powder
- ¼ tsp red pepper flakes
- ¼ cup Vegan butter
- 2 cups onions, sliced

Directions:
1. Place baking pan in position 2 in the oven. Lightly spray fryer basket with cooking spray.
2. Pat the beans with paper towel to get them as dry as possible.
3. Heat a medium skillet over med-high heat. Add mushrooms and cook, stirring frequently, until almost no moisture remains.
4. Add mushrooms, beans, rice, oats, and seasonings to a food processor. Pulse to chop and combine ingredients. Do not over blend. Let mixture rest 20 minutes.

5. Melt butter in a large skillet over medium heat. Add onions and cook until browned and tender.
6. Form mushroom mixture into 4 patties and place in the fryer basket. Place in oven and set to air fry on 350°F for 10 minutes. Cook burgers 8-10 minutes, until nicely browned, turning over halfway through cooking time.
7. Serve on toasted buns topped with cooked onions.
- **Nutrition Info:** Calories 351, Total Fat 15g, Saturated Fat 8g, Total Carbs 44g, Net Carbs 37g, Protein 10g, Sugar 4g, Fiber 7g, Sodium 704mg, Potassium 604mg, Phosphorus 286mg

350.Cottage Cheese Flat Cakes

Servings:x
Cooking Time:x
Ingredients:
- 2 or 3 green chilies finely chopped
- 1 ½ tbsp. lemon juice
- Salt and pepper to taste
- 2 tbsp. garam masala
- 2 cups sliced cottage cheese
- 3 tsp. ginger finely chopped
- 1-2 tbsp. fresh coriander leaves

Directions:
1. Mix the ingredients in a clean bowl and add water to it. Make sure that the paste is not too watery but is enough to apply on the cottage cheese slices.
2. Pre heat the oven at 160 degrees Fahrenheit for 5 minutes. Place the French Cuisine Galettes in the fry basket and let them cook for another 25 minutes at the same temperature. Keep rolling them over to get a uniform cook. Serve either with mint sauce or ketchup.

351.Parmesan Cabbage With Blue Cheese Sauce

Servings:4
Cooking Time: 25 Minutes
Ingredients:
- ½ head cabbage, cut into wedges
- 2 cups Parmesan cheese, chopped
- 4 tbsp butter, melted
- Salt and black pepper to taste
- ½ cup blue cheese sauce

Directions:
1. Drizzle cabbage wedges with butter and coat with Parmesan cheese. Place them in the frying basket and cook for 20 minutes at 380 F on AirFry setting. Serve topped with blue cheese sauce.

352.Balsamic Asparagus

Servings:4

Cooking Time: 10 Minutes
Ingredients:
- 4 tablespoons olive oil, plus more for greasing
- 4 tablespoons balsamic vinegar
- 1½ pounds (680 g) asparagus spears, trimmed
- Salt and freshly ground black pepper, to taste

Directions:
1. Grease the air fryer basket with olive oil.
2. In a shallow bowl, stir together the 4 tablespoons of olive oil and balsamic vinegar to make a marinade.
3. Put the asparagus spears in the bowl so they are thoroughly covered by the marinade and allow to marinate for 5 minutes.
4. Put the asparagus in the greased basket in a single layer and season with salt and pepper.
5. Put the air fryer basket on the baking pan and slide into Rack Position 2, select Air Fry, set temperature to 350ºF (180ºC), and set time to 10 minutes.
6. Flip the asparagus halfway through the cooking time.
7. When done, the asparagus should be tender and lightly browned. Cool for 5 minutes before serving.

353.Caramelized Eggplant With Yogurt Sauce

Servings:2
Cooking Time: 15 Minutes
Ingredients:
- 1 medium eggplant, quartered and cut crosswise into ½-inch-thick slices
- 2 tablespoons vegetable oil
- Kosher salt and freshly ground black pepper, to taste
- ½ cup plain yogurt (not Greek)
- 2 tablespoons harissa paste
- 1 garlic clove, grated
- 2 teaspoons honey

Directions:
1. Toss the eggplant slices with the vegetable oil, salt, and pepper in a large bowl until well coated.
2. Lay the eggplant slices in the air fryer basket.
3. Put the air fryer basket on the baking pan and slide into Rack Position 2, select Air Fry, set temperature to 400ºF (205ºC), and set time to 15 minutes.
4. Stir the slices two to three times during cooking.

5. Meanwhile, make the yogurt sauce by whisking together the yogurt, harissa paste, and garlic in a small bowl.
6. When cooking is complete, the eggplant slices should be golden brown. Spread the yogurt sauce on a platter, and pile the eggplant slices over the top. Serve drizzled with the honey.

354.Cauliflower Momo's Recipe

Servings:x
Cooking Time:x
Ingredients:
- 2 tsp. ginger-garlic paste
- 2 tsp. soya sauce
- 2 tsp. vinegar
- 1 ½ cup all-purpose flour
- ½ tsp. salt
- 5 tbsp. water
- 2 cups grated cauliflower
- 2 tbsp. oil

Directions:
1. Squeeze the dough and cover it with plastic wrap and set aside. Next, cook the ingredients for the filling and try to ensure that the cauliflower is covered well with the sauce.
2. Roll the dough and cut it into a square. Place the filling in the center. Now, wrap the dough to cover the filling and pinch the edges together.
3. Pre heat the oven at 200° F for 5 minutes. Place the gnocchi's in the fry basket and close it. Let them cook at the same temperature for another 20 minutes. Recommended sides are chili sauce or ketchup

355.Onion Rings

Servings: 4
Cooking Time: 10 Minutes
Ingredients:
- 1 large spanish onion
- 1/2 cup buttermilk
- 2 eggs, lightly beaten
- 3/4 cups unbleached all-purpose flour
- 3/4 cups panko bread crumbs
- 1/2 teaspoon baking powder
- 1/2 teaspoon Cayenne pepper, to taste
- Salt

Directions:
1. Preparing the Ingredients. Start by cutting your onion into 1/2 thick rings and separate. Smaller pieces can be discarded or saved for other recipes.
2. Beat the eggs in a large bowl and mix in the buttermilk, then set it aside.
3. In another bowl combine flour, pepper, bread crumbs, and baking powder.

4. Use a large spoon to dip a whole ring in the buttermilk, then pull it through the flour mix on both sides to completely coat the ring.
5. Air Frying. Cook about 8 rings at a time in your air fryer oven for 8-10 minutes at 360 degrees shaking half way through.
- **Nutrition Info:** CALORIES: 225; FAT: 3.8G; PROTEIN:19G; FIBER:2.4G

356.Black Gram French Cuisine Galette

Servings:x
Cooking Time:x
Ingredients:
- 2 or 3 green chilies finely chopped
- 1 ½ tbsp. lemon juice
- Salt and pepper to taste
- 2 cup black gram
- 2 medium potatoes boiled and mashed
- 1 ½ cup coarsely crushed peanuts
- 3 tsp. ginger finely chopped
- 1-2 tbsp. fresh coriander leaves

Directions:
1. Mix the ingredients in a clean bowl.
2. Mold this mixture into round and flat French Cuisine Galettes.
3. Wet the French Cuisine Galettes slightly with water.
4. Pre heat the oven at 160 degrees Fahrenheit for 5 minutes. Place the French Cuisine Galettes in the fry basket and let them cook for another 25 minutes at the same temperature. Keep rolling them over to get a uniform cook. Serve either with mint sauce or ketchup.

357.Classic Ratatouille

Servings: 2
Cooking Time: 30 Minutes
Ingredients:
- 1 tbsp olive oil
- 3 roma tomatoes, thinly sliced
- 2 garlic cloves, minced
- 1 zucchini, thinly sliced
- 2 yellow bell peppers, sliced
- 1 tbsp red wine vinegar
- 2 tbsp herbs de Provence
- Salt and black pepper to taste

Directions:
1. Preheat on Air Fry function to 390 F. In a bowl, mix together olive oil, garlic, vinegar, herbs, salt, and pepper. Add in tomatoes, zucchini, and bell peppers and toss to coat.
2. Arrange the vegetables in a baking dish and cook for 15 minutes, shaking occasionally. Let sit for 5 more minutes after the timer goes off. Serve.

358.Mushroom Club Sandwich

Servings:x
Cooking Time:x
Ingredients:
- ¼ tbsp. Worcestershire sauce
- ½ tsp. olive oil
- ½ flake garlic crushed
- ¼ cup chopped onion
- ¼ tbsp. red chili sauce
- ½ cup water
- 2 slices of white bread
- 1 tbsp. softened butter
- 1 cup minced mushroom
- 1 small capsicum

Directions:
1. Take the slices of bread and remove the edges. Now cut the slices horizontally.
2. Cook the ingredients for the sauce and wait till it thickens. Now, add the mushroom to the sauce and stir till it obtains the flavors. Roast the capsicum and peel the skin off. Cut the capsicum into slices. Apply the sauce on the slices.
3. Pre-heat the oven for 5 minutes at 300 Fahrenheit. Open the basket of the Fryer and place the prepared Classic Sandwiches in it such that no two Classic Sandwiches are touching each other. Now keep the fryer at 250 degrees for around 15 minutes. Turn the Classic Sandwiches in between the cooking process to cook both slices. Serve the Classic Sandwiches with tomato ketchup or mint sauce.

359.Korean Tempeh Steak With Broccoli

Servings: 4
Cooking Time: 15 Minutes + Marinating Time
Ingredients:
- 16 oz tempeh, cut into 1 cm thick pieces
- 1 pound broccoli, cut into florets
- ⅓ cup fermented soy sauce
- 2 tbsp sesame oil
- ⅓ cup sherry
- 1 tsp soy sauce
- 1 tsp white sugar
- 1 tsp cornstarch
- 1 tbsp olive oil
- 1 garlic clove, minced

Directions:
1. In a bowl, mix cornstarch, sherry, fermented soy sauce, sesame oil, soy sauce, sugar, and tempeh pieces. Marinate for 45 minutes.
2. Then, add in garlic, olive oil, and ginger. Place in the basket and fit in the baking tray; cook for 10 minutes at 390 F on Air Fry function, turning once halfway through. Serve.

360.Cayenne Spicy Green Beans

Servings: 4
Cooking Time: 20 Minutes
Ingredients:
- 1 cup panko breadcrumbs
- 2 whole eggs, beaten
- ½ cup Parmesan cheese, grated
- ½ cup flour
- 1 tsp cayenne pepper
- 1 ½ pounds green beans
- Salt to taste

Directions:
1. In a bowl, mix panko breadcrumbs, Parmesan cheese, cayenne pepper, salt, and pepper. Roll the green beans in flour and dip in eggs. Dredge beans in the parmesan-panko mix. Place the prepared beans in the greased cooking basket and fit in the baking tray; cook for 15 minutes on Air Fry function at 350 F, shaking once. Serve and enjoy!

361.Okra Flat Cakes

Servings:x
Cooking Time:x
Ingredients:
- 2 or 3 green chilies finely chopped
- 1 ½ tbsp. lemon juice
- Salt and pepper to taste
- 2 tbsp. garam masala
- 2 cups sliced okra
- 3 tsp. ginger finely chopped
- 1-2 tbsp. fresh coriander leaves

Directions:
1. Mix the ingredients in a clean bowl and add water to it. Make sure that the
2. paste is not too watery but is enough to apply on the okra.
3. Pre heat the oven at 160 degrees Fahrenheit for 5 minutes. Place the French Cuisine Galettes in the fry basket and let them cook for another 25 minutes at the same temperature. Keep rolling them over to get a uniform cook. Serve either with mint sauce or ketchup.

362.Cream Cheese Stuffed Bell Peppers

Servings:2
Cooking Time: 15 Minutes
Ingredients:
- 2 bell peppers, tops and seeds removed
- Salt and pepper, to taste
- $^2/_3$ cup cream cheese
- 2 tablespoons mayonnaise
- 1 tablespoon chopped fresh celery stalks
- Cooking spray

Directions:
1. Spritz the air fryer basket with cooking spray.

2. Place the peppers in the air fryer basket.
3. Put the air fryer basket on the baking pan and slide into Rack Position 2, select Roast, set temperature to 400ºF (205ºC) and set time to 10 minutes.
4. Flip the peppers halfway through.
5. When cooking is complete, the peppers should be crisp-tender.
6. Remove from the oven to a plate and season with salt and pepper.
7. Mix the cream cheese, mayo, and celery in a small bowl and stir to incorporate. Evenly stuff the roasted peppers with the cream cheese mixture with a spoon. Serve immediately.

363.Pineapple Spicy Lemon Kebab

Servings:x
Cooking Time:x
Ingredients:
- 4 tbsp. chopped coriander
- 3 tbsp. cream
- 3 tbsp. chopped capsicum
- 3 eggs
- 2 ½ tbsp. white sesame seeds
- 2 cups cubed pineapples
- 3 onions chopped
- 5 green chilies-roughly chopped
- 1 ½ tbsp. ginger paste
- 1 ½ tsp. garlic paste
- 1 ½ tsp. salt
- 3 tsp. lemon juice
- 2 tsp. garam masala

Directions:
1. Grind the ingredients except for the egg and form a smooth paste. Coat the pineapples in the paste. Now, beat the eggs and add a little salt to it.
2. Dip the coated vegetables in the egg mixture and then transfer to the sesame seeds and coat the pineapples well. Place the vegetables on a stick.
3. Pre heat the oven at 160 degrees Fahrenheit for around 5 minutes. Place the sticks in the basket and let them cook for another 25 minutes at the same temperature. Turn the sticks over in between the cooking process to get a uniform cook.

364.Cinnamon Celery Roots

Servings:4
Cooking Time: 20 Minutes
Ingredients:
- 2 celery roots, peeled and diced
- 1 teaspoon extra-virgin olive oil
- 1 teaspoon butter, melted
- ½ teaspoon ground cinnamon

- Sea salt and freshly ground black pepper, to taste

Directions:
1. Line the baking pan with aluminum foil.
2. Toss the celery roots with the olive oil in a large bowl until well coated. Transfer them to the prepared baking pan.
3. Slide the baking pan into Rack Position 2, select Roast, set temperature to 350ºF (180ºC), and set time to 20 minutes.
4. When done, the celery roots should be very tender. Remove from the oven to a serving bowl. Stir in the butter and cinnamon and mash them with a potato masher until fluffy.
5. Season with salt and pepper to taste. Serve immediately.

365.Simple Ratatouille

Servings:2
Cooking Time: 16 Minutes
Ingredients:
- 2 Roma tomatoes, thinly sliced
- 1 zucchini, thinly sliced
- 2 yellow bell peppers, sliced
- 2 garlic cloves, minced
- 2 tablespoons olive oil
- 2 tablespoons herbes de Provence
- 1 tablespoon vinegar
- Salt and black pepper, to taste

Directions:
1. Place the tomatoes, zucchini, bell peppers, garlic, olive oil, herbes de Provence, and vinegar in a large bowl and toss until the vegetables are evenly coated. Sprinkle with salt and pepper and toss again. Pour the vegetable mixture into the baking pan.
2. Slide the baking pan into Rack Position 2, select Roast, set temperature to 390ºF (199ºC) and set time to 16 minutes.
3. Stir the vegetables halfway through.
4. When cooking is complete, the vegetables should be tender.
5. Let the vegetable mixture stand for 5 minutes in the oven before removing and serving.

366.Roasted Asparagus With Eggs And Tomatoes

Servings:4
Cooking Time: 12 Minutes
Ingredients:
- 2 pounds (907 g) asparagus, trimmed
- 3 tablespoons extra-virgin olive oil, divided
- 1 teaspoon kosher salt, divided
- 1 pint cherry tomatoes
- 4 large eggs
- ¼ teaspoon freshly ground black pepper

Directions:

1. Put the asparagus in the baking pan and drizzle with 2 tablespoons of olive oil, tossing to coat. Season with ½ teaspoon of kosher salt.
2. Slide the baking pan into Rack Position 2, select Roast, set temperature to 375ºF (190ºC), and set time to 12 minutes.
3. Meanwhile, toss the cherry tomatoes with the remaining 1 tablespoon of olive oil in a medium bowl until well coated.
4. After 6 minutes, remove the pan and toss the asparagus. Evenly spread the asparagus in the middle of the pan. Add the tomatoes around the perimeter of the pan. Return the pan to the oven and continue cooking.
5. After 2 minutes, remove from the oven.
6. Carefully crack the eggs, one at a time, over the asparagus, spacing them out. Season with the remaining ½ teaspoon of kosher salt and the pepper. Return the pan to the oven and continue cooking. Cook for an additional 3 to 7 minutes, or until the eggs are cooked to your desired doneness.
7. When done, divide the asparagus and eggs among four plates. Top each plate evenly with the tomatoes and serve.

367.Mushroom Homemade Fried Sticks

Servings:x
Cooking Time:x
Ingredients:
- One or two poppadums'
- 4 or 5 tbsp. corn flour
- 1 cup of water
- 2 cups whole mushrooms
- 1 big lemon-juiced
- 1 tbsp. ginger-garlic paste
- For seasoning, use salt and red chili powder in small amounts
- ½ tsp. carom

Directions:
1. Make a mixture of lemon juice, red chili powder, salt, ginger garlic paste and carom to use as a marinade. Let the cottage cheese pieces marinate in the mixture for some time and then roll them in dry corn flour. Leave them aside for around 20 minutes.
2. Take the poppadum into a pan and roast them. Once they are cooked, crush them into very small pieces. Now take another container and pour around 100 ml of water into it. Dissolve 2 tbsp. of corn flour in this water. Dip the cottage cheese pieces in this solution of corn flour and roll them on to the pieces of crushed poppadum so that the poppadum sticks to the cottage cheese.
3. Pre heat the oven for 10 minutes at 290 Fahrenheit. Then open the basket of the fryer and place the cottage cheese pieces inside it. Close the basket properly. Let the

fryer stay at 160 degrees for another 20 minutes. Halfway through, open the basket and toss the cottage cheese around a bit to allow for uniform cooking. Once they are done, you can serve it either with ketchup or mint sauce. Another recommended side is mint sauce.

368.Cheesy Asparagus And Potato Platter

Servings:5
Cooking Time: 26 Minutes
Ingredients:
- 4 medium potatoes, cut into wedges
- Cooking spray
- 1 bunch asparagus, trimmed
- 2 tablespoons olive oil
- Salt and pepper, to taste
- Cheese Sauce:
- ¼ cup crumbled cottage cheese
- ¼ cup buttermilk
- 1 tablespoon whole-grain mustard
- Salt and black pepper, to taste

Directions:
1. Spritz the air fryer basket with cooking spray.
2. Put the potatoes in the air fryer basket.
3. Put the air fryer basket on the baking pan and slide into Rack Position 2, select Roast, set temperature to 400ºF (205ºC) and set time to 20 minutes.
4. Stir the potatoes halfway through.
5. When cooking is complete, the potatoes should be golden brown.
6. Remove the potatoes from the oven to a platter. Cover the potatoes with foil to keep warm. Set aside.
7. Place the asparagus in the air fryer basket and drizzle with the olive oil. Sprinkle with salt and pepper.
8. Put the air fryer basket on the baking pan and slide into Rack Position 2, select Roast, set temperature to 400ºF (205ºC) and set time to 6 minutes. Stir the asparagus halfway through.
9. When cooking is complete, the asparagus should be crispy.
10. Meanwhile, make the cheese sauce by stirring together the cottage cheese, buttermilk, and mustard in a small bowl. Season as needed with salt and pepper.
11. Transfer the asparagus to the platter of potatoes and drizzle with the cheese sauce. Serve immediately.

369.Roasted Brussels Sprouts With Parmesan

Servings:4
Cooking Time: 20 Minutes
Ingredients:

- 1 pound (454 g) fresh Brussels sprouts, trimmed
- 1 tablespoon olive oil
- ½ teaspoon salt
- ⅛ teaspoon pepper
- ¼ cup grated Parmesan cheese

Directions:
1. In a large bowl, combine the Brussels sprouts with olive oil, salt, and pepper and toss until evenly coated.
2. Spread the Brussels sprouts evenly in the air fryer basket.
3. Put the air fryer basket on the baking pan and slide into Rack Position 2, select Air Fry, set temperature to 330ºF (166ºC), and set time to 20 minutes.
4. Stir the Brussels sprouts twice during cooking.
5. When cooking is complete, the Brussels sprouts should be golden brown and crisp. Sprinkle the grated Parmesan cheese on top and serve warm.

370.Teriyaki Cauliflower

Servings:4
Cooking Time: 14 Minutes
Ingredients:
- ½ cup soy sauce
- $^1/_3$ cup water
- 1 tablespoon brown sugar
- 1 teaspoon sesame oil
- 1 teaspoon cornstarch
- 2 cloves garlic, chopped
- ½ teaspoon chili powder
- 1 big cauliflower head, cut into florets

Directions:
1. Make the teriyaki sauce: In a small bowl, whisk together the soy sauce, water, brown sugar, sesame oil, cornstarch, garlic, and chili powder until well combined.
2. Place the cauliflower florets in a large bowl and drizzle the top with the prepared teriyaki sauce and toss to coat well.
3. Put the cauliflower florets in the air fryer basket.
4. Put the air fryer basket on the baking pan and slide into Rack Position 2, select Air Fry, set temperature to 340ºF (171ºC) and set time to 14 minutes.
5. Stir the cauliflower halfway through.
6. When cooking is complete, the cauliflower should be crisp-tender.
7. Let the cauliflower cool for 5 minutes before serving.

371.Roasted Vegetables With Rice

Servings:4
Cooking Time: 12 Minutes
Ingredients:

- 2 teaspoons melted butter
- 1 cup chopped mushrooms
- 1 cup cooked rice
- 1 cup peas
- 1 carrot, chopped
- 1 red onion, chopped
- 1 garlic clove, minced
- Salt and black pepper, to taste
- 2 hard-boiled eggs, grated
- 1 tablespoon soy sauce

Directions:
1. Coat the baking pan with melted butter.
2. Stir together the mushrooms, cooked rice, peas, carrot, onion, garlic, salt, and pepper in a large bowl until well mixed. Pour the mixture into the prepared baking pan.
3. Slide the baking pan into Rack Position 2, select Roast, set temperature to 380ºF (193ºC), and set time to 12 minutes.
4. When cooking is complete, remove from the oven. Divide the mixture among four plates. Serve warm with a sprinkle of grated eggs and a drizzle of soy sauce.

372.Maple And Pecan Granola

Servings:4
Cooking Time: 20 Minutes
Ingredients:
- 1½ cups rolled oats
- ¼ cup maple syrup
- ¼ cup pecan pieces
- 1 teaspoon vanilla extract
- ½ teaspoon ground cinnamon

Directions:
1. Line a baking sheet with parchment paper.
2. Mix together the oats, maple syrup, pecan pieces, vanilla, and cinnamon in a large bowl and stir until the oats and pecan pieces are completely coated. Spread the mixture evenly in the baking pan.
3. Slide the baking pan into Rack Position 1, select Convection Bake, set temperature to 300ºF (150ºC), and set time to 20 minutes.
4. Stir once halfway through the cooking time.
5. When done, remove from the oven and cool for 30 minutes before serving. The granola may still be a bit soft right after removing, but it will gradually firm up as it cools.

373.Speedy Vegetable Pizza

Servings: 1
Cooking Time: 15 Minutes
Ingredients:
- 1 ½ tbsp tomato paste
- ¼ cup grated cheddar cheese
- ¼ cup grated mozzarella cheese
- 1 tbsp cooked sweet corn
- 4 zucchini slices
- 4 eggplant slices

- 4 red onion rings
- ½ green bell pepper, chopped
- 3 cherry tomatoes, quartered
- 1 pizza crust
- ¼ tsp basil
- ¼ tsp oregano

Directions:
1. Preheat on Bake function to 350 F. Spread the tomato paste on the pizza crust. Top with zucchini and eggplant slices first, then green peppers, and onion rings. Cover with cherry tomatoes and scatter the corn. Sprinkle with oregano and basil and sprinkle with cheddar and mozzarella cheeses. Cook for 10-12 minutes until golden brown on top. Serve.

374.Stuffed Capsicum Baskets

Servings:x
Cooking Time:x
Ingredients:
- 1 green chili finely chopped
- 2 or 3 large potatoes boiled and mashed
- 1 ½ tbsp. chopped coriander leaves
- 1 tsp. fenugreek
- 1 tsp. dried mango powder
- 3-4 long capsicum
- ½ tsp. salt
- ½ tsp. pepper powder
- For filling:
- 1 medium onion finely chopped
- 1 tsp. cumin powder
- Salt and pepper to taste
- 3 tbsp. grated cheese
- 1 tsp. red chili flakes
- ½ tsp. oregano
- ½ tsp. basil
- ½ tsp. parsley

Directions:
1. Take all the ingredients under the heading "Filling" and mix them together in a bowl.
2. Remove the stem of the capsicum. Cut off the caps. Remove the seeds as well. Sprinkle some salt and pepper on the inside of the capsicums. Leave them aside for some time.
3. Now fill the hollowed-out capsicums with the filling prepared but leave a small space at the top. Sprinkle grated cheese and also add the seasoning.
4. Pre heat the oven at 140 degrees Fahrenheit for 5 minutes. Put the capsicums in the fry basket and close it. Let them cook at the same temperature for another 20 minutes. Turn them over in between to prevent over cooking.

375.Lemony Wax Beans

Servings:4
Cooking Time: 12 Minutes

Ingredients:
- 2 pounds (907 g) wax beans
- 2 tablespoons extra-virgin olive oil
- Salt and freshly ground black pepper, to taste
- Juice of ½ lemon, for serving

Directions:
1. Line the air fryer basket with aluminum foil.
2. Toss the wax beans with the olive oil in a large bowl. Lightly season with salt and pepper.
3. Spread out the wax beans in the basket.
4. Put the air fryer basket on the baking pan and slide into Rack Position 2, select Roast, set temperature to 400ºF (205ºC), and set time to 12 minutes.
5. When done, the beans will be caramelized and tender. Remove from the oven to a plate and serve sprinkled with the lemon juice.

376.Baked Turnip And Zucchini

Servings:4
Cooking Time: 18 Minutes
Ingredients:
- 3 turnips, sliced
- 1 large zucchini, sliced
- 1 large red onion, cut into rings
- 2 cloves garlic, crushed
- 1 tablespoon olive oil
- Salt and black pepper, to taste

Directions:
1. Put the turnips, zucchini, red onion, and garlic in the baking pan. Drizzle the olive oil over the top and sprinkle with the salt and pepper.
2. Slide the baking pan into Rack Position 1, select Convection Bake, set temperature to 330ºF (166ºC), and set time to 18 minutes.
3. When cooking is complete, the vegetables should be tender. Remove from the oven and serve on a plate.

377.Cabbage Flat Cakes

Servings:x
Cooking Time:x
Ingredients:
- 2 or 3 green chilies finely chopped
- 1 ½ tbsp. lemon juice
- Salt and pepper to taste
- 2 tbsp. garam masala
- 2 cups halved cabbage leaves
- 3 tsp. ginger finely chopped
- 1-2 tbsp. fresh coriander leaves

Directions:
1. Mix the ingredients in a clean bowl and add water to it. Make sure that the paste is not too watery but is enough to apply on the cabbage.

2. Pre heat the oven at 160 degrees Fahrenheit for 5 minutes. Place the French Cuisine Galettes in the fry basket and let them cook for another 25 minutes at the same temperature. Keep rolling them over to get a uniform cook. Serve either with mint sauce or ketchup.

378.Roasted Fall Veggies

Servings: 6
Cooking Time: 30 Minutes
Ingredients:
- 2 cups sweet potatoes, cubed
- 2 cups Brussel sprouts, halved
- 3 cups button mushrooms, halved
- ½ red onion, chopped
- 3 cloves garlic, chopped fine
- 4 sage leaves, chopped
- 2 sprigs rosemary, chopped
- 2 sprigs thyme, chopped
- 1 tsp garlic powder
- 1 tsp onion powder
- ½ tsp salt
- ¼ tsp pepper
- 3 tbsp. balsamic vinegar
- Nonstick cooking spray

Directions:
1. Chop vegetables so that they are as close to equal in size as possible. Roughly chop the herbs.
2. In a large bowl, toss vegetables, herbs, and spices to mix. Drizzle vinegar overall and toss to coat.
3. Spray the baking pan with cooking spray. Set oven to bake on 350°F for 35 minutes.
4. Transfer the vegetable mixture to the baking pan and after 5 minutes, place in the oven in position 1. Bake vegetables 25-30 minutes or until vegetables are tender. Turn them over halfway through cooking. Serve immediately.
- **Nutrition Info:** Calories 76, Total Fat 0g, Saturated Fat 0g, Total Carbs 16g, Net Carbs 13g, Protein 3g, Sugar 5g, Fiber 3g, Sodium 231mg, Potassium 455mg, Phosphorus 92mg

379.Easy Cheesy Vegetable Quesadilla

Servings:1
Cooking Time: 10 Minutes
Ingredients:
- 1 teaspoon olive oil
- 2 flour tortillas
- ¼ zucchini, sliced
- ¼ yellow bell pepper, sliced
- ¼ cup shredded gouda cheese
- 1 tablespoon chopped cilantro
- ½ green onion, sliced

Directions:

1. Coat the air fryer basket with 1 teaspoon of olive oil.
2. Arrange a flour tortilla in the basket and scatter the top with zucchini, bell pepper, gouda cheese, cilantro, and green onion. Place the other flour tortilla on top.
3. Put the air fryer basket on the baking pan and slide into Rack Position 2, select Air Fry, set temperature to 390ºF (199ºC), and set time to 10 minutes.
4. When cooking is complete, the tortillas should be lightly browned and the vegetables should be tender. Remove from the oven and cool for 5 minutes before slicing into wedges.

380.Balsamic Eggplant Caviar

Servings:4
Cooking Time: 20 Minutes
Ingredients:
- 3 medium eggplants
- ½ red onion, chopped and blended
- 2 tbsp balsamic vinegar
- 1 tbsp olive oil
- Salt to taste

Directions:
1. Arrange the eggplants on the basket and cook them in the oven for 15 minutes at 380 F on Bake function. Let cool. Cut the eggplants in half, lengthwise and empty their insides.
2. Pulse the onion the inside of the eggplants in a blender. Add in vinegar, olive oil, and salt, then blend again. Serve cool with bread and tomato sauce or ketchup.

381.Eggplant Patties With Mozzarella

Servings:1
Cooking Time: 10 Minutes
Ingredients:
- 1 hamburger bun
- 2-inch eggplant slices, cut along the round axis
- 1 mozzarella cheese slice
- 3 red onion rings
- 1 lettuce leaf
- ½ tbsp tomato sauce
- 1 pickle, sliced

Directions:
1. Preheat on Bake function to 330 F. Cook in the eggplant slices to roast for 6 minutes. Place the mozzarella slice on top of the eggplant and cook for 30 more seconds. Spread tomato sauce on one half of the bun.
2. Place the lettuce leaf on top of the sauce. Place the cheesy eggplant on top of the lettuce. Top with onion rings and pickles, and then with the other bun half and enjoy.

382.Palak French Cuisine Galette

Servings:x
Cooking Time:x
Ingredients:
- 1-2 tbsp. fresh coriander leaves
- 2 or 3 green chilies finely chopped
- 1 ½ tbsp. lemon juice
- Salt and pepper to taste
- 2 tbsp. garam masala
- 2 cups Palak leaves
- 1 ½ cup coarsely crushed peanuts
- 3 tsp. ginger finely chopped

Directions:
1. Mix the ingredients in a clean bowl.
2. Mold this mixture into round and flat French Cuisine Galettes.
3. Wet the French Cuisine Galettes slightly with water. Coat each French Cuisine Galette with the crushed peanuts.
4. Pre heat the oven at 160 degrees Fahrenheit for 5 minutes. Place the French Cuisine Galettes in the fry basket and let them cook for another 25 minutes at the same temperature. Keep rolling them over to get a uniform cook. Serve either with mint sauce or ketchup.

383.Stuffed Peppers With Beans And Rice

Servings:4
Cooking Time: 18 Minutes
Ingredients:
- 4 medium red, green, or yellow bell peppers, halved and deseeded
- 4 tablespoons extra-virgin olive oil, divided
- ½ teaspoon kosher salt, divided
- 1 (15-ounce / 425-g) can chickpeas
- 1½ cups cooked white rice
- ½ cup diced roasted red peppers
- ¼ cup chopped parsley
- ½ small onion, finely chopped
- 3 garlic cloves, minced
- ½ teaspoon cumin
- ¼ teaspoon freshly ground black pepper
- ¾ cup panko bread crumbs

Directions:
1. Brush the peppers inside and out with 1 tablespoon of olive oil. Season the insides with ¼ teaspoon of kosher salt. Arrange the peppers in the air fryer basket, cut side up.
2. Place the chickpeas with their liquid into a large bowl. Lightly mash the beans with a potato masher. Sprinkle with the remaining ¼ teaspoon of kosher salt and 1 tablespoon of olive oil. Add the rice, red peppers, parsley, onion, garlic, cumin, and black pepper to the bowl and stir to incorporate.
3. Divide the mixture among the bell pepper halves.

4. Stir together the remaining 2 tablespoons of olive oil and panko in a small bowl. Top the pepper halves with the panko mixture.
5. Put the air fryer basket on the baking pan and slide into Rack Position 2, select Roast, set temperature to 375ºF (190ºC), and set time to 18 minutes.
6. When done, the peppers should be slightly wrinkled, and the panko should be golden brown.
7. Remove from the oven and serve on a plate.

384.Fenugreek French Cuisine Galette

Servings:x
Cooking Time:x
Ingredients:
- 2 or 3 green chilies finely chopped
- 1 ½ tbsp. lemon juice
- Salt and pepper to taste
- 2 cups fenugreek
- 2 medium potatoes boiled and mashed
- 3 tsp. ginger finely chopped
- 1-2 tbsp. fresh coriander leaves

Directions:
1. Mix the ingredients in a clean bowl.
2. Mold this mixture into round and flat French Cuisine Galettes.
3. Wet the French Cuisine Galettes slightly with water.
4. Pre heat the oven at 160 degrees Fahrenheit for 5 minutes. Place the French Cuisine Galettes in the fry basket and let them cook for another 25 minutes at the same temperature. Keep rolling them over to get a uniform cook. Serve either with mint sauce or ketchup.

385.Crispy Veggies With Halloumi

Servings:2
Cooking Time: 14 Minutes
Ingredients:
- 2 zucchinis, cut into even chunks
- 1 large eggplant, peeled, cut into chunks
- 1 large carrot, cut into chunks
- 6 ounces (170 g) halloumi cheese, cubed
- 2 teaspoons olive oil
- Salt and black pepper, to taste
- 1 teaspoon dried mixed herbs

Directions:
1. Combine the zucchinis, eggplant, carrot, cheese, olive oil, salt, and pepper in a large bowl and toss to coat well.
2. Spread the mixture evenly in the air fryer basket.
3. Put the air fryer basket on the baking pan and slide into Rack Position 2, select Air Fry, set temperature to 340ºF (171ºC), and set time to 14 minutes.
4. Stir the mixture once during cooking.

5. When cooking is complete, they should be crispy and golden. Remove from the oven and serve topped with mixed herbs.

386.Buffalo Cauliflower

Servings: 2
Cooking Time: 15 Minutes
Ingredients:
- Cauliflower:
- 1 C. panko breadcrumbs
- 1 tsp. salt
- 4 C. cauliflower florets
- Buffalo Coating:
- ¼ C. Vegan Buffalo sauce
- ¼ C. melted vegan butter

Directions:
1. Preparing the Ingredients. Melt butter in microwave and whisk in buffalo sauce.
2. Dip each cauliflower floret into buffalo mixture, ensuring it gets coated well. Hold over a bowl till floret is done dripping.
3. Mix breadcrumbs with salt.
4. Air Frying. Dredge dipped florets into breadcrumbs and place into the air fryer oven. Set the temperature to 350°F, and set time to 15 minutes. When slightly browned, they are ready to eat!
5. Serve with your favorite keto dipping sauce!
- **Nutrition Info:** CALORIES: 194; FAT: 17G; PROTEIN:10G; SUGAR:

387.Vegetable And Cheese Stuffed Tomatoes

Servings:4
Cooking Time: 18 Minutes
Ingredients:
- 4 medium beefsteak tomatoes, rinsed
- ½ cup grated carrot
- 1 medium onion, chopped
- 1 garlic clove, minced
- 2 teaspoons olive oil
- 2 cups fresh baby spinach
- ¼ cup crumbled low-sodium feta cheese
- ½ teaspoon dried basil

Directions:
1. On your cutting board, cut a thin slice off the top of each tomato. Scoop out a ¼- to ½-inch-thick tomato pulp and place the tomatoes upside down on paper towels to drain. Set aside.
2. Stir together the carrot, onion, garlic, and olive oil in the baking pan.
3. Slide the baking pan into Rack Position 1, select Convection Bake, set temperature to 350ºF (180ºC) and set time to 5 minutes.
4. Stir the vegetables halfway through.
5. When cooking is complete, the carrot should be crisp-tender.
6. Remove from the oven and stir in the spinach, feta cheese, and basil.

7. Spoon ¼ of the vegetable mixture into each tomato and transfer the stuffed tomatoes to the oven. Set time to 13 minutes.
8. When cooking is complete, the filling should be hot and the tomatoes should be lightly caramelized.
9. Let the tomatoes cool for 5 minutes and serve.

388.Mexican Burritos

Servings:x
Cooking Time:x
Ingredients:
- 1 tbsp. Olive oil
- 1 medium onion finely sliced
- 3 flakes garlic crushed
- 1 tsp. freshly ground peppercorns
- ½ cup pickled jalapenos (Chop them up finely)
- 2 carrots (Cut in to long thin slices)
- 1-2 lettuce leaves shredded.
- 1 or 2 spring onions chopped finely. Also cut the greens.
- Take one tomato. Remove the seeds and chop it into small pieces.
- ½ cup French beans (Slice them lengthwise into thin and long slices)
- ½ cup mushrooms thinly sliced
- 1 cup cottage cheese cut in too long and slightly thick Oregano Fingers
- ½ cup shredded cabbage
- 1 tbsp. coriander, chopped
- 1 tbsp. vinegar
- 1 tsp. white wine
- ½ cup red kidney beans (soaked overnight)
- ½ small onion chopped
- 1 tbsp. olive oil
- 2 tbsp. tomato puree
- ¼ tsp. red chili powder
- 1 tsp. of salt to taste
- 4-5 flour tortillas
- A pinch of salt to taste
- ½ tsp. red chili flakes
- 1 green chili chopped.
- 1 cup of cheddar cheese grated.

Directions:
1. Cook the beans along with the onion and garlic and mash them finely. Now, make the sauce you will need for the burrito. Ensure that you create a slightly thick sauce.
2. For the filling, you will need to cook the ingredients well in a pan and ensure that the vegetables have browned on the outside.
3. To make the salad, toss the ingredients together.

389.Rosemary Squash With Cheese

Servings: 2
Cooking Time: 20 Minutes
Ingredients:
- 1 pound (454 g) butternut squash, cut into wedges

- 2 tablespoons olive oil
- 1 tablespoon dried rosemary
- Salt, to salt
- 1 cup crumbled goat cheese
- 1 tablespoon maple syrup

Directions:
1. Toss the squash wedges with the olive oil, rosemary, and salt in a large bowl until well coated.
2. Transfer the squash wedges to the air fryer basket, spreading them out in as even a layer as possible.
3. Put the air fryer basket on the baking pan and slide into Rack Position 2, select Air Fry, set temperature to 350ºF (180ºC), and set time to 20 minutes.
4. After 10 minutes, remove from the oven and flip the squash. Return the pan to the oven and continue cooking for 10 minutes.
5. When cooking is complete, the squash should be golden brown. Remove from the oven. Sprinkle the goat cheese on top and serve drizzled with the maple syrup.

390.Air Fried Kale Chips

Servings: 6
Cooking Time: 10 Minutes
Ingredients:
- ¼ tsp. Himalayan salt
- 3 tbsp. yeast
- Avocado oil
- 1 bunch of kale

Directions:
1. Preparing the Ingredients. Rinse kale and with paper towels, dry well.
2. Tear kale leaves into large pieces. Remember they will shrink as they cook so good sized pieces are necessary.
3. Place kale pieces in a bowl and spritz with avocado oil till shiny. Sprinkle with salt and yeast.
4. With your hands, toss kale leaves well to combine.
5. Air Frying. Pour half of the kale mixture into the air fryer oven, set temperature to 350°F, and set time to 5 minutes. Remove and repeat with another half of kale.
- **Nutrition Info:** CALORIES: 55; FAT: 10G; PROTEIN: 1G; SUGAR:0G

391.Cottage Cheese Fingers

Servings:x
Cooking Time:x
Ingredients:
- 2 tsp. salt
- 1 tsp. pepper powder
- 1 tsp. red chili powder
- 6 tbsp. corn flour
- 4 eggs
- 2 cups cottage cheese Oregano Fingers
- 2 cup dry breadcrumbs
- 2 tsp. oregano

- 1 ½ tbsp. ginger-garlic paste
- 4 tbsp. lemon juice

Directions:
1. Mix all the ingredients for the marinade and put the chicken Oregano Fingers inside and let it rest overnight.
2. Mix the breadcrumbs, oregano and red chili flakes well and place the marinated Oregano Fingers on this mixture. Cover it with plastic wrap and leave it till right before you serve to cook.
3. Pre heat the oven at 160 degrees Fahrenheit for 5 minutes. Place the Oregano Fingers in the fry basket and close it. Let them cook at the same temperature for another 15 minutes or so. Toss the Oregano Fingers well so that they are cooked uniformly.

392.Green Chili Flat Cakes

Servings:x
Cooking Time:x
Ingredients:
- 2 or 3 green chilies finely chopped
- 1 ½ tbsp. lemon juice
- Salt and pepper to taste
- 2 tbsp. garam masala
- 10–12 green chilies
- 3 tsp. ginger finely chopped
- 1-2 tbsp. fresh coriander leaves

Directions:
1. Mix the ingredients in a clean bowl and add water to it. Make sure that the paste is not too watery but is enough to apply to the green chilies.
2. Pre heat the oven at 160 degrees Fahrenheit for 5 minutes. Place the French Cuisine Galettes in the fry basket and let them cook for another 25 minutes at the same temperature. Keep rolling them over to get a uniform cook. Serve either with mint sauce or ketchup.

393.Garlicky Vermouth Mushrooms

Servings: 4
Cooking Time: 20 Minutes
Ingredients:
- 2 lb portobello mushrooms, sliced
- 2 tbsp vermouth
- ½ tsp garlic powder
- 1 tbsp olive oil
- 2 tsp herbs
- 1 tbsp duck fat, softened

Directions:
1. In a bowl, mix the duck fat, garlic powder, and herbs. Rub the mushrooms with the mixture and place them in a baking tray. Drizzle with vermouth and cook in your for 15 minutes on Bake function at 350 F. Serve.

394.Carrot & Chickpea Oat Balls With Cashews

Servings:4
Cooking Time: 30 Minutes
Ingredients:
- 2 tbsp olive oil
- 2 tbsp soy sauce
- 1 tbsp flax meal
- 2 cups canned chickpeas, drained
- ½ cup sweet onions, diced
- ½ cup carrots, grated
- ½ cup cashews, toasted
- Juice of 1 lemon
- ½ tsp turmeric
- 1 tsp cumin
- 1 tsp garlic powder
- 1 cup rolled oats

Directions:
1. Preheat on AirFry function to 380 F. Heat olive oil in a skillet and sauté onions and carrots for 5 minutes. Ground the oats and cashews in a food processor. Transfer to a bowl.
2. Place the chickpeas, lemon juice, and soy sauce in the food processor and process until smooth. Add them to the bowl as well. Mix in the onions and carrots.
3. Stir in the remaining ingredients until fully incorporated. Make balls out of the mixture. Place them in the frying basket and press Start. Cook for 12 minutes. Serve warm.

395.Garlic Stuffed Mushrooms

Servings:2
Cooking Time: 12 Minutes
Ingredients:
- 18 medium-sized white mushrooms
- 1 small onion, peeled and chopped
- 4 garlic cloves, peeled and minced
- 2 tablespoons olive oil
- 2 teaspoons cumin powder
- A pinch ground allspice
- Fine sea salt and freshly ground black pepper, to taste

Directions:
1. On a clean work surface, remove the mushroom stems. Using a spoon, scoop out the mushroom gills and discard.
2. Thoroughly combine the onion, garlic, olive oil, cumin powder, allspice, salt, and pepper in a mixing bowl. Stuff the mushrooms evenly with the mixture.
3. Place the stuffed mushrooms in the air fryer basket.
4. Put the air fryer basket on the baking pan and slide into Rack Position 2, select Roast, set temperature to 345ºF (174ºC) and set time to 12 minutes.
5. When cooking is complete, the mushroom should be browned.
6. Cool for 5 minutes before serving.

396.Vegan Meatloaf

Servings: 8
Cooking Time: 65 Minutes
Ingredients:
- Nonstick cooking spray
- 3 1/3 cups chickpeas, cooked
- 1 onion, chopped fine
- 2 stalks celery, chopped
- 2 carrots, chopped fine
- 2 cloves garlic diced fine
- 2 cups panko bread crumbs
- ½ cup almond milk, unsweetened
- 3 tbsp. vegan Worcestershire sauce
- 3 tbsp. soy sauce, divided
- 2 tbsp. olive oil
- 2 tbsp. flax seeds, ground
- ¼ cup + 2 tbsp. tomato paste
- 1 tsp liquid smoke
- ¼ tsp pepper
- 2 tbsp. maple syrup
- 2 tbsp. apple cider vinegar
- 1 tsp paprika

Directions:
1. Place rack in position Lightly spray a 9-inch loaf pan with cooking spray.
2. Place chickpeas, onion, celery, carrots, cloves, bread crumbs, milk, Worcestershire, 2 tablespoons soy sauce, oil, flax seeds, 2 tablespoons tomato paste, liquid smoke, and pepper in a food processor, you may need to do this in batches. Pulse until ingredients are combined but don't over blend. Transfer each batch to a large bowl, then mix together.
3. Set oven to bake on 375°F for 35 minutes.
4. Press mixture into the prepared pan. After the oven has preheated 5 minutes, add loaf pan to the oven and bake 30 minutes.
5. In a small bowl, whisk together remaining tomato paste and soy sauce, along with the syrup, vinegar, and paprika until smooth.
6. When the timer goes off, remove the loaf from the oven. Spoon glaze over top and bake another 20-25 minutes. Let cool 10 minutes before slicing and serving.
- **Nutrition Info:** Calories 623, Total Fat 11g, Saturated Fat 2g, Total Carbs 83g, Net Carbs 70g, Protein 23g, Sugar 18g, Fiber 13g, Sodium 501mg, Potassium 969mg, Phosphorus 317mg

397.Stuffed Portobello Mushrooms With Vegetables

Servings:4
Cooking Time: 8 Minutes
Ingredients:
- 4 portobello mushrooms, stem removed
- 1 tablespoon olive oil
- 1 tomato, diced
- ½ green bell pepper, diced
- ½ small red onion, diced
- ½ teaspoon garlic powder

- Salt and black pepper, to taste
- ½ cup grated Mozzarella cheese

Directions:
1. Using a spoon to scoop out the gills of the mushrooms and discard them. Brush the mushrooms with the olive oil.
2. In a mixing bowl, stir together the remaining ingredients except the Mozzarella cheese. Using a spoon to stuff each mushroom with the filling and scatter the Mozzarella cheese on top.
3. Arrange the mushrooms in the air fryer basket.
4. Put the air fryer basket on the baking pan and slide into Rack Position 2, select Roast, set temperature to 330ºF (166ºC) and set time to 8 minutes.
5. When cooking is complete, the cheese should be melted.
6. Serve warm.

398.Jalapeño & Tomato Gratin

Servings: 4
Cooking Time: 35 Minutes
Ingredients:
- 1 (16 oz) can jalapeño peppers
- 1 cup cheddar cheese, shredded
- 1 cup Monterey Jack cheese, shredded
- 2 tbsp all-purpose flour
- 2 large eggs, beaten
- ½ cup milk
- 1 can tomato sauce

Directions:
1. Preheat on Air Fry function to 380 F. Arrange the jalapeño peppers on the greased Air Fryer baking pan and top with half of the cheese.
2. In a medium bowl, combine the eggs, milk, and flour and pour the mixture over the chilies. Cook in your for 20 minutes. Take out the chilies and pour the tomato sauce over them. Return and cook for 15 more minutes. Sprinkle with the remaining cheese and serve.

399.Cheese And Bean Enchiladas

Servings:x
Cooking Time:x
Ingredients:
- A pinch of salt or to taste
- A few red chili flakes to sprinkle
- 1 tsp. of oregano
- 2 tbsp. oil
- 2 tsp. chopped garlic
- 2 onions chopped finely
- 2 capsicums chopped finely
- 2 cups of readymade baked beans
- Flour tortillas (as many as required)
- 4 tbsp. of olive oil
- A pinch of salt
- 1 tsp. oregano
- ½ tsp. pepper
- 1 ½ tsp. red chili flakes or to taste
- 1 tbsp. of finely chopped jalapenos
- 1 cup grated pizza cheese (mix mozzarella and cheddar cheeses)
- 1 ½ tsp. of garlic that has been chopped
- 1 ½ cups of readymade tomato puree
- 3 medium tomatoes. Puree them in a mixer
- 1 tsp. of sugar
- A few drops of Tabasco sauce
- 1 cup crumbled or roughly mashed cottage cheese (cottage cheese)
- 1 cup grated cheddar cheese

Directions:
1. Prepare the flour tortillas. Now move on to making the red sauce. In a pan, pour around 2 tbsp. of oil and heat. Add some garlic. Add the rest of the ingredients mentioned under the heading "For the sauce".
2. Keep stirring. Cook until the sauce reduces and becomes thick. For the filling, heat one tbsp. of oil in another pan. Add onions and garlic and cook until the onions are caramelized or attain a golden-brown color. Add the rest of the ingredients required for the filling and cook for two to three minutes.
3. Take the pan off the flame and grate some cheese over the sauce. Mix it well and let it sit for a while. Let us start assembling the dish. Take a tortilla and spread some of the sauce on the surface. Now place the filling at the center in a line. Roll up the tortilla carefully. Do the same for all the tortillas. Now place all the tortillas in a tray and sprinkle them with grated cheese. Cover this with an aluminum foil. Pre heat the oven at 160° C for 4-5 minutes. Open the basket and place the tray inside.
4. Keep the fryer at the same temperature for another 15 minutes. Turn the tortillas over in between to get a uniform cook.

SNACKS AND DESSERTS RECIPES

400.Cheese Garlic Dip

Servings: 12
Cooking Time: 20 Minutes
Ingredients:
- 4 garlic cloves, minced
- 5 oz Asiago cheese, shredded
- 1 cup sour cream
- 1 cup mozzarella cheese, shredded
- 8 oz cream cheese, softened

Directions:
1. Fit the oven with the rack in position
2. Add all ingredients into the mixing bowl and mix until well combined.
3. Pour mixture into the baking dish.
4. Set to bake at 350 F for 25 minutes. After 5 minutes place the baking dish in the preheated oven.
5. Serve and enjoy.
- **Nutrition Info:** Calories 157 Fat 14.4 g Carbohydrates 1.7 g Sugar 0.1 g Protein 5.7 g Cholesterol 41 mg

401.Vegetables Balls

Servings: 6
Cooking Time: 10 Minutes
Ingredients:
- 2 cups cauliflower florets
- 1 tsp paprika
- 1 tsp chives
- 2 tsp garlic
- 1 medium Parsnip
- 1 medium carrot
- 1 cup breadcrumbs
- 1/2 cup desiccated coconut
- 2 tsp oregano
- 1 tsp mixed spice
- 1/2 cup sweet potato
- Pepper
- Salt

Directions:
1. Fit the oven with the rack in position
2. Add all vegetables into the food processor and process until resemble breadcrumbs.
3. Add process vegetables into the mixing bowl.
4. Add all remaining ingredients into the bowl and mix well until combine.
5. Make small balls from the mixture and place in the air fryer basket then place an air fryer basket in the baking pan.
6. Place a baking pan on the oven rack. Set to air fry at 400 F for 10 minutes.
7. Serve and enjoy.
- **Nutrition Info:** Calories 131 Fat 2.7 g Carbohydrates 23.6 g Sugar 4.5 g Protein 4 g Cholesterol 0 mg

402.Air Fried Lemon-pepper Wings

Servings:10
Cooking Time: 24 Minutes
Ingredients:
- 2 pounds (907 g) chicken wings
- 4½ teaspoons salt-free lemon pepper seasoning
- 1½ teaspoons baking powder
- 1½ teaspoons kosher salt

Directions:
1. In a large bowl, toss together all the ingredients until well coated. Place the wings in the air fryer basket, making sure they don't crowd each other too much.
2. Put the air fryer basket on the baking pan and slide into Rack Position 2, select Air Fry, set temperature to 375ºF (190ºC) and set time to 24 minutes.
3. After 12 minutes, remove from the oven. Use tongs to turn the wings over. Return to the oven to continue cooking.
4. When cooking is complete, the wings should be dark golden brown and a bit charred in places. Remove from the oven and let rest for 5 minutes before serving.

403.Glazed Lemon Cupcakes

Servings: 6
Cooking Time: 30 Minutes
Ingredients:
- 1 cup flour
- ½ cup sugar
- 1 small egg
- 1 tsp lemon zest
- ¾ tsp baking powder
- ¼ tsp baking soda
- ½ tsp salt
- 2 tbsp vegetable oil
- ½ cup milk
- ½ tsp vanilla extract
- Glaze:
- ½ cup powdered sugar
- 2 tsp lemon juice

Directions:
1. Preheat on Bake function to 350 F. In a bowl, combine dry ingredients. In another bowl, whisk together the wet ingredients. Gently combine the two mixtures. Divide the batter between 6 greased muffin tins. Place them in the baking tray and cook for 13-16 minutes.
2. Meanwhile, whisk the powdered sugar with the lemon juice. Spread the glaze over the muffins.

404.Chocolate And Coconut Cake

Servings:6

Cooking Time: 15 Minutes
Ingredients:
- ½ cup unsweetened chocolate, chopped
- ½ stick butter, at room temperature
- 1 tablespoon liquid stevia
- 1½ cups coconut flour
- 2 eggs, whisked
- ½ teaspoon vanilla extract
- A pinch of fine sea salt
- Cooking spray

Directions:
1. Place the chocolate, butter, and stevia in a microwave-safe bowl. Microwave for about 30 seconds until melted.
2. Let the chocolate mixture cool for 5 to 10 minutes.
3. Add the remaining ingredients to the bowl of chocolate mixture and whisk to incorporate.
4. Lightly spray the baking pan with cooking spray.
5. Scrape the chocolate mixture into the prepared baking pan.
6. Slide the baking pan into Rack Position 1, select Convection Bake, set temperature to 330ºF (166ºC), and set time to 15 minutes.
7. When cooking is complete, the top should spring back lightly when gently pressed with your fingers.
8. Let the cake cool for 5 minutes and serve.

405.Spicy Snack Mix

Servings:x
Cooking Time:x
Ingredients:
- ½ cup butter, melted
- 3 tablespoons Worcestershire sauce
- 2 teaspoons dried Italian seasoning
- ½ teaspoon crushed red pepper flakes
- 2 cups salted mixed nuts
- 2 cups small pretzels
- 2 cups potato sticks
- teaspoon white pepper

Directions:
1. Preheat oven to 300ºF. Pour nuts, pretzels, and potato sticks onto two cookie sheets with sides. In small saucepan, combine melted butter with remaining ingredients. Drizzle over the nut mixture. Toss to coat. Bake at 300ºF for 20 to 25 minutes, or until mixture is glazed and fragrant, stirring once during baking.
2. Cool snack mix and pack into zipper-lock bags. Label bags and freeze.
3. To thaw and reheat: Thaw at room temperature for 1 to 3 hours. Spread on baking sheet and reheat in 300ºF oven for 5 to 8 minutes, until crisp.

406.Healthy Carrot Fries

Servings: 4
Cooking Time: 25 Minutes
Ingredients:
- 4 medium carrots, peel and cut into fries shape
- 1/2 tbsp paprika
- 1 1/2 tbsp olive oil
- 1/2 tsp salt

Directions:
1. Fit the oven with the rack in position
2. Add carrots, paprika, oil, and salt into the mixing bowl and toss well.
3. Transfer carrot fries in baking pan.
4. Set to bake at 450 F for 30 minutes. After 5 minutes place the baking pan in the preheated oven.
5. Serve and enjoy.
- **Nutrition Info:** Calories 73 Fat 5.4 g Carbohydrates 6.5 g Sugar 3.1 g Protein 0.6 g Cholesterol 0 mg

407.Tangy Fried Pickle Spears

Servings:6
Cooking Time: 15 Minutes
Ingredients:
- 2 jars sweet and sour pickle spears, patted dry
- 2 medium-sized eggs
- $^1/_3$ cup milk
- 1 teaspoon garlic powder
- 1 teaspoon sea salt
- ½ teaspoon shallot powder
- $^1/_3$ teaspoon chili powder
- $^1/_3$ cup all-purpose flour
- Cooking spray

Directions:
1. Spritz the air fryer basket with cooking spray.
2. In a bowl, beat together the eggs with milk. In another bowl, combine garlic powder, sea salt, shallot powder, chili powder and all-purpose flour until well blended.
3. One by one, roll the pickle spears in the powder mixture, then dredge them in the egg mixture. Dip them in the powder mixture a second time for additional coating.
4. Place the coated pickles in the basket.
5. Put the air fryer basket on the baking pan and slide into Rack Position 2, select Air Fry, set temperature to 385ºF (196ºC), and set time to 15 minutes.
6. Stir the pickles halfway through the cooking time.
7. When cooking is complete, they should be golden and crispy. Transfer to a plate and let cool for 5 minutes before serving.

408.Fudge Pie

Servings:8
Cooking Time: 26 Minutes
Ingredients:
- 1½ cups sugar
- ½ cup self-rising flour
- $^1/_3$ cup unsweetened cocoa powder
- 3 large eggs, beaten
- 12 tablespoons (1½ sticks) butter, melted
- 1½ teaspoons vanilla extract
- 1 (9-inch) unbaked pie crust
- ¼ cup confectioners' sugar (optional)

Directions:
1. Thoroughly combine the sugar, flour, and cocoa powder in a medium bowl. Add the beaten eggs and butter and whisk to combine. Stir in the vanilla.
2. Pour the prepared filling into the pie crust and transfer to the baking pan.
3. Slide the baking pan into Rack Position 1, select Convection Bake, set temperature to 350ºF (180ºC), and set time to 26 minutes.
4. When cooking is complete, the pie should be set.
5. Allow the pie to cool for 5 minutes. Sprinkle with the confectioners' sugar, if desired. Serve warm.

409.Air Fryer Pepperoni Chips

Servings: 6
Cooking Time: 8 Minutes
Ingredients:
- 6 oz pepperoni slices

Directions:
1. Fit the oven with the rack in position 2.
2. Place pepperoni slices in an air fryer basket then place an air fryer basket in baking pan.
3. Place a baking pan on the oven rack. Set to air fry at 360 F for 8 minutes.
4. Serve and enjoy.
- **Nutrition Info:** Calories 51 Fat 1 g Carbohydrates 2 g Sugar 0 g Protein 9.1 g Cholesterol 0 mg

410.Famous New York Cheesecake

Servings: 8
Cooking Time: 15 Minutes
Ingredients:
- 1 ½ cups almond flour
- 3 ounces swerve
- 1/2 stick butter, melted
- 20 ounces full-fat cream cheese
- 1/2 cup heavy cream
- 1 ¼ cups granulated swerve
- 3 eggs, at room temperature
- 1 tablespoon vanilla essence
- 1 teaspoon grated lemon zest

Directions:
1. Coat the sides and bottom of a baking pan with a little flour.
2. In a mixing bowl, combine the almond flour and swerve. Add the melted butter and mix until your mixture looks like breadcrumbs.
3. Press the mixture into the bottom of the prepared pan to form an even layer. Bake at 330 degrees F for 7 minutes until golden brown. Allow it to cool completely on a wire rack.
4. Meanwhile, in a mixer fitted with the paddle attachment, prepare the filling by mixing the soft cheese, heavy cream, and granulated swerve; beat until creamy and fluffy.
5. Crack the eggs into the mixing bowl, one at a time; add the vanilla and lemon zest and continue to mix until fully combined.
6. Pour the prepared topping over the cooled crust and spread evenly.
7. Bake in the preheated Air Fryer at 330 degrees F for 25 to 30 minutes; leave it in the Air Fryer to keep warm for another 30 minutes.
8. Cover your cheesecake with plastic wrap. Place in your refrigerator and allow it to cool at least 6 hours or overnight. Serve well chilled.
- **Nutrition Info:** 245 Calories; 22g Fat; 5g Carbs; 8g Protein; 1g Sugars; 5g Fiber

411.Blackberry And Peach Cobbler

Servings:4
Cooking Time: 20 Minutes
Ingredients:
- Filling:
- 1 (6-ounce / 170-g) package blackberries
- 1½ cups chopped peaches, cut into ½-inch thick slices
- 2 teaspoons arrowroot or cornstarch
- 2 tablespoons coconut sugar
- 1 teaspoon lemon juice
- Topping:
- 2 tablespoons sunflower oil
- 1 tablespoon maple syrup
- 1 teaspoon vanilla
- 3 tablespoons coconut sugar
- ½ cup rolled oats
- $^1/_3$ cup whole-wheat pastry flour
- 1 teaspoon cinnamon
- ¼ teaspoon nutmeg
- ⅛ teaspoon sea salt
- Make the Filling:

Directions:
1. Combine the blackberries, peaches, arrowroot, coconut sugar, and lemon juice in the baking pan.
2. Using a rubber spatula, stir until well incorporated. Set aside.

3. Make the Topping:
4. Combine the oil, maple syrup, and vanilla in a mixing bowl and stir well. Whisk in the remaining ingredients. Spread this mixture evenly over the filling.
5. Slide the baking pan into Rack Position 1, select Convection Bake, set temperature to 320ºF (160ºC), and set time to 20 minutes.
6. When cooked, the topping should be crispy and golden brown. Serve warm

412.Delicious Cauliflower Hummus

Servings: 8
Cooking Time: 35 Minutes
Ingredients:
- 1 cauliflower head, cut into florets
- 3 tbsp olive oil
- 1/2 tsp ground cumin
- 2 tbsp fresh lemon juice
- 1/3 cup tahini
- 1 tsp garlic, chopped
- Pepper
- Salt

Directions:
1. Fit the oven with the rack in position
2. Spread cauliflower florets in baking pan.
3. Set to bake at 400 F for 40 minutes. After 5 minutes place the baking dish in the preheated oven.
4. Transfer roasted cauliflower into the food processor along with remaining ingredients and process until smooth.
5. Serve and enjoy.
- **Nutrition Info:** Calories 115 Fat 10.7 g Carbohydrates 4.2 g Sugar 0.9 g Protein 2.4 g Cholesterol 0 mg

413.Bacon Wrapped Brie

Servings: 8
Cooking Time: 15 Minutes
Ingredients:
- 1 (8-oz.round Brie
- 4 slices sugar-free bacon.

Directions:
1. Place two slices of bacon to form an X. Place the third slice of bacon horizontally across the center of the X. Place the fourth slice of bacon vertically across the X. It should look like a plus sign (+on top of an X. Place the Brie in the center of the bacon
2. Wrap the bacon around the Brie, securing with a few toothpicks. Cut a piece of parchment to fit your air fryer basket and place the bacon-wrapped Brie on top. Place inside the air fryer basket.
3. Adjust the temperature to 400 Degrees F and set the timer for 10 minutes. When 3 minutes remain on the timer, carefully flip Brie

4. When cooked, bacon will be crispy and cheese will be soft and melty. To serve; cut into eight slices.
- **Nutrition Info:** Calories: 116; Protein: 7g; Fiber: 0g; Fat: 9g; Carbs: 2g

414.Mushroom And Spinach calzones

Servings:4
Cooking Time: 26 To 27 Minutes
Ingredients:
- 2 tablespoons olive oil
- 1 onion, chopped
- 2 garlic cloves, minced
- ¼ cup chopped mushrooms
- 1 pound (454 g) spinach, chopped
- 1 tablespoon Italian seasoning
- ½ teaspoon oregano
- Salt and black pepper, to taste
- 1½ cups marinara sauce
- 1 cup ricotta cheese, crumbled
- 1 (13-ounce / 369-g) pizza crust
- Cooking spray

Directions:
1. Make the Filling:
2. Heat the olive oil in a pan over medium heat until shimmering.
3. Add the onion, garlic, and mushrooms and sauté for 4 minutes, or until softened.
4. Stir in the spinach and sauté for 2 to 3 minutes, or until the spinach is wilted. Sprinkle with the Italian seasoning, oregano, salt, and pepper and mix well.
5. Add the marinara sauce and cook for about 5 minutes, stirring occasionally, or until the sauce is thickened.
6. Remove the pan from the heat and stir in the ricotta cheese. Set aside.
7. Make the Calzones:
8. Spritz the air fryer basket with cooking spray. Set aside.
9. Roll the pizza crust out with a rolling pin on a lightly floured work surface, then cut it into 4 rectangles.
10. Spoon ¼ of the filling into each rectangle and fold in half. Crimp the edges with a fork to seal. Mist them with cooking spray. Transfer the calzones to the basket.
11. Put the air fryer basket on the baking pan and slide into Rack Position 2, select Air Fry, set temperature to 375ºF (190ºC), and set time to 15 minutes.
12. Flip the calzones halfway through the cooking time.
13. When cooking is complete, the calzones should be golden brown and crisp. Transfer the calzones to a paper towel-lined plate and serve.

415.Lemon-raspberry Muffins

Servings:6
Cooking Time: 15 Minutes
Ingredients:
- 2 cups almond flour
- ¾ cup Swerve
- 1¼ teaspoons baking powder
- $^1/_3$ teaspoon ground allspice
- $^1/_3$ teaspoon ground anise star
- ½ teaspoon grated lemon zest
- ¼ teaspoon salt
- 2 eggs
- 1 cup sour cream
- ½ cup coconut oil
- ½ cup raspberries

Directions:
1. Line a muffin pan with 6 paper liners.
2. In a mixing bowl, mix the almond flour, Swerve, baking powder, allspice, anise, lemon zest, and salt.
3. In another mixing bowl, beat the eggs, sour cream, and coconut oil until well mixed. Add the egg mixture to the flour mixture and stir to combine. Mix in the raspberries.
4. Scrape the batter into the prepared muffin cups, filling each about three-quarters full.
5. Put the muffin pan into Rack Position 1, select Convection Bake, set temperature to 345ºF (174ºC), and set time to 15 minutes.
6. When cooking is complete, the tops should be golden and a toothpick inserted in the middle should come out clean.
7. Allow the muffins to cool for 10 minutes in the muffin pan before removing and serving.

416.Bacon Cheese Jalapeno Poppers

Servings: 5
Cooking Time: 5 Minutes
Ingredients:
- 10 fresh jalapeno peppers, cut in half and remove seeds
- 1/4 cup cheddar cheese, shredded
- 5 oz cream cheese, softened
- ¼ tsp paprika
- 2 bacon slices, cooked and crumbled

Directions:
1. Fit the oven with the rack in position 2.
2. In a bowl, mix bacon, cream cheese, paprika and cheddar cheese.
3. Stuff cheese mixture into each jalapeno.
4. Place stuffed jalapeno halved in air fryer basket then place air fryer basket in baking pan.
5. Place a baking pan on the oven rack. Set to air fry at 370 F for 5 minutes.
6. Serve and enjoy.
- **Nutrition Info:** Calories 176 Fat 15.7 g Carbohydrates 3.2 g Sugar 1 g Protein 6.2 g Cholesterol 47 mg

417.Delicious Banana Cake

Servings: 8
Cooking Time: 40 Minutes
Ingredients:
- 2 large eggs, beaten
- 1 tsp baking powder
- 1 1/2 cup sugar, granulated
- 1 tsp vanilla extract
- 1/2 cup butter
- 1 cup milk
- 2 cups all-purpose flour
- 2 bananas, mashed
- 1 tsp baking soda

Directions:
1. Fit the oven with the rack in position
2. In a mixing bowl, beat together sugar and butter until creamy. Add beaten eggs and mix well.
3. Add milk, vanilla extract, baking soda, baking powder, flour, and mashed bananas into the mixture and beat for 2 minutes. Mix well.
4. Pour batter into the greased baking dish.
5. Set to bake at 350 F for 45 minutes. After 5 minutes place the baking dish in the preheated oven.
6. Slices and serve.
- **Nutrition Info:** Calories 418 Fat 13.8 g Carbohydrates 80 g Sugar 42.7 g Protein 6.2 g Cholesterol 80 mg

418.Blueberry Lemon Muffins

Servings: 12
Cooking Time: 10 Minutes
Ingredients:
- 1 tsp. vanilla
- Juice and zest of 1 lemon
- 2 eggs
- 1 C. blueberries
- ½ C. cream
- ¼ C. avocado oil
- ½ C. monk fruit
- 2 ½ C. almond flour

Directions:
1. Preparing the Ingredients. Mix monk fruit and flour together.
2. In another bowl, mix vanilla, egg, lemon juice, and cream together. Add mixtures together and blend well.
3. Spoon batter into cupcake holders.
4. Air Frying. Place in the air fryer oven. Bake 10 minutes at 320 degrees, checking at 6 minutes to ensure you don't overbake them.
- **Nutrition Info:** CALORIES: 317; FAT:11G; PROTEIN:3G; SUGAR:5G

419.Moist Chocolate Brownies

Servings: 16
Cooking Time: 20 Minutes

Ingredients:
- 1 1/3 cups all-purpose flour
- 1/2 tsp baking powder
- 1/3 cup cocoa powder
- 1 cup of sugar
- 1/2 tsp vanilla
- 1/2 cup vegetable oil
- 1/2 cup water
- 1/2 tsp salt

Directions:
1. Fit the oven with the rack in position
2. In a large mixing bowl, mix together flour, baking powder, cocoa powder, sugar, and salt.
3. In a small bowl, whisk together oil, water, and vanilla.
4. Pour oil mixture into the flour mixture and mix until well combined.
5. Pour batter into the greased baking dish.
6. Set to bake at 350 F for 25 minutes. After 5 minutes place the baking dish in the preheated oven.
7. Slice and serve.
- **Nutrition Info:** Calories 150 Fat 7.1 g Carbohydrates 21.5 g Sugar 12.6 g Protein 1.4 g Cholesterol 0 mg

420.Vanilla Banana Brownies

Servings: 12
Cooking Time: 20 Minutes
Ingredients:
- 1 egg
- 1 cup all-purpose flour
- 4 oz white chocolate
- 1/4 cup butter
- 1 tsp vanilla extract
- 1/2 cup granulated sugar
- 2 medium bananas, mashed
- 1/4 tsp salt

Directions:
1. Fit the oven with the rack in position
2. Add white chocolate and butter in a microwave-safe bowl and microwave for 30 seconds. Stir until melted.
3. Stir in sugar. Add mashed bananas, eggs, vanilla, and salt and mix until combined.
4. Add flour and mix until just combined.
5. Pour batter into the greased baking dish.
6. Set to bake at 350 F for 25 minutes. After 5 minutes place the baking dish in the preheated oven.
7. Slice and serve.
- **Nutrition Info:** Calories 178 Fat 7.4 g Carbohydrates 26.4 g Sugar 16.4 g Protein 2.3 g Cholesterol 26 mg

421.Date Bread

Servings: 10
Cooking Time: 20 Minutes

Ingredients:
- ¼ cup of butter
- 1½ cups of flour
- 1 teaspoon of baking powder
- ½ teaspoon of salt
- 2½ cup of dates, pitted and chopped
- 1 cup of hot water
- ½ cup of brown sugar
- 1 teaspoon of baking soda
- 1 egg

Directions:
1. Set the Instant Vortex on Air fryer to 340 degrees F for 20 minutes. Combine dates with butter and hot water in a bowl. Strain together brown sugar, flour, baking powder, baking soda, and salt in another bowl. Fold the brown sugar mixture and egg in the date's mixture. Place the mixture on the cooking tray. Insert the cooking tray in the Vortex when it displays "Add Food". Flip the sides when it displays "Turn Food". Remove from the oven when cooking time is complete. Slice into desired pieces to serve.
- **Nutrition Info:** Calories: 269 Cal Total Fat: 5.4 g Saturated Fat: 0 g Cholesterol: 0 mg Sodium: 0 mg Total Carbs: 55.1 g Fiber: 0 g Sugar: 0 g Protein: 3.6 g

422.Plum Cream(2)

Servings: 4
Cooking Time: 15 Minutes
Ingredients:
- 1 lb. plums, pitted and chopped.
- 1 ½ cups heavy cream
- ¼ cup swerve
- 1 tbsp. lemon juice

Directions:
1. Take a bowl and mix all the ingredients and whisk really well.
2. Divide this into 4 ramekins, put them in the air fryer and cook at 340°F for 20 minutes. Serve cold
- **Nutrition Info:** Calories: 171; Fat: 4g; Fiber: 2g; Carbs: 4g; Protein: 4g

423.Cinnamon Fried Bananas

Servings: 2-3
Cooking Time: 10 Minutes
Ingredients:
- 1 C. panko breadcrumbs
- 3 tbsp. cinnamon
- ½ C. almond flour
- 3 egg whites
- 8 ripe bananas
- 3 tbsp. vegan coconut oil

Directions:
1. Preparing the Ingredients. Heat coconut oil and add breadcrumbs. Mix around 2-3 minutes until golden. Pour into bowl.

2. Peel and cut bananas in half. Roll each bananas half into flour, eggs, and crumb mixture.
3. Air Frying. Place into the air fryer oven. Cook 10 minutes at 280 degrees.
4. A great addition to a healthy banana split!
- **Nutrition Info:** CALORIES: 219; FAT:10G; PROTEIN:3G; SUGAR:5G

424.Shrimp Cheese Quiches

Servings:x
Cooking Time:x
Ingredients:
- 1 (6-ounce) can tiny shrimp, drained
- ½ teaspoon dried marjoram leaves
- ½ teaspoon salt
- ½ teaspoon pepper
- ¾ cup shredded Havarti cheese
- 2 9-inch Pie Crusts
- ½ cup chopped leek, rinsed
- 1 tablespoon olive oil
- 2 eggs
- ½ cup cream

Directions:
1. Using a 2-inch cookie cutter, cut 36 rounds from pie crusts. Place each in a 1¾-inch mini muffin cup, pressing to bottom and sides. Set aside.
2. Sauté leek in olive oil until tender. Beat eggs with cream in medium bowl. Add drained shrimp, cooked leek, marjoram, salt, and pepper, and mix well.
3. Sprinkle 1 teaspoon cheese into each muffin cup and fill cups with shrimp mixture. Bake at 375ºF for 15 to 18 minutes or until pastry is golden and filling is set. Cool in refrigerator until cold, then freeze.
4. Freeze in single layer on baking sheet. When frozen solid, pack in rigid containers, using waxed paper to separate layers. Label and freeze.
5. To reheat: Place frozen quiches on baking sheet and bake at 375ºF for 8 to 11 minutes or until hot.

425.Almond Flour Blackberry Muffins

Servings:8
Cooking Time: 12 Minutes
Ingredients:
- ½ cup fresh blackberries
- Dry Ingredients:
- 1½ cups almond flour
- 1 teaspoon baking powder
- ½ teaspoon baking soda
- ½ cup Swerve
- ¼ teaspoon kosher salt
- Wet Ingredients:
- 2 eggs
- ¼ cup coconut oil, melted
- ½ cup milk
- ½ teaspoon vanilla paste

Directions:
1. Line an 8-cup muffin tin with paper liners.
2. Thoroughly combine the almond flour, baking powder, baking soda, Swerve, and salt in a mixing bowl.
3. Whisk together the eggs, coconut oil, milk, and vanilla in a separate mixing bowl until smooth.
4. Add the wet mixture to the dry and fold in the blackberries. Stir with a spatula just until well incorporated.
5. Spoon the batter into the prepared muffin cups, filling each about three-quarters full.
6. Put the muffin tin into Rack Position 1, select Convection Bake, set temperature to 350ºF (180ºC), and set time to 12 minutes.
7. When done, the tops should be golden and a toothpick inserted in the middle should come out clean.
8. Allow the muffins to cool in the muffin tin for 10 minutes before removing and serving

426.Rosemary Roasted Almonds

Servings: 12
Cooking Time: 20 Minutes
Ingredients:
- 2 1/2 cups almonds
- 1 tbsp fresh rosemary, chopped
- 1 tbsp olive oil
- 2 ½ tbsp maple syrup
- 1/4 tsp cayenne
- 1/4 tsp ground coriander
- 1/4 tsp cumin
- 1/4 tsp chili powder
- Pinch of salt

Directions:
1. Fit the oven with the rack in position
2. Spray a baking tray with cooking spray and set aside.
3. In a mixing bowl, whisk together oil, cayenne, coriander, cumin, chili powder, rosemary, maple syrup, and salt.
4. Add almond and stir to coat.
5. Spread almonds in baking pan.
6. Set to bake at 325 F for 20 minutes. After 5 minutes place the baking pan in the preheated oven.
7. Serve and enjoy.
- **Nutrition Info:** Calories 137 Fat 11.2 g Carbohydrates 7.3 g Sugar 3.3 g Protein 4.2 g Cholesterol 0 mg

427.Tuna Melts With Scallions

Servings:6
Cooking Time: 6 Minutes
Ingredients:

- 2 (5- to 6-ounce / 142- to 170-g) cans oil-packed tuna, drained
- 1 large scallion, chopped
- 1 small stalk celery, chopped
- $^1/_3$ cup mayonnaise
- 1 tablespoon chopped fresh dill
- 1 tablespoon capers, drained
- ¼ teaspoon celery salt
- 12 slices cocktail rye bread
- 2 tablespoons butter, melted
- 6 slices sharp Cheddar cheese

Directions:
1. In a medium bowl, stir together the tuna, scallion, celery, mayonnaise, dill, capers and celery salt.
2. Brush one side of the bread slices with the butter. Arrange the bread slices in the baking pan, buttered-side down. Scoop a heaping tablespoon of the tuna mixture on each slice of bread, spreading it out evenly to the edges.
3. Cut the cheese slices to fit the dimensions of the bread and place a cheese slice on each piece.
4. Slide the baking pan into Rack Position 2, select Roast, set temperature to 375ºF (190ºC) and set time to 6 minutes.
5. After 4 minutes, remove from the oven and check the tuna melts. The tuna melts are done when the cheese has melted and the tuna is heated through. If needed, continue cooking.
6. When cooking is complete, remove from the oven. Use a spatula to transfer the tuna melts to a clean work surface and slice each one in half diagonally. Serve warm.

428.Apple Chips

Servings: 4
Cooking Time: 8 Minutes
Ingredients:
- 4 large sliced apples
- ¼ tsp. apple cider vinegar
- ½ tsp. olive oil
- 2 tsps. sugar

Directions:
1. In a bowl add chips with vinegar and sugar, toss to combine.
2. Preheat Air Fryer to a temperature of 400°F (200°C).
3. Place chips into fryer basket, drizzle with a ½ tsp. of olive oil and cook for 8 minutes.
4. Serve!
- **Nutrition Info:** Calories: 126 Protein: 0.58 g Fat: 0.95 g Carbohydrates: 32.08 g

429.Crispy Coated Peaches

Servings: 1
Cooking Time: 10 Minutes
Ingredients:
- Nonstick cooking spray
- ¼ cup panko bread crumbs
- 1 tsp sugar
- ¼ tsp cinnamon
- 1/8 tsp salt
- 2 egg whites
- ¼ tsp vanilla
- 1 peach, pitted and cut in ½-inch thick slices

Directions:
1. Place baking pan in position 2. Lightly spray fryer basket with cooking spray.
2. In a medium bowl, combine bread crumbs, sugar, cinnamon, and salt.
3. In a separate medium bowl, whisk together egg whites and vanilla.
4. Add peaches to egg mixture and stir to coat. One at a time, shake off excess egg and coat with crumb mixture. Place in basket in a single layer.
5. Place basket on the baking pan and set oven to air fry on 390°F for 8 minutes. Cook until golden brown and crispy. Serve immediately topped with yogurt or whip cream.
- **Nutrition Info:** Calories 222, Total Fat 2g, Saturated Fat 0g, Total Carbs 39g, Net Carbs 35g, Protein 12g, Sugar 19g, Fiber 4g, Sodium 617mg, Potassium 450mg, Phosphorus 85mg

430.Crispy Asian Green Beans

Servings:x
Cooking Time:x
Ingredients:
- ½ tsp toasted sesame oil
- 1 tsp peanut oil
- 1-pound green beans, ends trimmed
- 2 cloves garlics, minced
- Coarse sea salt, to taste

Directions:
1. Heat oven on medium heat and add peanut oil until it shimmers.
2. Add garlic and cook about 30 seconds.
3. Add green beans and salt to the pan and roast until golden brown. I
4. At the last minute of cooking, drizzle on toasted sesame oil.

431.Cheese And Ham Stuffed Baby Bella

Servings:8
Cooking Time: 12 Minutes
Ingredients:
- 4 ounces (113 g) Mozzarella cheese, cut into pieces
- ½ cup diced ham
- 2 green onions, chopped
- 2 tablespoons bread crumbs

- ½ teaspoon garlic powder
- ¼ teaspoon ground oregano
- ¼ teaspoon ground black pepper
- 1 to 2 teaspoons olive oil
- 16 fresh Baby Bella mushrooms, stemmed removed

Directions:
1. Process the cheese, ham, green onions, bread crumbs, garlic powder, oregano, and pepper in a food processor until finely chopped.
2. With the food processor running, slowly drizzle in 1 to 2 teaspoons olive oil until a thick paste has formed. Transfer the mixture to a bowl.
3. Evenly divide the mixture into the mushroom caps and lightly press down the mixture.
4. Lay the mushrooms in the air fryer basket in a single layer.
5. Put the air fryer basket on the baking pan and slide into Rack Position 2, select Roast, set temperature to 390ºF (199ºC), and set time to 12 minutes.
6. When cooking is complete, the mushrooms should be lightly browned and tender. Remove from the oven to a plate. Let the mushrooms cool for 5 minutes and serve warm.

432.Oaty Chocolate Chip Cookies

Servings: 4 Dozen (1-by-1½-inch) Bars
Cooking Time: 20 Minutes
Ingredients:
- 1 cup unsalted butter, at room temperature
- 1 cup dark brown sugar
- ½ cup granulated sugar
- 2 large eggs
- 1 tablespoon vanilla extract
- Pinch salt
- 2 cups old-fashioned rolled oats
- 1½ cups all-purpose flour
- 1 teaspoon baking powder
- 1 teaspoon baking soda
- 2 cups chocolate chips

Directions:
1. Stir together the butter, brown sugar, and granulated sugar in a large mixing bowl until smooth and light in color.
2. Crack the eggs into the bowl, one at a time, mixing after each addition. Stir in the vanilla and salt.
3. Mix together the oats, flour, baking powder, and baking soda in a separate bowl. Add the mixture to the butter mixture and stir until mixed. Stir in the chocolate chips.
4. Spread the dough into the baking pan in an even layer.

5. Slide the baking pan into Rack Position 1, select Convection Bake, set temperature to 350ºF (180ºC), and set time to 20 minutes.
6. After 15 minutes, check the cookie. Continue cooking for a total of 18 to 20 minutes or until golden brown.
7. When cooking is complete, remove from the oven and allow to cool completely before slicing and serving.

433.Air Fryer Biscuit Donuts

Servings: 4
Cooking Time: 5 Minutes
Ingredients:
- Coconut oil
- 1 can of biscuit dough, premade
- 1/2 cup of white sugar
- 1/2 cup of powdered sugar
- 2 tablespoons of melted butter
- 2 teaspoons of cinnamon

Directions:
1. Set the Instant Vortex on Air fryer to 350 degrees F for 5 minutes. Cut the dough with the biscuit cutter. Brush the coconut oil on the cooking tray and place the biscuits on it. Insert the cooking tray in the Vortex when it displays "Add Food". Flip the sides when it displays "Turn Food". Remove from the oven when cooking time is complete. Drizzle the melted butter over the donuts and coat with either the cinnamon-sugar mixture or the powdered sugar. Serve warm.
- **Nutrition Info:** Calories: 301 Cal Total Fat: 32.2 g Saturated Fat: 0 g Cholesterol: 0 mg Sodium: 0 mg Total Carbs: 25 g Fiber: 0 g Sugar: 0 g Protein: 8.8 g

434.Tasty Jalapeno Poppers

Servings: 4
Cooking Time: 13 Minutes
Ingredients:
- 4 jalapeno peppers, slice in half and deseeded
- 4 oz goat cheese, crumbled
- 1/4 tsp chili powder
- 2 tbsp chunky salsa
- Pepper
- Salt

Directions:
1. Fit the oven with the rack in position 2.
2. In a small bowl, mix together cheese, chunky salsa, chili powder, pepper, and salt.
3. Stuff cheese mixture into each jalapeno half and place in the air fryer basket then place the air fryer basket in the baking pan.
4. Place a baking pan on the oven rack. Set to air fry at 350 F for 13 minutes.
5. Serve and enjoy.

- **Nutrition Info:** Calories 68 Fat 5.1 g Carbohydrates 2.5 g Sugar 1.6 g Protein 3.6 g Cholesterol 20 mg

435.Fudge Brownies

Servings: 8
Cooking Time: 20 Minutes
Ingredients:
- 1 cup sugar
- ½ cup butter, melted
- ½ cup flour
- 1/3 cup cocoa powder
- 1 teaspoon baking powder
- 2 eggs
- 1 teaspoon vanilla extract

Directions:
1. Grease a baking pan.
2. In a large bowl, add the sugar, and butter and whisk until light and fluffy.
3. Add the remaining ingredients and mix until well combined.
4. Place mixture into the prepared pan and with the back of spatula, smooth the top surface.
5. Press "Power Button" of Air Fry Oven and turn the dial to select the "Air Fry" mode.
6. Press the Time button and again turn the dial to set the cooking time to 20 minutes.
7. Now push the Temp button and rotate the dial to set the temperature at 350 degrees F.
8. Press "Start/Pause" button to start.
9. When the unit beeps to show that it is preheated, open the lid.
10. Arrange the pan in "Air Fry Basket" and insert in the oven.
11. Place the baking pan onto a wire rack to cool completely.
12. Cut into 8 equal-sized squares and serve.
- **Nutrition Info:** Calories 250 Total Fat 13.2 g Saturated Fat 7.9 g Cholesterol 71 mg Sodium 99 mg Total Carbs 33.4 g Fiber 1.3 g Sugar 25.2 g Protein 3 g

436.Coconut Butter Apple Bars

Servings: 8
Cooking Time: 45 Minutes
Ingredients:
- 1 tbsp ground flax seed
- 1/4 cup coconut butter, softened
- 1 cup pecans
- 1 cup of water
- 1/4 cup dried apples
- 1 1/2 tsp baking powder
- 1 1/2 tsp cinnamon
- 1 tsp vanilla
- 2 tbsp swerve

Directions:
1. Fit the oven with the rack in position

2. Add all ingredients into the blender and blend until smooth.
3. Pour blended mixture into the greased baking dish.
4. Set to bake at 350 F for 50 minutes. After 5 minutes place the baking dish in the preheated oven.
5. Slice and serve.
- **Nutrition Info:** Calories 161 Fat 15 g Carbohydrates 6 g Sugar 2 g Protein 2 g Cholesterol 0 mg

437.Coconut Pineapple Sticks

Servings:4
Cooking Time: 10 Minutes
Ingredients:
- ½ fresh pineapple, cut into sticks
- ¼ cup desiccated coconut

Directions:
1. Place the desiccated coconut on a plate and roll the pineapple sticks in the coconut until well coated.
2. Lay the pineapple sticks in the air fryer basket.
3. Put the air fryer basket on the baking pan and slide into Rack Position 2, select Air Fry, set temperature to 400ºF (205ºC), and set time to 10 minutes.
4. When cooking is complete, the pineapple sticks should be crisp-tender.
5. Serve warm.

438.Plum Cake

Servings: 8
Cooking Time: 30 Minutes
Ingredients:
- ½ cup butter, soft
- 3 eggs
- ½ cup swerve
- ¼ teaspoon almond extract
- 1 tablespoon vanilla extract
- 1 and ½ cups almond flour
- ½ cup coconut flour
- 2 teaspoons baking powder
- ¾ cup almond milk
- 4 plums, pitted and chopped

Directions:
1. In a bowl, mix all the ingredients and whisk well.
2. Pour this into a cake pan that fits the air fryer after you've lined it with parchment paper, put the pan in the machine and cook at 370 degrees F for 30 minutes.
3. Cool the cake down, slice and serve.
- **Nutrition Info:** calories 183, fat 4, fiber 3, carbs 4, protein 7

439.Avocado Chips

Servings:4

Cooking Time: 10 Minutes
Ingredients:
- 1 egg
- 1 tablespoon lime juice
- ⅛ teaspoon hot sauce
- 2 tablespoons flour
- ¾ cup panko bread crumbs
- ¼ cup cornmeal
- ¼ teaspoon salt

Directions:
1. 1 large avocado, pitted, peeled, and cut into ½-inch slices
2. Cooking spray
3. Whisk together the egg, lime juice, and hot sauce in a small bowl.
4. On a sheet of wax paper, place the flour. In a separate sheet of wax paper, combine the bread crumbs, cornmeal, and salt.
5. Dredge the avocado slices one at a time in the flour, then in the egg mixture, finally roll them in the bread crumb mixture to coat well.
6. Place the breaded avocado slices in the air fryer basket and mist them with cooking spray.
7. Put the air fryer basket on the baking pan and slide into Rack Position 2, select Air Fry, set temperature to 390ºF (199ºC), and set time to 10 minutes.
8. When cooking is complete, the slices should be nicely browned and crispy. Transfer the avocado slices to a plate and serve.

440.Cinnamon Maple Glazed Carrot Fries

Servings: 4
Cooking Time: 12 Minutes
Ingredients:
- 1 teaspoon of olive oil
- 1/2 teaspoon of ground cinnamon
- 1 teaspoon of maple syrup
- Salt, to taste
- 1 pound of carrots, cut into sticks

Directions:
1. Set the Instant Vortex on Air fryer to 400 degrees F for 12 minutes. Mix carrots with olive oil, cinnamon, maple syrup, and salt in a bowl. Place the carrots on the cooking tray. Insert the cooking tray in the Vortex when it displays "Add Food". Flip the sides when it displays "Turn Food". Remove from the oven when cooking time is complete. Serve warm.
- **Nutrition Info:** Calories: 62 Cal Total Fat: 1 g Saturated Fat: 0 g Cholesterol: 0 mg Sodium: 0 mg Total Carbs: 12 g Fiber: 0 g Sugar: 0 g Protein: 1 g

441.Margherita Pizza

Servings: 4

Cooking Time: 18 Minutes
Ingredients:
- 1 whole-wheat pizza crust
- 1/2 cup mozzarella cheese, grated
- 1/2 cup can tomatoes
- 2 tbsp olive oil
- 3 Roma tomatoes, sliced
- 10 basil leaves

Directions:
1. Fit the oven with the rack in position
2. Roll out whole wheat pizza crust using a rolling pin. Make sure the crust is ½-inch thick.
3. Sprinkle olive oil on top of pizza crust.
4. Spread can tomatoes over pizza crust.
5. Arrange sliced tomatoes and basil on pizza crust. Sprinkle grated cheese on top.
6. Place pizza on top of the oven rack and set to bake at 425 F for 23 minutes.
7. Slice and serve.
- **Nutrition Info:** Calories 126 Fat 7.9 g Carbohydrates 11.3 g Sugar 4.2 g Protein 3.6 g Cholesterol 2 mg

442.Parmesan Green Beans

Servings: 4
Cooking Time: 15 Minutes
Ingredients:
- 1 lb green beans
- 4 tbsp parmesan cheese
- 2 tbsp olive oil
- Pinch of salt

Directions:
1. Fit the oven with the rack in position
2. Add green beans in a large bowl.
3. Add remaining ingredients on top of green beans and toss to coat.
4. Spread green beans in baking pan.
5. Set to bake at 400 F for 20 minutes. After 5 minutes place the baking pan in the preheated oven.
6. Serve and enjoy.
- **Nutrition Info:** Calories 114 Fat 8.4 g Carbohydrates 8.3 g Sugar 1.6 g Protein 4 g Cholesterol 4 mg

443.Currant Pudding

Servings: 6
Cooking Time: 15 Minutes
Ingredients:
- 1 cup red currants, blended
- 1 cup coconut cream
- 1 cup black currants, blended
- 3 tbsp. stevia

Directions:
1. In a bowl, combine all the ingredients and stir well.
2. Divide into ramekins, put them in the fryer and cook at 340°F for 20 minutes

3. Serve the pudding cold.
- **Nutrition Info:** Calories: 200; Fat: 4g; Fiber: 2g; Carbs: 4g; Protein: 6g

444.Cheese-stuffed Mushrooms With Pimientos

Servings:12
Cooking Time: 18 Minutes
Ingredients:
- 24 medium raw white button mushrooms, rinsed and drained
- 4 ounces (113 g) shredded extra-sharp Cheddar cheese
- 2 ounces (57 g) cream cheese, at room temperature
- 1 ounce (28 g) chopped jarred pimientos
- 2 tablespoons grated onion
- ⅛ teaspoon smoked paprika
- ⅛ teaspoon hot sauce
- 2 tablespoons butter, melted, divided
- $^1/_3$ cup panko bread crumbs
- 2 tablespoons grated Parmesan cheese

Directions:
1. Gently pull out the stems of the mushrooms and discard. Set aside.
2. In a medium bowl, stir together the Cheddar cheese, cream cheese, pimientos, onion, paprika and hot sauce.
3. Brush the baking pan with 1 tablespoon of the melted butter. Arrange the mushrooms evenly on the pan, hollow-side up.
4. Place the cheese mixture into a large heavy plastic bag and cut off the end. Fill the mushrooms with the cheese mixture.
5. In a small bowl, whisk together the remaining 1 tablespoon of the melted butter, bread crumbs and Parmesan cheese. Sprinkle the panko mixture over each mushroom.
6. Slide the baking pan into Rack Position 2, select Roast, set temperature to 350ºF (180ºC) and set time to 18 minutes.
7. When cooking is complete, let the stuffed mushrooms rest for 2 minutes before serving.

445.Turkey Bacon-wrapped Dates

Servings: 16 Appetizers
Cooking Time: 6 Minutes
Ingredients:
- 16 whole dates, pitted
- 16 whole almonds
- 6 to 8 strips turkey bacon, cut in half
- Special Equipment:
- 16 toothpicks, soaked in water for at least 30 minutes

Directions:
1. On a flat work surface, stuff each pitted date with a whole almond.
2. Wrap half slice of bacon around each date and secure it with a toothpick.
3. Place the bacon-wrapped dates in the air fryer basket.
4. Put the air fryer basket on the baking pan and slide into Rack Position 2, select Air Fry, set temperature to 390ºF (199ºC), and set time to 6 minutes.
5. When cooking is complete, transfer the dates to a paper towel-lined plate to drain. Serve hot.

446.Crispy Eggplant Bites

Servings: 4
Cooking Time: 20 Minutes
Ingredients:
- 1 eggplant, cut into 1-inch pieces
- 1 tsp garlic powder
- 2 tbsp olive oil
- 1/2 tsp Italian seasoning
- 1 tsp paprika
- 1/2 tsp red pepper

Directions:
1. Fit the oven with the rack in position 2.
2. Add all ingredients into the large mixing bowl and toss well.
3. Transfer eggplant mixture in air fryer basket then places air fryer basket in baking pan.
4. Place a baking pan on the oven rack. Set to air fry at 375 F for 20 minutes.
5. Serve and enjoy.
- **Nutrition Info:** Calories 99 Fat 7.5 g Carbohydrates 8.7 g Sugar 4.5 g Protein 1.5 g Cholesterol 0 mg

447.Orange Sponge Cake

Servings:6
Cooking Time: 50 Minutes
Ingredients:
- 1 cup sugar
- 1 cup self-rising flour
- 1 cup butter
- 3 eggs
- 1 tsp baking powder
- 1 tsp vanilla extract
- Zest of 1 orange
- Frosting:
- 4 egg whites
- 1 orange, zested and juiced
- 1 tsp orange food coloring
- 7 oz superfine sugar

Directions:
1. Preheat on Bake function to 360 F. Beat all the cake ingredients in a bowl with an electric mixer. Transfer half of the batter into a greased cake pan and press Start. Bake for 15 minutes. Repeat the process for the other half of the batter.

2. Meanwhile, prepare the frosting by beating all frosting ingredients together. Spread the frosting mixture on top of one cake. Top with the other cake.

448.Caramelized Fruit Kebabs

Servings:4
Cooking Time: 4 Minutes
Ingredients:
- 2 peaches, peeled, pitted, and thickly sliced
- 3 plums, halved and pitted
- 3 nectarines, halved and pitted
- 1 tablespoon honey
- ½ teaspoon ground cinnamon
- ¼ teaspoon ground allspice
- Pinch cayenne pepper
- Special Equipment:
- 8 metal skewers

Directions:
1. Thread, alternating peaches, plums, and nectarines onto the metal skewers.
2. Thoroughly combine the honey, cinnamon, allspice, and cayenne in a small bowl. Brush generously the glaze over the fruit skewers.
3. Transfer the fruit skewers to the air fryer basket.
4. Put the air fryer basket on the baking pan and slide into Rack Position 2, select Air Fry, set temperature to 400ºF (205ºC), and set time to 4 minutes.
5. When cooking is complete, the fruit should be caramelized.
6. Remove the fruit skewers from the oven and let rest for 5 minutes before serving.

449.Walnut Brownies

Servings: 4
Cooking Time: 22 Minutes
Ingredients:
- ½ cup chocolate, roughly chopped
- 1/3 cup butter
- 5 tablespoons sugar
- 1 egg, beaten
- 1 teaspoon vanilla extract
- Pinch of salt
- 5 tablespoons self-rising flour
- ¼ cup walnuts, chopped

Directions:
1. In a microwave-safe bowl, add the chocolate and butter. Microwave on high heat for about 2 minutes, stirring after every 30 seconds.
2. Remove from microwave and set aside to cool.
3. In another bowl, add the sugar, egg, vanilla extract, and salt and whisk until creamy and light.
4. Add the chocolate mixture and whisk until well combined.

5. Add the flour, and walnuts and mix until well combined.
6. Line a baking pan with a greased parchment paper.
7. Place mixture evenly into the prepared pan and with the back of spatula, smooth the top surface.
8. Press "Power Button" of Air Fry Oven and turn the dial to select the "Air Fry" mode.
9. Press the Time button and again turn the dial to set the cooking time to 20 minutes.
10. Now push the Temp button and rotate the dial to set the temperature at 355 degrees F.
11. Press "Start/Pause" button to start.
12. When the unit beeps to show that it is preheated, open the lid.
13. Arrange the pan in "Air Fry Basket" and insert in the oven.
14. Place the baking pan onto a wire rack to cool completely.
15. Cut into 4 equal-sized squares and serve.
- **Nutrition Info:** Calories 407 Total Fat 27.4g Saturated Fat 14.7 g Cholesterol 86 mg Sodium 180 mg Total Carbs 35.9 g Fiber 1.5 g Sugar 26.2 g Protein 6 g

450.Crustless Pizza

Servings: 1
Cooking Time: 15 Minutes
Ingredients:
- 2 slices sugar-free bacon; cooked and crumbled
- 7 slices pepperoni
- ½ cup shredded mozzarella cheese
- ¼ cup cooked ground sausage
- 2 tbsp. low-carb, sugar-free pizza sauce, for dipping
- 1 tbsp. grated Parmesan cheese

Directions:
1. Cover the bottom of a 6-inch cake pan with mozzarella. Place pepperoni, sausage and bacon on top of cheese and sprinkle with Parmesan
2. Place pan into the air fryer basket. Adjust the temperature to 400 Degrees F and set the timer for 5 minutes.
3. Remove when cheese is bubbling and golden. Serve warm with pizza sauce for dipping.
- **Nutrition Info:** Calories: 466; Protein: 21g; Fiber: 5g; Fat: 30g; Carbs: 2g

451.Crème Coffee Brûlée

Servings: 3
Cooking Time: 10 Minutes
Ingredients:
- ½ teaspoon of vanilla extract
- 3 tablespoons of superfine sugar
- 1 cup of water

- 4 egg yolks
- 1 cup of heavy cream
- ½ teaspoon of coffee powder
- Pinch of salt
- ¼ cup of granulated sugar

Directions:
1. Set the Instant Vortex on Air fryer to 375 degrees F for 10 minutes. Whip the egg yolks with granulated sugar, coffee powder, heavy cream, vanilla extract, and salt in a bowl. Pour this mixture into 3 ramekins. Place the ramekins on the cooking tray. Insert the cooking tray in the Vortex when it displays "Add Food". Remove from the oven when cooking time is complete. Sprinkle the superfine sugar on the Crème Coffee Brûlée and refrigerate for about 2 hours. Use a blow torch to burn the sprinkled sugar to serve.
- **Nutrition Info:** Calories: 337 Cal Total Fat: 20.8 g Saturated Fat: 0 g Cholesterol: 0 mg Sodium: 0 mg Total Carbs: 35.4 g Fiber: 0 g Sugar: 0 g Protein: 4.4 g

452.Shrimp Toasts With Sesame Seeds

Servings:4 To 6
Cooking Time: 8 Minutes
Ingredients:
- ½ pound (227 g) raw shrimp, peeled and deveined
- 1 egg, beaten
- 2 scallions, chopped, plus more for garnish
- 2 tablespoons chopped fresh cilantro
- 2 teaspoons grated fresh ginger
- 1 to 2 teaspoons sriracha sauce
- 1 teaspoon soy sauce
- ½ teaspoon toasted sesame oil
- 6 slices thinly sliced white sandwich bread
- ½ cup sesame seeds
- Cooking spray
- Thai chili sauce, for serving

Directions:
1. In a food processor, add the shrimp, egg, scallions, cilantro, ginger, sriracha sauce, soy sauce and sesame oil, and pulse until chopped finely. You'll need to stop the food processor occasionally to scrape down the sides. Transfer the shrimp mixture to a bowl.
2. On a clean work surface, cut the crusts off the sandwich bread. Using a brush, generously brush one side of each slice of bread with shrimp mixture.
3. Place the sesame seeds on a plate. Press bread slices, shrimp-side down, into sesame seeds to coat evenly. Cut each slice diagonally into quarters.

4. Spritz the air fryer basket with cooking spray. Spread the coated slices in a single layer in the basket.
5. Put the air fryer basket on the baking pan and slide into Rack Position 2, select Air Fry, set temperature to 400ºF (205ºC), and set time to 8 minutes.
6. Flip the bread slices halfway through.
7. When cooking is complete, they should be golden and crispy. Remove from the oven to a plate and let cool for 5 minutes. Top with the chopped scallions and serve warm with Thai chili sauce.

453.Baked Plums

Servings: 6
Cooking Time: 20 Minutes
Ingredients:
- 6 plums, cut into wedges
- 1 teaspoon ginger, ground
- ½ teaspoon cinnamon powder
- Zest of 1 lemon, grated
- 2 tablespoons water
- 10 drops stevia

Directions:
1. In a pan that fits the air fryer, combine the plums with the rest of the ingredients, toss gently, put the pan in the air fryer and cook at 360 degrees F for 20 minutes.
2. Serve cold.
- **Nutrition Info:** calories 170, fat 5, fiber 1, carbs 3, protein 5

454.Tiny Filled Puffs

Servings:x
Cooking Time:x
Ingredients:
- 3 eggs
- ½ cup grated Parmesan cheese
- 1 tablespoon dried chives
- 1 cup water
- ½ cup butter
- ½ teaspoon salt
- 1 cup flour

Directions:
1. Preheat oven to 375ºF. Line baking sheet with parchment paper and set aside. In heavy saucepan, combine water and butter. Bring to a rolling boil that cannot be stirred down. Add salt and flour all at once. Cook and stir over medium heat until dough forms a ball and cleans sides of pan. Remove from heat and beat in eggs, one at a time, until well combined. Stir in cheese and chives.
2. Drop dough by teaspoons onto prepared baking sheet. Bake at 375ºF for 18 to 22 minutes or until dough is puffed, golden

brown, and firm. Remove from baking sheet
and cool on wire rack.
3. Flash freeze puffs in single layer on baking
sheet. Then carefully pack into rigid
containers. Label puffs and freeze.
4. To reheat: Place frozen puffs on baking
sheet. Bake in preheated 400ºF oven for 5
to 8 minutes, until hot. Let cool slightly,
then cut puffs in half and fill with desired
filling.

455.Artichoke Cashews Spinach Dip

Servings: 10
Cooking Time: 20 Minutes
Ingredients:
- 28 oz can artichokes, drained and rinsed
- 1 small onion, diced
- 4 garlic cloves
- 1 1/2 cups cashews
- 1 tsp olive oil
- 4 cups fresh spinach
- 2 tbsp fresh lemon juice
- 1/4 cup nutritional yeast
- 1 1/2 cups milk
- 1 1/2 tsp salt

Directions:
1. Fit the oven with the rack in position 2.
2. Soak cashews in boiling water for 5 minutes.
   Drain well.
3. Heat oil in a pan over medium heat. Add
   onion and garlic and sauté for 2-3 minutes.
4. Remove pan from heat and set aside.
5. Add soaked cashews, milk, nutritional yeast,
   lemon juice, and salt into the blender and
   blend until smooth.

6. Add sautéed garlic onion, artichokes, and
   spinach and blend for few minutes until
   getting chunky texture.
7. Transfer blended mixture into the baking
   dish.
8. Set to bake at 425 F for 25 minutes. After 5
   minutes place the baking dish in the
   preheated oven.
9. Serve and enjoy.
- **Nutrition Info:** Calories 205 Fat 11.3 g
  Carbohydrates 21.4 g Sugar 3.9 g Protein 9
  g Cholesterol 3 mg

456.Carrot Chips

Servings:4
Cooking Time: 10 Minutes
Ingredients:
- 4 to 5 medium carrots, trimmed and thinly
  sliced
- 1 tablespoon olive oil, plus more for
  greasing
- 1 teaspoon seasoned salt

Directions:
1. Toss the carrot slices with 1 tablespoon of
   olive oil and salt in a medium bowl until
   thoroughly coated.
2. Grease the air fryer basket with the olive oil.
   Place the carrot slices in the greased pan.
3. Put the air fryer basket on the baking pan
   and slide into Rack Position 2, select Air Fry,
   set temperature to 390ºF (199ºC), and set
   time to 10 minutes.
4. Stir the carrot slices halfway through the
   cooking time.
5. When cooking is complete, the chips should
   be crisp-tender. Remove from the oven and
   allow to cool for 5 minutes before serving.

OTHER FAVORITE RECIPES

457.Jewish Blintzes

Servings: 8 Blintzes
Cooking Time: 10 Minutes
Ingredients:
- 2 (7½-ounce / 213-g) packages farmer cheese, mashed
- ¼ cup cream cheese
- ¼ teaspoon vanilla extract
- ¼ cup granulated white sugar
- 8 egg roll wrappers
- 4 tablespoons butter, melted

Directions:
1. Combine the farmer cheese, cream cheese, vanilla extract, and sugar in a bowl. Stir to mix well.
2. Unfold the egg roll wrappers on a clean work surface, spread ¼ cup of the filling at the edge of each wrapper and leave a ½-inch edge uncovering.
3. Wet the edges of the wrappers with water and fold the uncovered edge over the filling. Fold the left and right sides in the center, then tuck the edge under the filling and fold to wrap the filling.
4. Brush the wrappers with melted butter, then arrange the wrappers in a single layer in the air fryer basket, seam side down. Leave a little space between each two wrappers.
5. Put the air fryer basket on the baking pan and slide into Rack Position 2, select Air Fry, set temperature to 375ºF (190ºC) and set time to 10 minutes.
6. When cooking is complete, the wrappers will be golden brown.
7. Serve immediately.

458.Classic Marinara Sauce

Servings: About 3 Cups
Cooking Time: 30 Minutes
Ingredients:
- ¼ cup extra-virgin olive oil
- 3 garlic cloves, minced
- 1 small onion, chopped (about ½ cup)
- 2 tablespoons minced or puréed sun-dried tomatoes (optional)
- 1 (28-ounce / 794-g) can crushed tomatoes
- ½ teaspoon dried basil
- ½ teaspoon dried oregano
- ¼ teaspoon red pepper flakes

Directions:
1. 1 teaspoon kosher salt or ½ teaspoon fine salt, plus more as needed
2. Heat the oil in a medium saucepan over medium heat.
3. Add the garlic and onion and sauté for 2 to 3 minutes, or until the onion is softened. Add the sun-dried tomatoes (if desired) and cook for 1 minute until fragrant. Stir in the crushed tomatoes, scraping any brown bits from the bottom of the pot. Fold in the basil, oregano, red pepper flakes, and salt. Stir well.
4. Bring to a simmer. Cook covered for about 30 minutes, stirring occasionally.
5. Turn off the heat and allow the sauce to cool for about 10 minutes.
6. Taste and adjust the seasoning, adding more salt if needed.
7. Use immediately.

459.Kale Chips With Soy Sauce

Servings:2
Cooking Time: 5 Minutes
Ingredients:
- 4 medium kale leaves, about 1 ounce (28 g) each, stems removed, tear the leaves in thirds
- 2 teaspoons soy sauce
- 2 teaspoons olive oil

Directions:
1. Toss the kale leaves with soy sauce and olive oil in a large bowl to coat well. Place the leaves in the baking pan.
2. Put the air fryer basket on the baking pan and slide into Rack Position 2, select Air Fry, set temperature to 400ºF (205ºC) and set time to 5 minutes.
3. Flip the leaves with tongs gently halfway through.
4. When cooked, the kale leaves should be crispy. Remove from the oven and serve immediately.

460.Simple Butter Cake

Servings:8
Cooking Time: 20 Minutes
Ingredients:
- 1 cup all-purpose flour
- 1¼ teaspoons baking powder
- ¼ teaspoon salt
- ½ cup plus 1½ tablespoons granulated white sugar
- 9½ tablespoons butter, at room temperature
- 2 large eggs
- 1 large egg yolk
- 2½ tablespoons milk
- 1 teaspoon vanilla extract
- Cooking spray

Directions:
1. Spritz the baking pan with cooking spray.
2. Combine the flour, baking powder, and salt in a large bowl. Stir to mix well.

3. Whip the sugar and butter in a separate bowl with a hand mixer on medium speed for 3 minutes.
4. Whip the eggs, egg yolk, milk, and vanilla extract into the sugar and butter mix with a hand mixer.
5. Pour in the flour mixture and whip with hand mixer until sanity and smooth.
6. Scrape the batter into the baking pan and level the batter with a spatula.
7. Slide the baking pan into Rack Position 1, select Convection Bake, set temperature to 325ºF (163ºC) and set time to 20 minutes.
8. After 15 minutes, remove the pan from the oven. Check the doneness. Return the pan to the oven and continue cooking.
9. When done, a toothpick inserted in the center should come out clean.
10. Invert the cake on a cooling rack and allow to cool for 15 minutes before slicing to serve.

461.South Carolina Shrimp And Corn Bake

Servings:2
Cooking Time: 18 Minutes
Ingredients:
- 1 ear corn, husk and silk removed, cut into 2-inch rounds
- 8 ounces (227 g) red potatoes, unpeeled, cut into 1-inch pieces
- 2 teaspoons Old Bay Seasoning, divided
- 2 teaspoons vegetable oil, divided
- ¼ teaspoon ground black pepper
- 8 ounces (227 g) large shrimps (about 12 shrimps), deveined
- 6 ounces (170 g) andouille or chorizo sausage, cut into 1-inch pieces
- 2 garlic cloves, minced
- 1 tablespoon chopped fresh parsley

Directions:
1. Put the corn rounds and potatoes in a large bowl. Sprinkle with 1 teaspoon of Old Bay seasoning and drizzle with vegetable oil. Toss to coat well.
2. Transfer the corn rounds and potatoes into the baking pan.
3. Slide the baking pan into Rack Position 1, select Convection Bake, set temperature to 400ºF (205ºC) and set time to 18 minutes.
4. After 6 minutes, remove from the oven. Stir the corn rounds and potatoes. Return the pan to the oven and continue cooking.
5. Meanwhile, cut slits into the shrimps but be careful not to cut them through. Combine the shrimps, sausage, remaining Old Bay seasoning, and remaining vegetable oil in the large bowl. Toss to coat well.
6. After 6 minutes, remove the pan from the oven. Add the shrimps and sausage to the pan. Return the pan to the oven and

continue cooking for 6 minutes. Stir the shrimp mixture halfway through the cooking time.
7. When done, the shrimps should be opaque. Transfer the dish to a plate and spread with parsley before serving.

462.Chicken Sausage And Broccoli Casserole

Servings:8
Cooking Time: 20 Minutes
Ingredients:
- 10 eggs
- 1 cup Cheddar cheese, shredded and divided
- ¾ cup heavy whipping cream
- 1 (12-ounce / 340-g) package cooked chicken sausage
- 1 cup broccoli, chopped
- 2 cloves garlic, minced
- ½ tablespoon salt
- ¼ tablespoon ground black pepper
- Cooking spray

Directions:
1. Spritz the baking pan with cooking spray.
2. Whisk the eggs with Cheddar and cream in a large bowl to mix well.
3. Combine the cooked sausage, broccoli, garlic, salt, and ground black pepper in a separate bowl. Stir to mix well.
4. Pour the sausage mixture into the baking pan, then spread the egg mixture over to cover.
5. Slide the baking pan into Rack Position 1, select Convection Bake, set temperature to 400ºF (205ºC) and set time to 20 minutes.
6. When cooking is complete, the egg should be set and a toothpick inserted in the center should come out clean.
7. Serve immediately.

463.Citrus Avocado Wedge Fries

Servings: 12 Fries
Cooking Time: 8 Minutes
Ingredients:
- 1 cup all-purpose flour
- 3 tablespoons lime juice
- ¾ cup orange juice
- 1¼ cups plain dried bread crumbs
- 1 cup yellow cornmeal
- 1½ tablespoons chile powder
- 2 large Hass avocados, peeled, pitted, and cut into wedges
- Coarse sea salt, to taste
- Cooking spray

Directions:
1. Spritz the air fryer basket with cooking spray.

2. Pour the flour in a bowl. Mix the lime juice with orange juice in a second bowl. Combine the bread crumbs, cornmeal, and chile powder in a third bowl.
3. Dip the avocado wedges in the bowl of flour to coat well, then dredge the wedges into the bowl of juice mixture, and then dunk the wedges in the bread crumbs mixture. Shake the excess off.
4. Arrange the coated avocado wedges in a single layer in the basket. Spritz with cooking spray.
5. Put the air fryer basket on the baking pan and slide into Rack Position 2, select Air Fry, set temperature to 400ºF (205ºC) and set time to 8 minutes.
6. Stir the avocado wedges and sprinkle with salt halfway through the cooking time.
7. When cooking is complete, the avocado wedges should be tender and crispy.
8. Serve immediately.

464.Fast Cinnamon Toast

Servings:6
Cooking Time: 5 Minutes
Ingredients:
- 1½ teaspoons cinnamon
- 1½ teaspoons vanilla extract
- ½ cup sugar
- 2 teaspoons ground black pepper
- 2 tablespoons melted coconut oil
- 12 slices whole wheat bread

Directions:
1. Combine all the ingredients, except for the bread, in a large bowl. Stir to mix well.
2. Dunk the bread in the bowl of mixture gently to coat and infuse well. Shake the excess off. Arrange the bread slices in the air fryer basket.
3. Put the air fryer basket on the baking pan and slide into Rack Position 2, select Air Fry, set temperature to 400ºF (205ºC) and set time to 5 minutes.
4. Flip the bread halfway through.
5. When cooking is complete, the bread should be golden brown.
6. Remove the bread slices from the oven and slice to serve.

465.Golden Nuggets

Servings: 20 Nuggets
Cooking Time: 4 Minutes
Ingredients:
- 1 cup all-purpose flour, plus more for dusting
- 1 teaspoon baking powder
- ½ teaspoon butter, at room temperature, plus more for brushing
- ¼ teaspoon salt

- ¼ cup water
- ⅛ teaspoon onion powder
- ¼ teaspoon garlic powder
- ⅛ teaspoon seasoning salt
- Cooking spray

Directions:
1. Line the air fryer basket with parchment paper.
2. Mix the flour, baking powder, butter, and salt in a large bowl. Stir to mix well. Gradually whisk in the water until a sanity dough forms.
3. Put the dough on a lightly floured work surface, then roll it out into a ½-inch thick rectangle with a rolling pin.
4. Cut the dough into about twenty 1- or 2-inch squares, then arrange the squares in a single layer in the basket. Spritz with cooking spray.
5. Combine onion powder, garlic powder, and seasoning salt in a small bowl. Stir to mix well, then sprinkle the squares with the powder mixture.
6. Put the air fryer basket on the baking pan and slide into Rack Position 2, select Air Fry, set temperature to 370ºF (188ºC) and set time to 4 minutes.
7. Flip the squares halfway through the cooking time.
8. When cooked, the dough squares should be golden brown.
9. Remove the golden nuggets from the oven and brush with more butter immediately. Serve warm.

466.Golden Salmon And Carrot Croquettes

Servings:6
Cooking Time: 10 Minutes
Ingredients:
- 2 egg whites
- 1 cup almond flour
- 1 cup panko bread crumbs
- 1 pound (454 g) chopped salmon fillet
- $^2/_3$ cup grated carrots
- 2 tablespoons minced garlic cloves
- ½ cup chopped onion
- 2 tablespoons chopped chives
- Cooking spray

Directions:
1. Spritz the air fryer basket with cooking spray.
2. Whisk the egg whites in a bowl. Put the flour in a second bowl. Pour the bread crumbs in a third bowl. Set aside.
3. Combine the salmon, carrots, garlic, onion, and chives in a large bowl. Stir to mix well.
4. Form the mixture into balls with your hands. Dredge the balls into the flour, then egg, and then bread crumbs to coat well.

5. Arrange the salmon balls on the basket and spritz with cooking spray.
6. Put the air fryer basket on the baking pan and slide into Rack Position 2, select Air Fry, set temperature to 350ºF (180ºC) and set time to 10 minutes.
7. Flip the salmon balls halfway through cooking.
8. When cooking is complete, the salmon balls will be crispy and browned. Remove from the oven and serve immediately.

467.Ritzy Pimento And Almond Turkey Casserole

Servings:4
Cooking Time: 32 Minutes
Ingredients:
- 1 pound (454 g) turkey breasts
- 1 tablespoon olive oil
- 2 boiled eggs, chopped
- 2 tablespoons chopped pimentos
- ¼ cup slivered almonds, chopped
- ¼ cup mayonnaise
- ½ cup diced celery
- 2 tablespoons chopped green onion
- ¼ cup cream of chicken soup
- ¼ cup bread crumbs
- Salt and ground black pepper, to taste

Directions:
1. Put the turkey breasts in a large bowl. Sprinkle with salt and ground black pepper and drizzle with olive oil. Toss to coat well.
2. Transfer the turkey to the air fryer basket.
3. Put the air fryer basket on the baking pan and slide into Rack Position 2, select Air Fry, set temperature to 390ºF (199ºC) and set time to 12 minutes.
4. Flip the turkey halfway through.
5. When cooking is complete, the turkey should be well browned.
6. Remove the turkey breasts from the oven and cut into cubes, then combine the chicken cubes with eggs, pimentos, almonds, mayo, celery, green onions, and chicken soup in a large bowl. Stir to mix.
7. Pour the mixture into the baking pan, then spread with bread crumbs.
8. Slide the baking pan into Rack Position 1, select Convection Bake, set time to 20 minutes.
9. When cooking is complete, the eggs should be set.
10. Remove from the oven and serve immediately.

468.Crunchy And Beery Onion Rings

Servings:2 To 4
Cooking Time: 16 Minutes
Ingredients:
- ²/₃ cup all-purpose flour
- 1 teaspoon paprika
- ½ teaspoon baking soda
- 1 teaspoon salt
- ½ teaspoon freshly ground black pepper
- 1 egg, beaten
- ¾ cup beer
- 1½ cups bread crumbs
- 1 tablespoons olive oil
- 1 large Vidalia onion, peeled and sliced into ½-inch rings
- Cooking spray

Directions:
1. Spritz the air fryer basket with cooking spray.
2. Combine the flour, paprika, baking soda, salt, and ground black pepper in a bowl. Stir to mix well.
3. Combine the egg and beer in a separate bowl. Stir to mix well.
4. Make a well in the center of the flour mixture, then pour the egg mixture in the well. Stir to mix everything well.
5. Pour the bread crumbs and olive oil in a shallow plate. Stir to mix well.
6. Dredge the onion rings gently into the flour and egg mixture, then shake the excess off and put into the plate of bread crumbs. Flip to coat the both sides well. Arrange the onion rings in the basket.
7. Put the air fryer basket on the baking pan and slide into Rack Position 2, select Air Fry, set temperature to 360ºF (182ºC) and set time to 16 minutes.
8. Flip the rings and put the bottom rings to the top halfway through.
9. When cooked, the rings will be golden brown and crunchy. Remove from the oven and serve immediately.

469.Garlicky Spiralized Zucchini And Squash

Servings:4
Cooking Time: 10 Minutes
Ingredients:
- 2 large zucchini, peeled and spiralized
- 2 large yellow summer squash, peeled and spiralized
- 1 tablespoon olive oil, divided
- ½ teaspoon kosher salt
- 1 garlic clove, whole
- 2 tablespoons fresh basil, chopped
- Cooking spray

Directions:
1. Spritz the air fryer basket with cooking spray.
2. Combine the zucchini and summer squash with 1 teaspoon of the olive oil and salt in a large bowl. Toss to coat well.

3. Transfer the zucchini and summer squash to the basket and add the garlic.
4. Put the air fryer basket on the baking pan and slide into Rack Position 2, select Air Fry, set temperature to 360ºF (182ºC) and set time to 10 minutes.
5. Stir the zucchini and summer squash halfway through the cooking time.
6. When cooked, the zucchini and summer squash will be tender and fragrant. Transfer the cooked zucchini and summer squash onto a plate and set aside.
7. Remove the garlic from the oven and allow to cool for 5 minutes. Mince the garlic and combine with remaining olive oil in a small bowl. Stir to mix well.
8. Drizzle the spiralized zucchini and summer squash with garlic oil and sprinkle with basil. Toss to serve.

470.Riced Cauliflower Casserole

Servings:4
Cooking Time: 12 Minutes
Ingredients:
- 1 head cauliflower, cut into florets
- 1 cup okra, chopped
- 1 yellow bell pepper, chopped
- 2 eggs, beaten
- ½ cup chopped onion
- 1 tablespoon soy sauce
- 2 tablespoons olive oil
- Salt and ground black pepper,
- to taste Spritz the baking pan with cooking spray.

Directions:
1. Put the cauliflower in a food processor and pulse to rice the cauliflower.
2. Pour the cauliflower rice in the baking pan and add the remaining ingredients. Stir to mix well.
3. Slide the baking pan into Rack Position 1, select Convection Bake, set temperature to 380ºF (193ºC) and set time to 12 minutes.
4. When cooking is complete, the eggs should be set.
5. Remove from the oven and serve immediately.

471.Broccoli, Carrot, And Tomato Quiche

Servings:4
Cooking Time: 14 Minutes
Ingredients:
- 4 eggs
- 1 teaspoon dried thyme
- 1 cup whole milk
- 1 steamed carrots, diced
- 2 cups steamed broccoli florets
- 2 medium tomatoes, diced
- ¼ cup crumbled feta cheese
- 1 cup grated Cheddar cheese
- 1 teaspoon chopped parsley
- Salt and ground black pepper, to taste
- Cooking spray

Directions:
1. Spritz the baking pan with cooking spray.
2. Whisk together the eggs, thyme, salt, and ground black pepper in a bowl and fold in the milk while mixing.
3. Put the carrots, broccoli, and tomatoes in the prepared baking pan, then spread with feta cheese and ½ cup Cheddar cheese. Pour the egg mixture over, then scatter with remaining Cheddar on top.
4. Slide the baking pan into Rack Position 1, select Convection Bake, set temperature to 350ºF (180ºC) and set time to 14 minutes.
5. When cooking is complete, the egg should be set and the quiche should be puffed.
6. Remove the quiche from the oven and top with chopped parsley, then slice to serve.

472.Crispy Cheese Wafer

Servings:2
Cooking Time: 5 Minutes
Ingredients:
- 1 cup shredded aged Manchego cheese
- 1 teaspoon all-purpose flour
- ½ teaspoon cumin seeds
- ¼ teaspoon cracked black pepper

Directions:
1. Line the air fryer basket with parchment paper.
2. Combine the cheese and flour in a bowl. Stir to mix well. Spread the mixture in the pan into a 4-inch round.
3. Combine the cumin and black pepper in a small bowl. Stir to mix well. Sprinkle the cumin mixture over the cheese round.
4. Put the air fryer basket on the baking pan and slide into Rack Position 2, select Air Fry, set temperature to 375ºF (190ºC) and set time to 5 minutes.
5. When cooked, the cheese will be lightly browned and frothy.
6. Use tongs to transfer the cheese wafer onto a plate and slice to serve.

473.Sweet And Sour Peanuts

Servings:9
Cooking Time: 5 Minutes
Ingredients:
- 3 cups shelled raw peanuts
- 1 tablespoon hot red pepper sauce
- 3 tablespoons granulated white sugar

Directions:
1. Put the peanuts in a large bowl, then drizzle with hot red pepper sauce and sprinkle with sugar. Toss to coat well.

2. Pour the peanuts in the air fryer basket.
3. Put the air fryer basket on the baking pan and slide into Rack Position 2, select Air Fry, set temperature to 400ºF (205ºC) and set time to 5 minutes.
4. Stir the peanuts halfway through the cooking time.
5. When cooking is complete, the peanuts will be crispy and browned. Remove from the oven and serve immediately.

474.Roasted Carrot Chips

Servings: 3 Cups
Cooking Time: 15 Minutes
Ingredients:
- 3 large carrots, peeled and sliced into long and thick chips diagonally
- 1 tablespoon granulated garlic
- 1 teaspoon salt
- ¼ teaspoon ground black pepper
- 1 tablespoon olive oil
- 1 tablespoon finely chopped fresh parsley

Directions:
1. Toss the carrots with garlic, salt, ground black pepper, and olive oil in a large bowl to coat well. Place the carrots in the air fryer basket.
2. Put the air fryer basket on the baking pan and slide into Rack Position 2, select Roast, set temperature to 360ºF (182ºC) and set time to 15 minutes.
3. Stir the carrots halfway through the cooking time.
4. When cooking is complete, the carrot chips should be soft. Remove from the oven. Serve the carrot chips with parsley on top.

475.Cheddar Jalapeño Cornbread

Servings:8
Cooking Time: 20 Minutes
Ingredients:
- $^2/_3$ cup cornmeal
- $^1/_3$ cup all-purpose flour
- ¾ teaspoon baking powder
- 2 tablespoons buttery spread, melted
- ½ teaspoon kosher salt
- 1 tablespoon granulated sugar
- ¾ cup whole milk
- 1 large egg, beaten
- 1 jalapeño pepper, thinly sliced
- $^1/_3$ cup shredded sharp Cheddar cheese
- Cooking spray

Directions:
1. Spritz the baking pan with cooking spray.
2. Combine all the ingredients in a large bowl. Stir to mix well. Pour the mixture in the baking pan.

3. Slide the baking pan into Rack Position 1, select Convection Bake, set temperature to 300ºF (150ºC) and set time to 20 minutes.
4. When the cooking is complete, a toothpick inserted in the center of the bread should come out clean.
5. Remove the baking pan from the oven and allow the bread to cool for 5 minutes before slicing to serve.

476.Creamy Pork Gratin

Servings:4
Cooking Time: 21 Minutes
Ingredients:
- 2 tablespoons olive oil
- 2 pounds (907 g) pork tenderloin, cut into serving-size pieces
- 1 teaspoon dried marjoram
- ¼ teaspoon chili powder
- 1 teaspoon coarse sea salt
- ½ teaspoon freshly ground black pepper
- 1 cup Ricotta cheese
- 1½ cups chicken broth
- 1 tablespoon mustard
- Cooking spray

Directions:
1. Spritz the baking pan with cooking spray.
2. Heat the olive oil in a nonstick skillet over medium-high heat until shimmering.
3. Add the pork and sauté for 6 minutes or until lightly browned.
4. Transfer the pork to the prepared baking pan and sprinkle with marjoram, chili powder, salt, and ground black pepper.
5. Combine the remaining ingredients in a large bowl. Stir to mix well. Pour the mixture over the pork in the pan.
6. Slide the baking pan into Rack Position 1, select Convection Bake, set temperature to 350ºF (180ºC) and set time to 15 minutes.
7. Stir the mixture halfway through.
8. When cooking is complete, the mixture should be frothy and the cheese should be melted.
9. Serve immediately.

477.Chicken Divan

Servings:4
Cooking Time: 24 Minutes
Ingredients:
- 4 chicken breasts
- Salt and ground black pepper, to taste
- 1 head broccoli, cut into florets
- ½ cup cream of mushroom soup
- 1 cup shredded Cheddar cheese
- ½ cup croutons
- Cooking spray

Directions:

1. Spritz the air fryer basket with cooking spray.
2. Put the chicken breasts in the basket and sprinkle with salt and ground black pepper.
3. Put the air fryer basket on the baking pan and slide into Rack Position 2, select Air Fry, set temperature to 390ºF (199ºC) and set time to 14 minutes.
4. Flip the breasts halfway through the cooking time.
5. When cooking is complete, the breasts should be well browned and tender.
6. Remove the breasts from the oven and allow to cool for a few minutes on a plate, then cut the breasts into bite-size pieces.
7. Combine the chicken, broccoli, mushroom soup, and Cheddar cheese in a large bowl. Stir to mix well.
8. Spritz the baking pan with cooking spray. Pour the chicken mixture into the pan. Spread the croutons over the mixture.
9. Slide the baking pan into Rack Position 1, select Convection Bake, set time to 10 minutes.
10. When cooking is complete, the croutons should be lightly browned and the mixture should be set.
11. Remove from the oven and serve immediately.

478.Mediterranean Quiche

Servings:4
Cooking Time: 30 Minutes
Ingredients:
- 4 eggs
- ¼ cup chopped Kalamata olives
- ½ cup chopped tomatoes
- ¼ cup chopped onion
- ½ cup milk
- 1 cup crumbled feta cheese
- ½ tablespoon chopped oregano
- ½ tablespoon chopped basil
- Salt and ground black pepper, to taste
- Cooking spray

Directions:
1. Spritz the baking pan with cooking spray.
2. Whisk the eggs with remaining ingredients in a large bowl. Stir to mix well.
3. Pour the mixture into the prepared baking pan.
4. Slide the baking pan into Rack Position 1, select Convection Bake, set temperature to 340ºF (171ºC) and set time to 30 minutes.
5. When cooking is complete, the eggs should be set and a toothpick inserted in the center should come out clean.
6. Serve immediately.

479.Crunchy Green Tomatoes Slices

Servings: 12 Slices
Cooking Time: 8 Minutes
Ingredients:
- ½ cup all-purpose flour
- 1 egg
- ½ cup buttermilk
- 1 cup cornmeal
- 1 cup panko
- 2 green tomatoes, cut into ¼-inch-thick slices, patted dry
- ½ teaspoon salt
- ½ teaspoon ground black pepper
- Cooking spray

Directions:
1. Spritz a baking sheet with cooking spray.
2. Pour the flour in a bowl. Whisk the egg and buttermilk in a second bowl. Combine the cornmeal and panko in a third bowl.
3. Dredge the tomato slices in the bowl of flour first, then into the egg mixture, and then dunk the slices into the cornmeal mixture. Shake the excess off.
4. Transfer the well-coated tomato slices in the baking sheet and sprinkle with salt and ground black pepper. Spritz the tomato slices with cooking spray.
5. Put the air fryer basket on the baking pan and slide into Rack Position 2, select Air Fry, set temperature to 400ºF (205ºC) and set time to 8 minutes.
6. Flip the slices halfway through the cooking time.
7. When cooking is complete, the tomato slices should be crispy and lightly browned. Remove the baking sheet from the oven.
8. Serve immediately.

480.Air Fried Blistered Tomatoes

Servings:4 To 6
Cooking Time: 10 Minutes
Ingredients:
- 2 pounds (907 g) cherry tomatoes
- 2 tablespoons olive oil
- 2 teaspoons balsamic vinegar
- ½ teaspoon salt
- ½ teaspoon ground black pepper

Directions:
1. Toss the cherry tomatoes with olive oil in a large bowl to coat well. Pour the tomatoes in the baking pan.
2. Put the air fryer basket on the baking pan and slide into Rack Position 2, select Air Fry, set temperature to 400ºF (205ºC) and set time to 10 minutes.
3. Stir the tomatoes halfway through the cooking time.
4. When cooking is complete, the tomatoes will be blistered and lightly wilted.

5. Transfer the blistered tomatoes to a large
   bowl and toss with balsamic vinegar, salt,
   and black pepper before serving.

481.Apple Fritters With Sugary Glaze

Servings: 15 Fritters
Cooking Time: 8 Minutes
Ingredients:
- Apple Fritters:
- 2 firm apples, peeled, cored, and diced
- ½ teaspoon cinnamon
- Juice of 1 lemon
- 1 cup all-purpose flour
- 1½ teaspoons baking powder
- ½ teaspoon kosher salt
- 2 eggs
- ¼ cup milk
- 2 tablespoons unsalted butter, melted
- 2 tablespoons granulated sugar
- Cooking spray
- Glaze:
- ½ teaspoon vanilla extract
- 1¼ cups powdered sugar, sifted
- ¼ cup water

Directions:
1. Line the air fryer basket with parchment
   paper.
2. Combine the apples with cinnamon and
   lemon juice in a small bowl. Toss to coat
   well.
3. Combine the flour, baking powder, and salt
   in a large bowl. Stir to mix well.
4. Whisk the egg, milk, butter, and sugar in a
   medium bowl. Stir to mix well.
5. Make a well in the center of the flour
   mixture, then pour the egg mixture into the
   well and stir to mix well. Mix in the apple
   until a dough forms.
6. Use an ice cream scoop to scoop 15 balls
   from the dough onto the pan. Spritz with
   cooking spray.
7. Put the air fryer basket on the baking pan
   and slide into Rack Position 2, select Air Fry,
   set temperature to 360ºF (182ºC) and set
   time to 8 minutes.
8. Flip the apple fritters halfway through the
   cooking time.
9. Meanwhile, combine the ingredients for the
   glaze in a separate small bowl. Stir to mix
   well.
10. When cooking is complete, the apple fritters
   will be golden brown. Serve the fritters with
   the glaze on top or use the glaze for dipping.

482.Burgundy Beef And Mushroom Casserole

Servings:4
Cooking Time: 25 Minutes
Ingredients:
- 1½ pounds (680 g) beef steak
- 1 ounce (28 g) dry onion soup mix
- 2 cups sliced mushrooms
- 1 (14.5-ounce / 411-g) can cream of
  mushroom soup
- ½ cup beef broth
- ¼ cup red wine
- 3 garlic cloves, minced
- 1 whole onion, chopped

Directions:
1. Put the beef steak in a large bowl, then
   sprinkle with dry onion soup mix. Toss to
   coat well.
2. Combine the mushrooms with mushroom
   soup, beef broth, red wine, garlic, and onion
   in a large bowl. Stir to mix well.
3. Transfer the beef steak in the baking pan,
   then pour in the mushroom mixture.
4. Slide the baking pan into Rack Position 1,
   select Convection Bake, set temperature to
   360ºF (182ºC) and set time to 25 minutes.
5. When cooking is complete, the mushrooms
   should be soft and the beef should be well
   browned.
6. Remove from the oven and serve
   immediately.

483.Spanakopita

Servings:6
Cooking Time: 8 Minutes
Ingredients:
- ½ (10-ounce / 284-g) package frozen
  spinach, thawed and squeezed dry
- 1 egg, lightly beaten
- ¼ cup pine nuts, toasted
- ¼ cup grated Parmesan cheese
- ¾ cup crumbled feta cheese
- ⅛ teaspoon ground nutmeg
- ½ teaspoon salt
- Freshly ground black pepper, to taste
- 6 sheets phyllo dough
- ½ cup butter, melted

Directions:
1. Combine all the ingredients, except for the
   phyllo dough and butter, in a large bowl.
   Whisk to combine well. Set aside.
2. Place a sheet of phyllo dough on a clean
   work surface. Brush with butter then top
   with another layer sheet of phyllo. Brush
   with butter, then cut the layered sheets into
   six 3-inch-wide strips.
3. Top each strip with 1 tablespoon of the
   spinach mixture, then fold the bottom left
   corner over the mixture towards the right
   strip edge to make a triangle. Keep folding
   triangles until each strip is folded over.
4. Brush the triangles with butter and repeat
   with remaining strips and phyllo dough.
5. Place the triangles in the baking pan.

6. Put the air fryer basket on the baking pan and slide into Rack Position 2, select Air Fry, set temperature to 350ºF (180ºC) and set time to 8 minutes.
7. Flip the triangles halfway through the cooking time.
8. When cooking is complete, the triangles should be golden brown. Remove from the oven and serve immediately.

484.Keto Cheese Quiche

Servings:8
Cooking Time: 1 Hour
Ingredients:
- Crust:
- 1¼ cups blanched almond flour
- 1 large egg, beaten
- 1¼ cups grated Parmesan cheese
- ¼ teaspoon fine sea salt
- Filling:
- 4 ounces (113 g) cream cheese
- 1 cup shredded Swiss cheese
- $^1/_3$ cup minced leeks
- 4 large eggs, beaten
- ½ cup chicken broth
- ⅛ teaspoon cayenne pepper
- ¾ teaspoon fine sea salt
- 1 tablespoon unsalted butter, melted
- Chopped green onions, for garnish
- Cooking spray

Directions:
1. Spritz the baking pan with cooking spray.
2. Combine the flour, egg, Parmesan, and salt in a large bowl. Stir to mix until a satiny and firm dough forms.
3. Arrange the dough between two grease parchment papers, then roll the dough into a $^1/_{16}$-inch thick circle.
4. Make the crust: Transfer the dough into the prepared pan and press to coat the bottom.
5. Slide the baking pan into Rack Position 1, select Convection Bake, set temperature to 325ºF (163ºC) and set time to 12 minutes.
6. When cooking is complete, the edges of the crust should be lightly browned.
7. Meanwhile, combine the ingredient for the filling, except for the green onions in a large bowl.
8. Pour the filling over the cooked crust and cover the edges of the crust with aluminum foil.
9. Slide the baking pan into Rack Position 1, select Convection Bake, set time to 15 minutes.
10. When cooking is complete, reduce the heat to 300ºF (150ºC) and set time to 30 minutes.
11. When cooking is complete, a toothpick inserted in the center should come out clean.
12. Remove from the oven and allow to cool for 10 minutes before serving.

485.Butternut Squash With Hazelnuts

Servings: 3 Cups
Cooking Time: 23 Minutes
Ingredients:
- 2 tablespoons whole hazelnuts
- 3 cups butternut squash, peeled, deseeded and cubed
- ¼ teaspoon kosher salt
- ¼ teaspoon freshly ground black pepper
- 2 teaspoons olive oil
- Cooking spray

Directions:
1. Spritz the air fryer basket with cooking spray. Spread the hazelnuts in the pan.
2. Put the air fryer basket on the baking pan and slide into Rack Position 2, select Air Fry, set temperature to 300ºF (150ºC) and set time to 3 minutes.
3. When done, the hazelnuts should be soft. Remove from the oven. Chopped the hazelnuts roughly and transfer to a small bowl. Set aside.
4. Put the butternut squash in a large bowl, then sprinkle with salt and pepper and drizzle with olive oil. Toss to coat well. Transfer the squash to the lightly greased basket.
5. Put the air fryer basket on the baking pan and slide into Rack Position 2, select Air Fry, set temperature to 360ºF (182ºC) and set time to 20 minutes.
6. Flip the squash halfway through the cooking time.
7. When cooking is complete, the squash will be soft. Transfer the squash to a plate and sprinkle with the chopped hazelnuts before serving.

486.Greek Frittata

Servings:2
Cooking Time: 8 Minutes
Ingredients:
- 1 cup chopped mushrooms
- 2 cups spinach, chopped
- 4 eggs, lightly beaten
- 3 ounces (85 g) feta cheese, crumbled
- 2 tablespoons heavy cream
- A handful of fresh parsley, chopped
- Salt and ground black pepper, to taste
- Cooking spray

Directions:
1. Spritz the baking pan with cooking spray.

2. Whisk together all the ingredients in a large bowl. Stir to mix well.
3. Pour the mixture in the prepared baking pan.
4. Slide the baking pan into Rack Position 1, select Convection Bake, set temperature to 350ºF (180ºC) and set time to 8 minutes.
5. Stir the mixture halfway through.
6. When cooking is complete, the eggs should be set.
7. Serve immediately.

487.Baked Cherry Tomatoes With Basil

Servings:2
Cooking Time: 5 Minutes
Ingredients:
- 2 cups cherry tomatoes
- 1 clove garlic, thinly sliced
- 1 teaspoon olive oil
- ⅛ teaspoon kosher salt
- 1 tablespoon freshly chopped basil, for topping
- Cooking spray

Directions:
1. Spritz the baking pan with cooking spray and set aside.
2. In a large bowl, toss together the cherry tomatoes, sliced garlic, olive oil, and kosher salt. Spread the mixture in an even layer in the prepared pan.
3. Slide the baking pan into Rack Position 1, select Convection Bake, set temperature to 360ºF (182ºC) and set time to 5 minutes.
4. When cooking is complete, the tomatoes should be the soft and wilted.
5. Transfer to a bowl and rest for 5 minutes. Top with the chopped basil and serve warm.

488.Caesar Salad Dressing

Servings: About ²/₃ Cup
Cooking Time: 0 Minutes
Ingredients:
- ½ cup extra-virgin olive oil
- 2 tablespoons freshly squeezed lemon juice
- 1 teaspoon anchovy paste
- ¼ teaspoon kosher salt or ⅛ teaspoon fine salt
- ¼ teaspoon minced or pressed garlic
- 1 egg, beaten
- Add all the ingredients to a tall, narrow container.

Directions:
1. Purée the mixture with an immersion blender until smooth.
2. Use immediately.

489.Chocolate And Coconut Macaroons

Servings: 24 Macaroons
Cooking Time: 8 Minutes

Ingredients:
- 3 large egg whites, at room temperature
- ¼ teaspoon salt
- ¾ cup granulated white sugar
- 4½ tablespoons unsweetened cocoa powder
- 2¼ cups unsweetened shredded coconut

Directions:
1. Line the air fryer basket with parchment paper.
2. Whisk the egg whites with salt in a large bowl with a hand mixer on high speed until stiff peaks form.
3. Whisk in the sugar with the hand mixer on high speed until the mixture is thick. Mix in the cocoa powder and coconut.
4. Scoop 2 tablespoons of the mixture and shape the mixture in a ball. Repeat with remaining mixture to make 24 balls in total.
5. Arrange the balls in a single layer in the basket and leave a little space between each two balls.
6. Put the air fryer basket on the baking pan and slide into Rack Position 2, select Air Fry, set temperature to 375ºF (190ºC) and set time to 8 minutes.
7. When cooking is complete, the balls should be golden brown.
8. Serve immediately.

490.Simple Baked Green Beans

Servings: 2 Cups
Cooking Time: 10 Minutes
Ingredients:
- ½ teaspoon lemon pepper
- 2 teaspoons granulated garlic
- ½ teaspoon salt
- 1 tablespoon olive oil
- 2 cups fresh green beans, trimmed and snapped in half

Directions:
1. Combine the lemon pepper, garlic, salt, and olive oil in a bowl. Stir to mix well.
2. Add the green beans to the bowl of mixture and toss to coat well.
3. Arrange the green beans in the the baking pan.
4. Slide the baking pan into Rack Position 1, select Convection Bake, set temperature to 370ºF (188ºC) and set time to 10 minutes.
5. Stir the green beans halfway through the cooking time.
6. When cooking is complete, the green beans will be tender and crispy. Remove from the oven and serve immediately.

491.Chocolate Buttermilk Cake

Servings:8
Cooking Time: 20 Minutes
Ingredients:

- 1 cup all-purpose flour
- $^2/_3$ cup granulated white sugar
- ¼ cup unsweetened cocoa powder
- ¾ teaspoon baking soda
- ¼ teaspoon salt
- $^2/_3$ cup buttermilk
- 2 tablespoons plus 2 teaspoons vegetable oil
- 1 teaspoon vanilla extract
- Cooking spray

Directions:
1. Spritz the baking pan with cooking spray.
2. Combine the flour, cocoa powder, baking soda, sugar, and salt in a large bowl. Stir to mix well.
3. Mix in the buttermilk, vanilla, and vegetable oil. Keep stirring until it forms a grainy and thick dough.
4. Scrape the chocolate batter from the bowl and transfer to the pan, level the batter in an even layer with a spatula.
5. Slide the baking pan into Rack Position 1, select Convection Bake, set temperature to 325ºF (163ºC) and set time to 20 minutes.
6. After 15 minutes, remove the pan from the oven. Check the doneness. Return the pan to the oven and continue cooking.
7. When done, a toothpick inserted in the center should come out clean.
8. Invert the cake on a cooling rack and allow to cool for 15 minutes before slicing to serve.

492.Traditional Latkes

Servings: 4 Latkes
Cooking Time: 10 Minutes
Ingredients:
- 1 egg
- 2 tablespoons all-purpose flour
- 2 medium potatoes, peeled and shredded, rinsed and drained
- ¼ teaspoon granulated garlic
- ½ teaspoon salt
- Cooking spray

Directions:
1. Spritz the air fryer basket with cooking spray.
2. Whisk together the egg, flour, potatoes, garlic, and salt in a large bowl. Stir to mix well.
3. Divide the mixture into four parts, then flatten them into four circles. Arrange the circles onto the basket and spritz with cooking spray.
4. Put the air fryer basket on the baking pan and slide into Rack Position 2, select Air Fry, set temperature to 380ºF (193ºC) and set time to 10 minutes.
5. Flip the latkes halfway through.

6. When cooked, the latkes will be golden brown and crispy. Remove from the oven and serve immediately.

493.Sausage And Colorful Peppers Casserole

Servings:6
Cooking Time: 25 Minutes
Ingredients:
- 1 pound (454 g) minced breakfast sausage
- 1 yellow pepper, diced
- 1 red pepper, diced
- 1 green pepper, diced
- 1 sweet onion, diced
- 2 cups Cheddar cheese, shredded
- 6 eggs
- Salt and freshly ground black pepper, to taste
- Fresh parsley, for garnish

Directions:
1. Cook the sausage in a nonstick skillet over medium heat for 10 minutes or until well browned. Stir constantly.
2. When the cooking is finished, transfer the cooked sausage to the baking pan and add the peppers and onion. Scatter with Cheddar cheese.
3. Whisk the eggs with salt and ground black pepper in a large bowl, then pour the mixture into the baking pan.
4. Slide the baking pan into Rack Position 1, select Convection Bake, set temperature to 360ºF (182ºC) and set time to 15 minutes.
5. When cooking is complete, the egg should be set and the edges of the casserole should be lightly browned.
6. Remove from the oven and top with fresh parsley before serving.

494.Smoked Trout And Crème Fraiche Frittata

Servings:4
Cooking Time: 17 Minutes
Ingredients:
- 2 tablespoons olive oil
- 1 onion, sliced
- 1 egg, beaten
- ½ tablespoon horseradish sauce
- 6 tablespoons crème fraiche
- 1 cup diced smoked trout
- 2 tablespoons chopped fresh dill
- Cooking spray

Directions:
1. Spritz the baking pan with cooking spray.
2. Heat the olive oil in a nonstick skillet over medium heat until shimmering.
3. Add the onion and sauté for 3 minutes or until translucent.

4. Combine the egg, horseradish sauce, and
   crème fraiche in a large bowl. Stir to mix
   well, then mix in the sautéed onion, smoked
   trout, and dill.
5. Pour the mixture in the prepared baking
   pan.
6. Slide the baking pan into Rack Position 1,
   select Convection Bake, set temperature to
   350ºF (180ºC) and set time to 14 minutes.
7. Stir the mixture halfway through.
8. When cooking is complete, the egg should
   be set and the edges should be lightly
   browned.
9. Serve immediately.

495.Roasted Mushrooms

Servings: About 1½ Cups
Cooking Time: 30 Minutes
Ingredients:
- 1 pound (454 g) button or cremini
  mushrooms, washed, stems trimmed, and
  cut into quarters or thick slices
- ¼ cup water
- 1 teaspoon kosher salt or ½ teaspoon fine
  salt
- 3 tablespoons unsalted butter, cut into
  pieces, or extra-virgin olive oil

Directions:
1. Place a large piece of aluminum foil on the
   sheet pan. Place the mushroom pieces in the
   middle of the foil. Spread them out into an
   even layer. Pour the water over them,
   season with the salt, and add the butter.
   Wrap the mushrooms in the foil.
2. Select Roast, set the temperature to 325ºF
   (163ºC), and set the time for 15 minutes.
   Select Start to begin preheating.
3. Once the unit has preheated, place the pan
   in the oven.
4. After 15 minutes, remove the pan from the
   oven. Transfer the foil packet to a cutting
   board and carefully unwrap it. Pour the
   mushrooms and cooking liquid from the foil
   onto the sheet pan.
5. Select Roast, set the temperature to 350ºF
   (180ºC), and set the time for 15 minutes.
   Return the pan to the oven. Select Start to
   begin.
6. After about 10 minutes, remove the pan
   from the oven and stir the mushrooms.
   Return the pan to the oven and continue
   cooking for anywhere from 5 to 15 more
   minutes, or until the liquid is mostly gone
   and the mushrooms start to brown.
7. Serve immediately.

496.Sweet Cinnamon Chickpeas

Servings:2
Cooking Time: 10 Minutes
Ingredients:
- 1 tablespoon cinnamon
- 1 tablespoon sugar
- 1 cup chickpeas, soaked in water overnight,
  rinsed and drained

Directions:
1. Combine the cinnamon and sugar in a bowl.
   Stir to mix well.
2. Add the chickpeas to the bowl, then toss to
   coat well.
3. Pour the chickpeas in the air fryer basket.
4. Put the air fryer basket on the baking pan
   and slide into Rack Position 2, select Air Fry,
   set temperature to 390ºF (199ºC) and set
   time to 10 minutes.
5. Stir the chickpeas three times during
   cooking.
6. When cooked, the chickpeas should be
   golden brown and crispy. Remove from the
   oven and serve immediately.

497.Spicy Air Fried Old Bay Shrimp

Servings: 2 Cups
Cooking Time: 10 Minutes
Ingredients:
- ½ teaspoon Old Bay Seasoning
- 1 teaspoon ground cayenne pepper
- ½ teaspoon paprika
- 1 tablespoon olive oil
- ⅛ teaspoon salt
- ½ pound (227 g) shrimps, peeled and
  deveined
- Juice of half a lemon

Directions:
1. Combine the Old Bay Seasoning, cayenne
   pepper, paprika, olive oil, and salt in a large
   bowl, then add the shrimps and toss to coat
   well.
2. Put the shrimps in the air fryer basket.
3. Put the air fryer basket on the baking pan
   and slide into Rack Position 2, select Air Fry,
   set temperature to 390ºF (199ºC) and set
   time to 10 minutes.
4. Flip the shrimps halfway through the
   cooking time.
5. When cooking is complete, the shrimps
   should be opaque. Serve the shrimps with
   lemon juice on top.

498.Pastrami Casserole

Servings:2
Cooking Time: 8 Minutes
Ingredients:
- 1 cup pastrami, sliced
- 1 bell pepper, chopped
- ¼ cup Greek yogurt
- 2 spring onions, chopped
- ½ cup Cheddar cheese, grated
- 4 eggs
- ¼ teaspoon ground black pepper

- Sea salt, to taste
- Cooking spray

Directions:
1. Spritz the baking pan with cooking spray.
2. Whisk together all the ingredients in a large bowl. Stir to mix well. Pour the mixture into the baking pan.
3. Slide the baking pan into Rack Position 1, select Convection Bake, set temperature to 330ºF (166ºC) and set time to 8 minutes.
4. When cooking is complete, the eggs should be set and the casserole edges should be lightly browned.
5. Remove from the oven and allow to cool for 10 minutes before serving.

499.Teriyaki Shrimp Skewers

Servings: 12 Skewered Shrimp
Cooking Time: 6 Minutes
Ingredients:
- 1½ tablespoons mirin
- 1½ teaspoons ginger juice
- 1½ tablespoons soy sauce
- 12 large shrimp (about 20 shrimps per pound), peeled and deveined
- 1 large egg
- ¾ cup panko bread crumbs
- Cooking spray

Directions:
1. Combine the mirin, ginger juice, and soy sauce in a large bowl. Stir to mix well.
2. Dunk the shrimp in the bowl of mirin mixture, then wrap the bowl in plastic and refrigerate for 1 hour to marinate.
3. Spritz the air fryer basket with cooking spray.
4. Run twelve 4-inch skewers through each shrimp.
5. Whisk the egg in the bowl of marinade to combine well. Pour the bread crumbs on a plate.
6. Dredge the shrimp skewers in the egg mixture, then shake the excess off and roll over the bread crumbs to coat well.
7. Arrange the shrimp skewers in the basket and spritz with cooking spray.
8. Put the air fryer basket on the baking pan and slide into Rack Position 2, select Air Fry, set temperature to 400ºF (205ºC) and set time to 6 minutes.
9. Flip the shrimp skewers halfway through the cooking time.
10. When done, the shrimp will be opaque and firm.
11. Serve immediately.

500.Simple Air Fried Edamame

Servings:6
Cooking Time: 7 Minutes
Ingredients:
- 1½ pounds (680 g) unshelled edamame
- 2 tablespoons olive oil
- 1 teaspoon sea salt

Directions:
1. Place the edamame in a large bowl, then drizzle with olive oil. Toss to coat well. Transfer the edamame to the air fryer basket.
2. Put the air fryer basket on the baking pan and slide into Rack Position 2, select Air Fry, set temperature to 400ºF (205ºC) and set time to 7 minutes.
3. Stir the edamame at least three times during cooking.
4. When done, the edamame will be tender and warmed through.
5. Transfer the cooked edamame onto a plate and sprinkle with salt. Toss to combine well and set aside for 3 minutes to infuse before serving.

9 781801 245586